"IT'S A FUNNY THING"

HOW THE PROFESSIONAL COMEDY BUSINESS MADE ME FAT AND BALD

A COMEDY MEMOIR

BY
MICHAEL ROWE

IT'S A FUNNY THING. Copyright © 2020 by Michael Rowe. All rights reserved. Printed in the United States of America. No part of this book may be used or reproduced in any manner whatsoever without written permission except in the case of brief quotations embodied in critical articles and reviews.

FIRST EDITION

Published in the USA by:
Published in the USA by:
BearManor Media
1317 Edgewater Dr #110
Orlando, FL 32804
www.bearmanormedia.com

Perfect ISBN 978-1-62933-686-2
Case ISBN 978-1-62933-687-9

BearManor Media, Orlando, Florida
Printed in the United States of America
Book design by Robbie Adkins, www.adkinsconsult.com
Cover design by Coco Shinomiya

It's A Funny Thing is a roadmap for you, the driven, the inspired, and the dreamer. At its core, it demystifies or at least uncovers many of the demons of uncertainty that stand in the way of you and your fullest potential.

TO DENISE, JACK AND NICK

CONTENTS

Foreword by Bob Odenkirk vii
1. Walt Disney Is Trying To Kill Me 1
2. The Seeds of Funny 9
3. Hollywood & Rowe 22
4. Dying Alone 30
5. The Launching Pad 39
6. Funny How? 51
7. Porn: A Love Story 64
8. When Do I Get My Sitcom? 77
9. New York Is Where I'd Rather Stay 86
10. I Consider Transitioning 92
11. I Was Having An Affair 98
12. How Ya Like Me Now, Motherfuckers? 105
13. A Fluffer's Journey 114
14. Writing A Sitcom Is Easy, Right? 121
15. The Ugly Truth About Star Search 126
16. When Comedy Was King 137
17. SNL, My Unrequited Love 142
18. A Hollywood Virgin 148
19. The Love Life of A Hapless Comedy Writer 155
20. Writing The Wrongs 160
21. A Farewell To Standup 163
22. The Birth of The Cool Comedy 167
23. Failing Up While Falling Down 174
24. Getting Fired Before You're Hired 183
25. Meet Them Before They Go, Please 188
26. Lost In A Fantasy 197
27. Futurama And My Future 205
28. The Burning Of Celebrities 213
29. I Almost Jumped 217
30. Heroes In Black-And-White 221
31. One Flew Over The Writers' Nest 225
32. So What Have We Learned? 232
Mike Rowe's Room Bits Explained 239
Acknowledgments 243
About The Author 245

FOREWORD

Bob Odenkirk

In November, 1987, I was hired as a writer at *SNL*. I wish someone had told *SNL*. Like nearly everyone else who got their big break at that storied institution, I was greeted with a kick-line of scowling faces, and the daily question, "What are YOU doing here?" - the unwelcome wagon that the show has become famous for in a billion showbiz bios. The show is notorious for offering a cold shoulder to its wide-eyed new hires, and I got the treatment. It's a place built for competition, in-fighting, fear, and intense feelings of all kinds, so I was just the latest hopeful to get the hope beat out of him.

Or maybe it was me.

I'm a pretty snarky guy. Critical. I hate a lot of things. That's one of the reasons, probably the main reason, I gravitated toward comedy. To make fun. Of you. And myself. Of everything.

But here I was in the big city, knowing almost no one, at an incredibly intimidating job where the intimidation factor seemed to grow by the day, cranked up by circumstance, and, I suspected, by the management, who must have thought that there was good motivation in everybody feeling ragged and on-edge all the time. I needed a break.

Where could I go in New York to get some love? How about a dingy, seen-better-days comedy club, located near the then-gross, scum-coated, Times Square... "The Original Improv" (not the shiny, as-seen-on-TV L.A. version). Yes, I was so bereft of love and warmth that a comedy club was a step up! That's saying something. Something sad.

But it was...a step up. The comics at the "Improv" in New York at the time – Mike Rowe, Larry David, Gilbert Gottfried, Mark Cohen, Jon Manfrellotti, among many, seemed to have a camaraderie that I did not find in the halls of 30 Rock (at least not until

Sandler and Spade showed up). This scene was unlike Chicago, as well, where I had many friends among the comics, but where there was a rougher, disinterested, backstage vibe. In New York, I was somehow supported by the other comics, who didn't bother watching my "act" – because mostly they seemed to not care all that much about each other's acts, but had more laughs and fun off to the side, or in the bar, or out on the street (there was no "backstage" at this club), shooting the shit and making *each other* laugh. Onstage, I did fine...better than I was doing at *SNL*, which is to say, I got some laughs. Relief...*I can still get a few, here and there. Okay. Maybe I'm not an abject failure*. But backstage, or, like I said, out in the street, we'd shoot the shit and I'd feel like a human being, sort of. Recognized. Of some value. Three dimensional. I also "got in" for occasional sets at "The Cellar" in the Village, and found the same vibe, if not more so. Take note...these comics could be rough on each other, but there was a connection there that I needed and was thankful to be readily included in.

Or maybe it was Mike Rowe.

Everybody liked Mike.

Like a lot of comics, Mike is funnier out of his act than he is in it. This is very common. Partly because he doesn't have to worry about hurting the other comic's sensitivities (just try to hurt another comic's sensitivities in that day and age – it couldn't be done! They had NO sensitivities!), and partly because among an audience of comics, there is such a deep appreciation of snarky, twisted, wise-assery, that every inflection and call-back, and reference point, is picked-up-on and dug-into. Mike is, as you will see, a student of comedy, who became a tenured professor before I got to New York when we were both still in our twenties. He can approach and appreciate comedy from every angle, which isn't true of every comic, and he's a nice person, which REALLY isn't true of every comic. Everybody liked Mike, and Mike was a good friend and comic confidant of everybody. His humanity didn't abandon him in the drive to conquer this twisted, sour, corner of showbiz.

Mike loves classic old school comedy stylings, as well as digging your most ground-breaking, absurdist, up-and-comer. In this way, we connect strongly. He is a one-man Friars Club, but one that would have welcomed Andy Kaufman with open arms. He can crack a corny joke, and revel in the corn like a fucking farmer in Des Moines on a July day, and he can talk about the weirdest, offbeat, comedy show from England (they were all from England until "Tim and Eric" showed up), and be just as jazzed by it. Mike introduced me around and that was all I needed to feel like a part of this scene. At least I was a part of something; it took me years at *SNL* to finally feel like I kinda, sorta, belonged there.

Mike was a friend when I needed one and we have remained friends for decades now. At some point I moved to L.A. At some point he moved to L.A. We wrote together, a funny homage to Blaxploitation films. We met Rudy Ray Moore once, together. Oh! We met George Burns once, together, too! How about that? I've known Mike so long that I have had time to evolve from a comedy wastrel into a shining beacon of dramatical artistry. At least, that's what my Mom calls me. Mike knows everyone, and is friends with everyone, and if you're not a friend of Mike's, then you need medication of some kind.

You don't get to be friends with the people Mike is friends with if you're not funny, so, the man is funny. But unlike many of us (including myself, sadly) there's more to him than just career striving. There's a real appreciation of being a part of this mad business, and I am sure you will feel it in this memoir.

WALT DISNEY IS TRYING TO KILL ME

I WAS SUITING UP for my first meeting with an actual TV showrunner. We'll call him Denny. A showrunner is the boss, and usually the creator of the show that he or she is running. Denny read my sample *Seinfeld* script (or spec script as they call it in the biz) and deemed it adequate enough to consider me as a writer for their ABC family sitcom. He asked my agent to ask me if I could meet him, face-to-face. This would help him determine if I had the comic capacity to keep up with him and his hotshot team at the "funny table." He also needed to make sure that I was a normal Joe and not a bug-infested, drug-addled vagabond. Good thing I shaved that morning.

I was considerably new to Hollywood, but not new to comedy. I had a decent ten-year run as a standup comic in New York City, and I was already on a few network and cable TV writing staffs. You, no doubt, remember these hit shows: *Hi Honey I'm Home, Nothing Upstairs, Mouth To Mouth*...No? ...Nothing? Anyway, those jobs came to me through my stand-up comedy connections. This meeting came to me by way of my amazing and world's funniest spec script.

All of the stories in my *Seinfeld* script were based on stuff that actually happened to me during my New York City days. For instance, a waitress thirty years my senior, at my favorite corner diner, The Money Tree, had an undying crush on me. She was so unrelenting that I had to stop going there, it became too awkward. Just outta bed at 12:30 in the afternoon, I'd wander in for my coffee and precious alone time with the *New York Post*. Instead, I had to deal with the waitress lingering at my booth, sharing never-ending stories about her darlin' kitty cats. After I vanished, she tracked me down and started calling me at home. So I felt like that situation was a viable story area for George Costanza and his favorite diner, Monks. Then, my bike was stolen and weeks later I saw it on a rack in front of a Chinese restaurant. It was in their fleet of food-delivery bikes. This smacked of *Seinfeld* territory. I imagined Kramer retrieving his stolen bike from a high-strung delivery boy. These stories, along with Elaine discovering her boyfriend lied about wearing a hairpiece, wove together nicely. That script opened a lot of doors for me in Hollywood. At one point, it was under consideration as an actual episode for the series. Nonetheless, it got me in the door for that TGIF interview on that day.

All I needed to do for this meeting was to muster up enough charm to sell my young self to this sitcom gatekeeper. I carefully selected my 1990s Hollywood writer's outfit; stonewashed, pleated and baggy jeans, ball cap and hip T-shirt. If you spent any time in Hollywood back then, us writer-types were easy to spot; pasty and doughy men and women shuffling lifelessly in a gaggle. That's us, squinting from the sun and hungry, as we searched, zombie-like, for the nearest sandwich hut. Most shows that I've been on lately, though, consist of polyethnic staffs, and somehow everyone's in shockingly good shape. Except, well, yours truly.

My meeting was on the Disney lot in Burbank. It felt like I was walking into an actual Disney cartoon. I was surrounded by quaint, single-story buildings, patches of green grass with smiling squirrels dashing about, and birds chirping merrily. I was instructed to go into the Dwarfs Building (political correctness wasn't as prevalent back then). It wasn't that hard to find. I spotted the seven of them, all fashioned from cement. They were positioned high up over the main entrance and looking worried as they valiantly held up the main frame of the building. As I crossed in under them, I swear I heard, "Hi-Ho, Hi-Ho/We hope you get this show."

The sitcom I was interviewing for had been on the air for a few years and was still holding a massive audience. It featured typical teens and their adult adversaries. I hadn't paid much attention to the show prior to this meeting, so I watched a few episodes the night before to collect enough recon to gush over it and carry on about how it was my favorite TV show ever. In truth, it wasn't the worst sitcom on TV, although it's not a show I would've programmed into my TiVo. Nonetheless, this was a big-deal ABC primetime sitcom. It was a much-needed steppingstone to what I hoped would be a wildly successful career as a sitcom writer. Dammit! I *had* to get this gig.

I walked through the hallowed Disney halls, wide-eyed, eager, and nervous. The walls were lined with original Disney animated movie cels. There were photos from the '30s showing animators sketching out early versions of classic Disney characters. I passed an over-sized framed portrait of Walt himself who, I swear, winked at me as if to say, "Welcome aboard, Mike!"

I found the offices where I'd meet Denny, my new boss-to-be. This job was gonna happen, I was sure of it. I mean, c'mon; I was charming, fresh-faced and, according to my mom, I was funny, so all is good. The young woman assistant at the front desk was busy wrangling a barrage of incoming phone calls. The office's white walls were covered with sit-comy posters of the cast; kids smiling mischievously while the adults shot them disapproving looks.

Typically, production offices in Hollywood are not all that glamorous, especially back in the 1990s. There were dead plants and random stacks of scripts on worn-out carpeting. Down and dirty is ideal; us writer-types clearly don't want any unnecessary distractions. These offices were our sanctuary where we rolled up our sleeves and readied ourselves to fight through hours of heated story ideas and pitch bone-crunchingly funny jokes. It was an artist's workshop where we'd plunge our hands into the comedy ball of clay and masterfully craft it into a hit, primetime TGIF sitcom.

I made my way to the assistant, who was still buried in incoming calls. I whispered, "I'm Mike Rowe...." She pulled the phone from her face and covered the mouthpiece, "Have a seat; he'll be with you shortly."

Sitting there nervously I could hear the electronics of the room buzzing; the clock, the fluorescent lights. The phone seemed to ring louder as the assistant answered it over and over, "He's not in. Can I take a message?"

Finally, Denny emerged from his private office. These moments aren't usually all that gracious. He just sort of stormed in and barked out orders to the assistant, "Call bellggyy and bavvah caaab. We need jajhh for the jabadada." Steeped in anxiety, that was all that my brain could digest. I sat there and smiled, unsure of what to do next. Do I stand? Nod knowingly? Maybe throw him a thumbs-up? Denny popped back into his office before I could decide. The assistant quietly mumbled, "It'll be a few more minutes." She went back to the ringing phones, "He's not in. Can I take a message?"

I sat there trying not to sweat as I flipped through an outdated *Hollywood Reporter*. The humming lights, I swear, adjusted themselves to a pitch designed to purposely play with my frayed nerves. After about fifteen minutes, the assistant got the call: "Yes. Okay..." She hung up and, with a painted smile, pointed to his office door: "Denny will see you now."

I was dealing with unrelenting, low-grade nervousness. It's that feeling you get just before stepping into the O.R. for minor surgery. I slinked into his office, youth-first. I was smiling, ready, and trying desperately to stay cool and calm and not let them see the pit-sweat.

Denny's office, I swear, was about the size of a drawer. It was a windowless space with floor-to-ceiling dark, 1980s wood paneling. I was standing in a casket. Denny was on the phone, harried and concerned, "Well tell Habavaa I need chachdaba right away! And I want wwhaazahaza to baba!" He hung up, looked at me and nodded. Then he yelled through the closed door, "Mary, get whishhhajayba on the phone, over at hhhezee." I heard her muzzled response through the door. He looked to me, "So what shows you work on?"

I went into my short resume while I situated myself into the hard chair, "I was on a Showtime comedy series about the Friars Club. Before that I was a standup in New York, so..."

Mary, the assistant, entered with paperwork and handed it over to Denny. I waited as he read through it, signed a page and handed it all back while telling her, "Don't let fhhavaa jaaby until 3. I'll need jimmbbco, ASAP. I have kaajabjba tomorrow." She darted out with confidence.

I kept going, "I wrote sketches for TV comedy shows in..."

The phone rang. He grabbed it, "Baaagy, fffassy kaba? ...Good." He hung up. I jumped back into my comedy bio, "But it was a great experience. I learned a lot, so..."

He was curt, "Okay, good. We wanted to see who was out there, so thanks for coming by."

Wait...What just happened? I was in that office less than one minute and I was getting the TGIF boot. I got up slowly and looked around, wondering if maybe it was a prank of some sort. It was painfully awkward. I mean, how could it not be? I mumbled as I ambled towards the door, "Uh, yeah...Okay, good. Uh...Thanks." I slunk out, lost and confused. Was my penis exposed? I checked my forehead for a carved-in swastika. When I exited the building and walked under the Dwarfs, I swear Doc shot me a look that said, "Wow, that's fucked!" I was like, "I know, right?"

I got home and called my agent to find out what happened. "Uh, yeah," he said with his pretend sad agent-voice, "Just got off the phone with Denny...Said you weren't funny."

"What...? I wasn't fu-- How could...?" No. Not cool. It wasn't right. My agent blew past this. It didn't even seem weird to him. He tossed out a perfunctory, "Don't worry, man. Onward, upward..."

Right then and there I learned a huge Hollywood comedy writer lesson: You had to go into every meeting with your funny guns a-blazin'.

Many months later, my agent called with some positive news, "Denny at Disney wants to meet you. He likes your script. He has a new series at ABC. He thinks you might be right for this." It was *him*, that same Denny, my former boss-to-be! Aw man, I am taking this meeting. I couldn't wait. I knew how this worked. I learned my lesson; I was a step ahead of the game. I was gonna load up my comedy six-shooters and go in, both guns firin'.

I hit the Disney lot and merrily headed back to the Dwarfs Building. They were still holding up the building, steadfast and unflinching. Dopey gave me a knowing nod, I was sure of it. I zipped through the same hallways, same office, same buzzing lights. Denny's new assistant escorted me right into his office. I sat down across from him at his desk. He wasn't signing anything and there were no incoming phone calls. I had his attention. With my charm at full tilt, I arranged my shirt, "Am I blousing okay...?" Snarky and charming. Nice start.

I don't actually remember what the fuck I said next to get the funny ball rolling, but I was there, I was present, and in the moment. I started yapping away with all the comedy aplomb of a Mel Brooks on Carson's *Tonight Show*.

Denny's first question, yet again: "So tell me the shows you worked on."

With huge heapings of gusto and vigor, I answered, "I was a standup comic in New York. That helped get me on staff at a Showtime series about the Friars Club. Then I wrote on a series with the creator of *Taxi*. That show's coming out this fall, so…"

He smiled as I prattled on like a boy on a first date. I had my first heavy-hitting casual-meeting joke ready to fire out of the chamber when, yep, he stopped me.

"Okay…Good. We wanted to see who's out there."

What-the-fuuuuck!? My only guess at that moment was, *"Denny is a ne'er-do-well relative of Walt's. He gave him this pretend office to conduct fake meetings so's to keep him busy and out of jail."* I left the building crushed and confused yet again. I found my way back to my car and drove home in a daze. I called my agent. He said Denny thought I wasn't right for the show. "But I talked to him for twenty seconds. I hardly got past hello."

My agent shrugged it off, "That show sucks anyway. You don't want to be on that piece of shit." I shook my head in disbelief.

That night, I hung out with my new comedy-writer friends and we laughed about my ridiculous meeting. In truth, that experience was an inflection point for me. This is where I realized that all the legendary stories about the insanity and heartlessness of Hollywood were true. Right then and there, I understood that if I didn't laugh at the ridiculousness of these insane showbiz moments, Hollywood would kill me. Or, at the very least, it would make me fat and bald.

Another year or so later, I got a call from my agent, "Denny at Disney read your script. He wants to meet with you. He's got a new series starting up."

I was angry: "*Really? Seriously?* Okay, that same fucking Denny-guy wants to meet me?!" No way he's going to make me do this dance again. If this was going to happen, it was happening on *my* terms. I signed on for the fucking meeting, but I had a plan and I *could not wait* to spring it on him. *Fuck this guy!* My strategy was simple: I'd step into his shitty little shoebox office, sit down and ask him, "So what shows have you worked on?" After about twenty seconds, I'd cut him off, stand up and coldly tell him, "Okay, I just wanted to see who's out there." Then I'd stomp off the lot victoriously. I was serious. I was ready.

Back at Disney, Dwarfs, winking Walt, buzzing lights...I sat and waited in the outer office, trying to hide my devilish smirk. I was finally called into...a different office. I stepped into a cozy room with huge windows that looked out onto a tree-lined little park. The sun was beaming down, blue birds were flitting about, squirrels were prancing happily on the tree limbs. I was in a warm and welcoming oasis where four young faces were happy to see me. They knew my resume. They didn't have to ask where I'd worked before. They commented on my spec script. They even quoted a few jokes and laughed.

Hmm, this was going to put a damper on my diabolical scheme. They apologized to me because Denny couldn't make it to the meeting, "He's in the middle of post [production]." *Great. Fuck that guy!* (Relax; I didn't say it out loud.) They asked me what I thought about their pilot. I did read it and I actually liked it -- a lot. We talked and laughed, as the Disney birds and squirrels began to sing and dance outside the window. I truly hit it off with everyone in that room.

My agent called me that afternoon. They were offering me a staff job on the series: "*Un-fucking-believable!*"

The next Monday, I showed up at the comedy round table and found the best seat (i.e., closest to the snack room), settled in with my new pencil in hand, and then Denny stepped in, "Welcome, everyone!"

DENNY! God-DAMN-it!

In the glory and excitement of getting the job, I forgot all about Denny!

My writing life was truly difficult when he showed up in the writers' room, which was often. He came in mostly to blow up our work and abandon us in the debris, expecting us to rebuild it all from scratch. The show stayed on the air for one season. This experience was indicative of what I'd go through during my comedy career. It's the roller coaster I begged to be on, and so far, it's been as harrowing, heartbreaking and as tremendous as I dreamt it'd be. So then how and why in the hell did I want to go on this ride? Well, let's take it from the top...

THE SEEDS OF FUNNY

My hometown, Waterbury, Connecticut, was once a thriving factory town. Now, after years of corrupt mayors, riots and widespread unemployment, it's a vast pit of burned-out and abandoned homes and tenements. The Brass City was its moniker from the 1940s to the 1960s, due to its wildly productive brass factories. As a kid, when my mom would drive my sisters, Tracy and Janis, and myself through downtown, I distinctly remember hearing the sounds of heavy machinery clanking and pounding through the century-old concrete walls and steel-framed windows of the massive industrial plants. My polluted hometown prided itself on manufacturing belt buckles, buttons, crescent wrenches and clock parts.

Career expectations were not all that high in Waterbury. Marry early, have some kids, get an OK paying job at the mall, a restaurant, the local tire-repair shop or some such place. Most considered that a noble way to live. I get that. Happiness through simplicity. Why not?

From around 1967 through 1970, my dad owned a bar on East Main Street, just a few miles from downtown Waterbury. He lovingly named it The Carousel. A corner tavern, to my kid-self, was the ultimate clubhouse. If my friends and I could've built a neat-o fort, this would've been it. It had that hearty stench of spilled beer and Dewar's whisky absorbed layers-deep into the soft wood of the bar. To this day, when I wander into an old neighborhood beer joint and I smell that same sweet smell, it instantly takes me back to my happy childhood, hanging with stinky and sweaty softball players, bums, pimps and alcoholics.

My dad said he named the bar The Carousel because of the semicircular shape of the bar, but I honestly think it was because he loved the movie musical *Carousel*. Many's the time I'd catch him alone on the front porch of our second-floor apartment, sitting quietly while losing himself in the LP of the soundtrack as it spun on my portable record player. It was hard to imagine that he liked musicals at all,

The Carousel (1968).

never mind having a favorite. I mean, he was a stocky, half-Italian, ex-Marine who was wounded while fighting in North Korea. He got out of the hospital, got his Purple Heart, and went back to fight overseas. So yeah, if any of his beer-swigging, gun-toting clientele asked him about the name Carousel, he'd tell 'em, "It's the shape of the bar. That's all."

The Carousel was adorned with year-round Christmas lights that hung haphazardly across the paneled walls. They lit up posters of Santana, Ali/Frazier, and crinkled Playboy centerfolds, along with assorted banners and pennants celebrating the '69 Red Sox. The bar had a jukebox that played Scopitones. They were the first attempt at music videos and were produced strictly for an adult audience. My dad refused to play them for me; they were too risqué for my tender age.

After a lot of haranguing, he eventually let me watch the tamest one, *"Yellow Polka-Dot Bikini."* A hottie in a polka-dot bikini grinded and shook her stuff, hoping to entice the schlubby food vendor for a free hot dog. The softcore pornographic imagery was lost on me. What my dad didn't realize was that I was more curious about the technology and machinery of it all; the sex and innuendo, not so much.

Elaborate breweriana touting ice-cold Budweiser, Piels and Rheingold hung on the walls and in the front windows. They were reminders that for thirty-five cents a glass, you could drink your pain away. Most of these glowing mementos of alcoholism would end up at home with me in my bedroom. My nine-year-old self would fall asleep to the comforting hum of my bedside nightlight: a spinning windmill advertising Heineken beer, imported from Holland.

Beer wasn't even a consideration for me until my late teens though. At The Carousel, I sat with the local drunks and drank myself silly with free Cokes. I played pool with pimps who, to me, were just cool black dudes. "What-up, little man?" they would ask.

It was a kid Fantasyland. I was addicted to the cowboy-themed pinball machine and the shuffle bowl that clacked and pinged and rang all night as it tallied up the strikes and spares. Typically, the bar was jammed with sweaty softball players on the heels of winning a game for my dad's beer league. These guys were twenty-somethings, just out of college for the summer and *man*, they were damn good athletes. My dad was a respected softball coach in Waterbury and had an eye for putting great bar teams together. At his peak, he assembled about eleven of them. He even played a few innings, now and again, as a slow-ball pitcher. According to league rules, the losing team was required to go to the winners' bar and buy drinks for both teams. The more The Carousel won, the better the bar business. But, with almost a dozen winning teams churning through the joint, The Carousel was still struggling.

I truly liked the players. They were silly, corny, sarcastic, and *really* funny. They especially loved to make each other laugh. One time, old, drunk Tony, a local, showed off a snapshot from his youth. Due to his lifelong bout with alcohol ("the suds" as they called it), his hand shook wildly as he held out the photo for all to see. One of the ball players took the photo and showed it to the others, shaking it as well. "Yeah, looks just like you." Everyone exploded with laughter.

"*Wow, poking fun at someone's affliction was fun,*" I thought. It was building, through laughter, an undying brotherhood right before my eyes. My dad wasn't afraid to participate, but his forte was not insults. He worked in corny jokes and puns the way some artists worked in oil or clay. When Schaefer introduced a beer can made of glass, he held it up for all to see, examined it and shot, "Hmm. Uncanny."

When you're a kid, there's nothing funnier than a hardcore pun.

Late into the 1960s, The Carousel still had hints of what it might've looked like in its heyday back in the 1940s. I distinctly remember wood cutouts of elegant top hats and martini glasses, dirty and worn out, but still attached to the back of the tattered and faded orange, gold and yellow booths. The records in the jukebox were in constant turn-around. When new hit records came in, the old ones would come home with me, so I got to play, over and over, all the Top 40 hits of the '60s and '70s. My dad demanded that the Sinatra and Dean Martin records stay in the jukebox, though. I was the hippest kid in my neighborhood "music scene," surprising friends with 45s of The Guess Who, Three Dog Night, Jackson 5, Temps and Tops, you name it. Cool, hip and funny, The Carousel was shaping little me into a sophisticated man.

My dad, steadfast behind his bar, was the captain of The Carousel. Many respected his command. In truth, he was above it all; he just didn't quite know it yet. I watched quietly as people would belly up to the bar hoping for a free shot and some comforting therapy from my dad. He would have heart-to-hearts with guys who had troubled relationships, money problems or concerns about their softball slumps.

Depression and alcoholism was a large part of the fuel that kept the lights on at The Carousel. Life's frustrations would get the best of some. They'd start fights for no reason: "Get da fuck outta here! Wille McCovey sucks!" Fists would fly. My dad, with his broom-handle bat, would dash out from behind the bar and start swinging.

A toolmaker from nearby Scovill Manufacturing was laid off without warning. He planted his ass at the bar and tried to drink himself into a better life. Way past his limit, the barmaid cut off his Cutty Sark. He felt she was mistaken and made his point with a small pistol and *Bam! Bam!* He shot drunkenly, landing a bullet in her hand. Wow! The Carousel was the Old West! Fantastic!

My dad hired a go-go dancer to perform at The Carousel on Tuesday nights at 9 p.m. How, you ask, could I possibly remember that? Damn, how could I not? Every single Tuesday night, I hoped and prayed my dad would let me stay long enough to see her get up and do her thing. The mystery of what she could be or do was all consuming. Was there nudity? Live sex of some sort? Did she read poems? *Fuck!* The more I thought about it, the more I needed to know.

One Tuesday, I saw the Schaefer Beer clock about to hit the nine o'clock hour. Typically, my dad would've had me out of the building and halfway home at this point. Did he forget? Or maybe he thought I was ready to behold the unbridled evil that was (or wasn't) going to happen? I hid partway behind the ice machine, hoping he'd forget I was there. I started to get clammy and a little woozy as the minutes ticked by.

A spotlight popped on to the little black riser up against the wall near the bathrooms. I scanned the place; my dad was nowhere in sight. Someone got behind the juke to turn the volume way up and then fed it a bunch of quarters. *Holy shit*, it was happening! I was getting scared. Maybe it'd be too much for me. I could pass out. Who knows, maybe this unknown imagery would forever taint my view of women or sex or even life itself. But there was no turning back now.

Three Dog Night's *"Mama Told Me Not To Come"* blasted out from the juke. The nine drunks in the place started to whoop.

A young woman came out of the dark and into the spotlight. She was perfect 1969 sexy, wearing scuffed white go-go boots and a green sequined bikini which really wasn't all that different than the bathing suits I saw on the beaches of Cape Cod during our family vacations. But this was different. *She* was different. I was both frightened and stimulated as I watched her dance slowly, working her body to the music. *"..that ain't the way to have fun, sonnnn!"* the song went on. Her sequins shimmied wildly as she picked up the pace. The spinning color wheel that my dad stole from our aluminum Christmas tree made her change colors, from red to green to blue. I felt my body fling into puberty. My voice even changed a few octaves in those first few minutes of what I considered to be my first sexual experience.

I was getting worried. If this was her starting point, where did she go from here? My system was already overheating. I was fevered and short of breath. Where was my dad? I started to feel abandoned. It turned out he was deep into the basement going through inventory and forgot I was there. He came back upstairs and saw his kid locked off and lost in the glory of hot, gyrating pulchritude. He dropped everything and yanked me out of there like a fireman saving a child from a burning building.

I'm still not sure why my dad exposed me to this environment at such a young age. Maybe he thought it'd toughen me up. Maybe he figured there were life lessons to be learned. Most of these nights on our car ride home, I'd hope for some sort of incisive, ethereal explanation. All I got was, "Don't tell your mother..."

My dad was raised by Nancy Petrunti, a very strict and demanding Italian mom. He told me stories of how she'd get mad at him for no real reason and often chase him around their apartment while whacking him really hard on the noggin with a giant wooden spoon. His dad, Charlie Rowe, was the complete opposite of her: Mellow, quiet and seriously funny. I remember visiting their house as a kid. My Grampie, while dead asleep, passed wind. With that, he instantly jumped off the couch and ran to look out the window. For my benefit, he played worried as he announced, "Holy Christ! Lightning just struck a shithouse!" Sadly, as a kid, my dad didn't really get to know his dad all that well. He was hardly at home, spending most days and some nights working multiple factory jobs.

My dad and his six kid sisters were expected to work as well. His first job was as a bowling-pin setter at the downtown Waterbury lanes. His mom gathered all their monies to help pay the bills, leaving my dad feeling more like an employee than a son. According to him, the only time his mom was motherly to her kids was when they were sick. It's probably why he often complained about not feeling well. It was, I'm guessing, a clarion call for motherly comfort. He was raised during the Depression, which I think left him with the feeling that he could lose everything in an instant. He was never able to shake this looming threat, so as a result, he lived much of his life worried about impending doom. Growing up, the stress from this permeated our home life and ultimately affected his marriage.

My mom, Joanne LeBlanc, had five brothers and four sisters. She was just twelve when she bravely moved down to Connecticut from Millinocket, Maine without her parents; just her older sisters. She too had a difficult childhood. When she was just six months old, her dad and his brother were on an ice fishing expedition. This took them to a lake deep in the woods of Maine where they were blindsided by a sudden and massive Nor'easter snowstorm. They tried desperately to find shelter through the blinding white snow. They were found the next day in a snow bank just a few hundred yards from their cabin. Both were dead from the freezing cold.

Like most of that generation, marriage was pretty much just one of the things you were supposed to do -- *especially* if you were a woman. You didn't question it, and no girl wanted to end up as what they used to call "an old maid." The checklist for women read: Go to school (hopefully graduate), learn a skill (as a homemaker), get married (hopefully to someone you love) and then drop some babies (and be a mother).

My dad fell in love with my mom. *She* fell in love with the idea of being in love and being married and taken care of by a capable and dutiful husband. She wasn't *IN* love with my dad, which she freely admits, but for her, thriving in a loving environment seemed like the right idea at the time.

My dad proposed to my mom a few times before she said yes. She was almost 23 and dad was 25 when they were married. Young by our standards, my mom actually *was* close to becoming a dreaded "old maid" -- perhaps another reason she felt the need to tie the knot. After two years of trying to get pregnant, my sister Tracy was born. I came along exactly one year later, on my sister's first birthday. Janis, the youngest, was born ten months later. Suddenly, my mom went from worrying she'd never have children to finding herself herding a house full of crying and cranky "Irish Triplets."

My dad lacked a college education, but he did have some toolmaking skills and was able to support his young family by working in one of the Waterbury factories, just like his dad did. In truth, there was no way my dad was going to spend his life crafting hammers at a metal lathe. Eventually the day-to-day tedium of it all became too much for him and he quit. He couldn't take it. He was suddenly flailing as he tried to find a new career that would bring some sense of accomplishment and perhaps a little joy into his life. A manageable paycheck that would take care of his new family would be pretty sweet, too. I remember him, early on, selling insurance. When that didn't work out, he partnered up in a butcher shop with an old Marine buddy. When that ended abruptly, he found work in an auto body repair shop.

These were tough rows to hoe, especially for a man who cared about how he was perceived by his peers. The "elites" he hoped to impress were his friends, the local lawyers, bankers and politicians. My dad always carried with him an unrelenting sense of pride and dignity. It was important for him to be seen as a pillar of success. This was evident at the local events, fundraisers and parties where he was the snappiest dresser, typically in his bright red or green blazers and white shoes. This was the cool, smart look of the mature adult male of the late 1960s.

John Rowe stylin' in the 60's.

His pride is what drove him to buy The Carousel and keep it up and running for almost six years. It was important to him to be seen as the owner/barkeep of the city's meeting place. He felt that the idea of owning his own business was the sign of a true entrepreneur. The bar was a struggle, but he kept up the good fight. Sadly, his deep frustration in trying to keep its lights on started to seep into our family dynamic.

At one point my dad stopped coming home. My mom told us kids that his back was bothering him again and that he found comfort sleeping on the hard, slate surface of his pool table down at the bar. He was gone for at least a few days, maybe weeks; it's hard to remember. My dad did have serious back issues that plagued him throughout his whole life, so there was no reason why my sisters and I would think this was odd. We were too young to understand that their marriage was in jeopardy.

Finally, my parents made a decision. They felt it was best that they stay married until we were older and ready to start our own lives. In retrospect, this decision may not have been the best. This dynamic brought with it a stressful household with some rage and combustibility and, at times, severe declarations of disappointment aimed at us kids. Those came mostly from my dad.

Me with Janis and Tracy (late 1960's).

My mom did her best to protect us from any verbal abuse. It was never extreme, but the subtly of it all can carry a lot of weight when it's inflicted at a tender young age. To this day, the residual stress of our childhood continues to affect my sisters and me. Luckily, Tracy, Janis and I figured out how to stay strong, find resolve, some success and happiness while struggling to stave off the remnants of those childhood demons.

Janis, since her teen days, was always surrounded by close friends. As kids, I hardly remember her being at home. She was always out and about and having a blast with her circle of pals. She was always cute, immediately likable and had a natural, quick, sarcastic wit. She's since raised an amazing daughter, Kristen, who lives in Connecticut with a young and wonderful family of her own.

Tracy has always been creative and a gifted and imaginative artist. After trying her hand at the corporate world, she soon learned that it's not where she wanted to be. She went back to school and studied theater. Not a lucrative career by any stretch, but she spent 25 years painting and designing sets in Hollywood and later in community theater in Connecticut. Like my mom, also a gifted artist who continues to win awards for her inspired oil paintings, my sister is a visual thinker.

So right about now, I bet you're asking, "Where are all the neato Hollywood stories?" Just relax a minute; I'm getting there…

As we all consider our childhoods and how they shaped us as adults, we see flashpoints or moments of clarity that help us understand who we truly are. When I was a kid, there were times when my family was truly calm, relaxed, and at their happiest. It was during our summer vacations in Cape Cod. Also, when we were crowded around the TV watching sitcoms. Those warm family gatherings started in the 1970s, during the days of the sitcoms *All In The Family, Welcome Back Kotter, MASH, Laverne and Shirley,* et al. Laughter by way of TV humor brought solace to our home. In fact, the moments where I felt most connected to my dad were while he and I sat on the couch together and watched standup comedians on TV. Our eyes would lock in on our fuzzy, color Zenith watching and screaming-laughing at Don Rickles: "Great, I'll drop my pants and light off a rocket." Norm Crosby: "Thank you for that standing ovulation," Charlie Callas: "Fert-fert!" and especially Henny Youngman: "Our anniversary my wife says, 'Take me somewhere I've never been before.' I said, 'How 'bout the kitchen?'" So at every facet of my kiddom, I was feeling and absorbing the bonding and healing power of comedy.

My mom and dad, in the middle of one of the worst periods of their marriage, went to see Mel Brooks' movie, *Blazing Saddles*. To them, it was the funniest movie ever made. They laughed their asses off every time they recounted, for friends and family, the campfire farting scene. It gave me hope that humor might reinvigorate their marriage.

Armed with the knowledge that comedy created calm, I tried it when the school bully waited to kick my ass on my walk home. He randomly picked me from the F. J. Kingsbury schoolyard and decided I'd be his next target. He warned me that it was time to "toughen up" as he menacingly closed in on me. I asked, unknowingly like Woody Allen, "Is it okay if I run home first for a change of clothes? These are new pants. If I rip 'em, my mom will kill me." He laughed and threw a light sucker punch to my shoulder. I ran home. He never bothered me again.

That was it! The power of humor was undeniable.

From then on, I became a joke collector the way kids at that age collected baseball cards. I admit I spent way too much time alone in my bedroom. Clicking through every of one of the four channels on my black-and-white portable TV, I was in search of anyone and anything that resembled a joke. Shy and awkward, I was gathering funny lines to memorize and tell in school and I needed them bad. Friendship, allegiance and respect through comedy; that was my m.o. at Kingsbury Elementary School. It was becoming clearer that jokes were my portal to friendships with the cool kids, the bullies, the 8th graders and, on occasion, the teachers. Comedy was power and I needed a source of undeniably funny stuff every damn school day.

When times were desperate, I'd even settle for jokes from *Mr. Goober*, the local morning kids show. A lovable thirty-something-year-old grandpa, with his wire-rim glasses, overalls, porkpie hat and a fuzzy, glued-on old codger-type white mustache, he'd fool us into thinking he was an actual old man. With the help of his band of puppets and misfit neighbors, he'd spread good morning wishes, happy birthdays and silly fun to us eight to thirteen-year-old kids as we got ourselves dressed for school. He was an overly happy old duffer with corny one-liners. Talking on his hand-cranked phone to set up his dentist appointment, he'd joke, "He's not there? Then who's filling in?" -- a line I still use at every opportunity.

At six o'clock every day, *Mr. Goober*, sans overalls, glasses and glued-on mustache, would reveal himself as Mike Warren, anchor for the local TV news. Confident and in command, he'd report on the local robbery of a downtown Hartford appliance store or some other news item. Years later, I performed on his afternoon talk show, *12 O'Clock Live*, a show that was, in fact, *LIVE*. There I was, on camera, standing alone doing observational jokes to no one in an echoey cavern of a studio for five long minutes. Regrettably, the show was broadcast to all of my relatives and everyone I'd ever met in my young life. I didn't care though: I got to be on TV with *Mr. Goober's* Clark Kent.

I was also building a joke arsenal from the fast-paced topical sketch show *Rowan and Martin's Laugh-In*, comedy records, sitcoms, old-time comedians from TV, and dirty jokes overheard in my dad's bar.

My comedy excavations continued into my teen years. I skipped the whole drinking and pot-smoking phase; jokes and goofy gags were my drug of choice. I was a comedy explorer. George Carlin, Steve Martin, Lenny Bruce and Franklyn Ajaye were my first hip '70s comedy records. I played those suckers over and over in my basement bedroom until they became a part of my DNA. I communicated to my friends in comedy-speak, "Yo, what'd it be like if Mickey got high at Disneyland?" My voice would go up as if Mickey were a slick 70's black dude, high on dope. "What up, Pluto? Slap me four!" Normal teens, back then, were partying and listening to classic rock LPs from Foghat and *Frampton Comes Alive*. I was alone spinning comedy records or glued to the TV watching popular talk and music shows like Merv Griffin, Johnny Carson, or *The Midnight Special*, searching for standup comedy.

Norm Crosby's Comedy Shop, a standup show hosted by, coincidentally, malaprop comic Norm Crosby, featured early appearances by Jay Leno, Jeff Altman and George Miller, among others. To me, they were the inspirational new breed; all were original, undeniably funny, and still honing their style in the L.A. comedy clubs. I captured them with my little cassette recorder and listened to them over and over, letting their comedy-speak and musicality seep permanently into the deepest recesses of my brain. These recordings became my master class in comedy.

I had yet to tell a single joke in front of an audience, but I was already imagining my national TV standup comedy debut. After my killer set on Carson's iconic, late-night *Tonight Show*, Johnny would, no doubt, wave me over to sit with him at the panel -- Johnny's highest compliment. Swingin' singer, Sammy Davis Jr., who I imagined as his other guest, would greet me and, with his cig hangin' from his fingers, pat me really hard on the shoulder and tell me, through his laugh, "Wow. You're a funny cat, man!" I was figuring out that if you did great for Johnny, you'd be launched from some dusty comedy club into the world of stardom.

Frustrated at my lack of practical experience, I was swelling up like a deer tick from absorbing so much of the comedy around me. I had to release funny from my system or I was going to pop. I was jonesing for my first big swing at standup. I *had* to somehow get up and tell jokes on a real stage in front of a living, breathing audience!

HOLLYWOOD & ROWE

It's 1978, my senior year at Warren F. Kaynor Regional Vocational High School. The halls were abuzz with chatter about the upcoming talent show. The lunch lady was gonna sing, the carpentry students were crafting a comedy sketch, the cool dudes on the basketball team had something, well, "cool" up their sleeves. What about *class clown* Mike Rowe? Where's the wannabe standup in all this?

I was hiding. My first time doing standup was NOT going to be in front of the entire student body.

My civics teacher took umbrage at this. He stopped me in the hall, grabbed me by the shirt collar, waved his finger in my face and demanded that I sign up for it "...and tell some of your goddamn jokes." He recognized my need. After all, he dealt with it every day in his classroom. I was that student in the back of the room firing off heckles in his general direction. Oddly, he would never shut me down. I was never disruptive, really. I'd pick my spots and deliver quick sharp hits off of something he'd say and it'd generate sweet laughs. He, basically, was Mr. Kotter from the '70s TV hit, *Welcome Back Kotter*, I was a little bit of every one of the Sweathogs.

There were nuggets like, "Mr. Rowe, what can you tell the class about the Louisiana Purchase?"

"It has a nice beat. It's easy to dance to."

Everyone erupted. Okay, sure, the classroom was an easy room, but still, it was intoxicating. Once I got a taste of the nectar of acceptance that a room full of laughter brings, I couldn't stop myself. Every school day, I'd leave his classroom dizzy, feverish and high from the adrenaline rush that comes from shooting off one-liners to a white-hot audience.

When discussing Napoleon, I raised my hand, "Yes, Mr. Rowe, question?"

Almost like Sweathog Arnold Horshack, I wondered, "Uh, yeah. When was the War of 1812?"

The room exploded with laughter.

This, you see, is why my teacher would have had me killed if I didn't perform in that talent show. But no way. Faced with actually living out my dream and getting on stage in front of real people suddenly seemed very wrong to me. It would be a mistake; I was sure of it!

In truth, fear was doing what it could to push me away from this opportunity. I soon realized that I couldn't let fear win. If I did, it would win every time.

So I was set to do my first-ever standup gig in the Kaynor Tech talent show. I was scared shitless. I had a few weeks to cobble something together, which really wasn't enough time. There was no turning back. I was committed. Students and teachers were stopping me in the halls, cheering me on, all expecting great things. A girl, for the first time ever, actually stopped me in the cafeteria to talk to me about it. Well, it was Judy Deleo and she had chronic chapped lips and Level 8 B.O., but still.

Panicked, I went to my cassette recordings. I decided I'd steal a few minutes of a Freddie Prinze routine. Freddie was pretty near my age and on the verge of super-comedy-stardom, so who better to steal from? I had to; his act was proven and already honed. Of course, I'd skip most of the parts about being a Puerto Rican. Freddie was the security blanket I needed to get up on that stage. The rest of my set needed to come from my own head.

I did a deep scan of my memory banks, trying desperately to remember stuff I'd said or done with my friends that garnered laughs. Carson! The guys in my electronics class laughed at my Johnny Carson impression. Okay -- I could do that!

Sitting at the cafeteria lunch table, I yucked it up with my fellow radio/TV repair nerds. I was commenting on the girls from fashion-design class as they walked by our table, "How's she walk in those giant platform shoes? If she trips, her fake eyelashes'll break the fall." The guys laughed. It's going into the act.

Brian, a classmate, saw my struggle to find original "funny." He reminded me about something I said that got a laugh: "My parents sent me to a vocational school so they'd know what kind of work I'd be out of." If Brian thinks it's funny -- it's goin' *in*!

I kept fishing around for thoughts, ideas and jokes and finally felt that I had enough to build out a full set. Night after night, I stood in my basement bedroom and talked into a broom handle as if it were a microphone. I repeated, out loud, my collection of gags, impressions and Freddie Prinze bits, trying my best to shape a hefty bowl of word salad into some form of cogency.

Show night. The Kaynor Tech cafeteria was packed with students, teacher and parents. My mom and dad were there, but to this day, my mom reminds me that she didn't alert friends and relatives about my premier. I was a quiet kid around the house, so she couldn't, for the life of her, imagine me taking command of a room full of people and getting them to laugh. She saw disaster on my horizon and figured, why bring in others to get singed by my horrific crash and burn?

The show was a hodgepodge of wild and esoteric moments. The guys on the basketball team dressed as cheerleaders and pom-pommed around the stage. They clumsily formed a human pyramid and toppled into a heap. There were singers – so many singers. The civics teacher -- the one who made sure I signed up for this show -- shot up from the back of the cafeteria and onto the stage as Elvis. He gyrated to *Hound Dog* in a green jumpsuit, to the delight of the students, especially the lunch ladies. I was cast as an extra in a comedy sketch written and performed by our electronics shop. I remember nothing about it except that the lead player, my friend Bill Hollywood (his real name) was undeniably hilarious.

I was next, right after Shelly Campner's "jazz dance." This was going to be it: my first time on stage as a stand-up comic. I was about to lose my comedy virginity and, as it goes when one loses their virginity, I was expecting buckets of nervous sweating, some crying, ending with a pathetic apology.

I hit the stage and instinct took over. I got into my Freddie Prinze routine, "There are no Puerto Rican astronauts. That's 'cause all the way to the moon, they'd blow the horn and play the radio." It went over great. Why wouldn't it? It killed when Freddie did it on *The Midnight Special*. I went into some of my own jokes, then segued into Johnny Carson, "It was so cold, I saw Karl Malden wearing TWO hats." The Kaynor crowd liked it all, bless their hearts. They were reacting, I think, to how I carried myself: Noticeably slick and somewhat professional. It came from the hundreds of hours I spent studying each and every aspect of comedy. My six minutes felt like five seconds. When I got off the stage, I basked in the glory of what would be the first of countless times I'd strut before a room full of strangers, trying with all of my comedy might to win their laughs.

I was still spinning. I just took the hardest first step into an impossible fantasy world. My parents were surprised, excited, and delighted about my performance. My mom said she didn't recognize who I was up there. She wondered where her quiet boy went to for all of those five minutes.

So, for all intents and purposes, my comedy life had officially started -- but then what? As a freshly minted standup in a small town, I had nowhere to go.

The Ground Round, a local burger and beer joint, was holding a talent contest. The winner would take home fifty bucks, a Ground Round T-shirt, and an ice cream float served in a small baseball helmet (your team of choice)! This was my opportunity to try standup in the truest sense of the form; in front of a room full of people who didn't know me or care about me. Despite my successful turn at Kaynor's *Talent Night '78*, I was still worried about getting in front of a real audience. I wasn't sure what to do.

I remembered how funny Bill Hollywood was in that comedy sketch. Hmmm, well there *is* safety in numbers. I cajoled Bill into signing on to the contest with me as my comedy partner. The team of Hollywood & Rowe was born!

Bill and I quickly built up an act together. It was a solid premise that utilized my ability to do dopey vocal sound effects with my mouth. I was able to recreate sirens, drums and exploding bombs. When hanging with friends, they were always delighted when I'd reproduce a siren so loud that drivers in passing cars would pull over and wait for an emergency vehicle that was never coming. Yeah, I'm gifted. Anyway, for a premise I thought, there are too many commercials on TV, so what if during a national emergency, the Emergency Broadcast System was interrupted by stupid commercials? Not a bad premise for a high-school kid.

During this time in my life, I was wholeheartedly into a sweet relationship with my high-school girlfriend, Suzanne. She was truly smart, creative and very patient with my comedy obsession. She, in fact, became a sounding board for Bill and me and helped us shape our comedy routine.

Suzanne and I met through mutual friends as sort of a blind date. My friend Bob lived in the same tenement as his cousin Doreen, Suzanne's friend. She figured Suzanne and I would make a nice couple, so she masterminded a night out with the four of us. When I got to Bob's apartment and met Suzanne, I instantly thought, "She is adorable and out of my league." In truth, this feeling took the pressure off. I decided that she'd have no interest in dating me, so I had nothing to lose. I was relaxed and ready to just have a fun night out with some friends.

I took everyone to The Lake Drive-In to see the low-budget exploitation movie, *Food of the Gods*. It was about rats that ate nuclear waste that inexplicably seeped from the hillsides of the city. This caused them to mutate into giant rats that assaulted an entire (cheap model of a) city. Actually, they really didn't do much; they just sort of hung out as rats do. Eventually, we all ended up lying out on the hood of my car. The movie was so dumb and horrible, my comedy instincts kicked in and I started heckling the rats. I just got on a roll and I had everyone laughing, especially Suzanne -- so much so that at one point, I felt everything change (at least in my mind). I looked at her and I could tell she thought I was adorable. The power of laughter comes though again. We started dating right away and little did she know she was about to get seriously caught up in the whirlwind of my showbiz fantasy.

Suzanne was at my side as Bill and I, in his living room, rehearsed our routine over and over. When we hit the infamous Ground Round stage, we were more than ready. We were the Skiles and Henderson of Waterbury (Google them). Bill Hollywood, with his fluffy red Afro and freckled face, yelled out the emergency announcements. My mouth created a cacophony of mayhem; blaring sirens, emergency vehicles zipping by and bombs blowing up around us.

Bill would throw it to a commercial and the chaos stopped cold. I was suddenly in a TV testimonial as a hapless white-trash dope praising a correspondence school that taught you how to drive a tractor-trailer "in the privacy of your own home!" I mimed driving an eighteen-wheel rig around the living room, breaking furniture and crashing through kitchen walls. Then, after more bombings and siren sounds, I would (slightly) transform into Elvis for a record offer featuring songs that he recorded *after* he was dead. I was an enchanting seventeen-year-old tour de force.

Hollywood and Rowe killing it at Waterbury's Ground Round Restaurant (1977).

I noticed, as we performed, that people from the bar side were pouring into the room, wondering where the racket was coming from. Then the cooks and waitresses had stopped what they were doing to watch us. I saw pockets of people forming around the room, watching, smiling and laughing. Excitement was building. I saw all of those laughing faces and figured right then and there that our super-stardom was imminent. That night, we were, no doubt, going to be whisked off the stage and put onto a jet and sent to Hollywood and right into our very own primetime TV sitcom. The routine ended with me imitating the sounds of the world blowing up. Bill and I flew off the stage, propelled by the mighty force of a standing ovation.

It would be the only one in my entire forty-whatever-year career.

I vaguely remember the others in competition with us on that night; a magician, some fat guy imitating Tom Jones, a folk singer with his clunky, acoustic-guitar version of *Amy* by Pure Prairie League. The host, in his powder-blue leisure suit, ambled to the stage to announce the winner. I was sitting nervously in the audience, like Richard Dreyfuss on Oscar night. We were a shoo-in, right? My mouth was already tasting that sweet Red Sox helmet full of ice cream. The place grew quiet: "Annnd the Ground Round winner is..."

We lost to the fat Tom Jones.

You know what? Fine. Whatever. Because, seriously, no matter what, losing did not take away from our audience reaction. In truth, my life changed that night. My desire to do standup comedy was fully injected into my DNA. There was no turning back. Oh, and by the way, that night, Hollywood & Rowe were still awarded the Ground Round T-shirts and they booked us to perform our nutty skit once a week for eight weeks at fifty bucks a pop! So Tom Jones can suck it!

Believe it or not, Hollywood & Rowe wasn't whisked away from Waterbury, Connecticut to TV stardom that night. After a summer of gigs at The Ground Round, Bill readied himself for an honorable career in electrical engineering and a blissful life

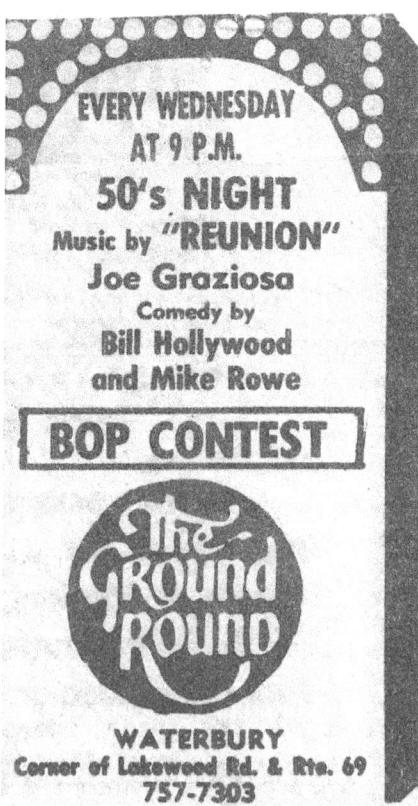

You've got to start somewhere...

with Katherine, his lovely high-school sweetheart. A Hollywood & Rowe breakup was inevitable. Just like when Dean and Jerry split, the country was about to be heartbroken all over again.

It was time for me to go it alone.

DYING ALONE

Throughout most of my teen years, I'd stay up late at night in my paneled basement bedroom to watch Johnny Carson's *Tonight Show*. For me, it was all about the comedians. Who was gonna step out and give kid-Rowe a six-minute master class in the art of standup? Carlin? Robert Klein? Pryor? Shit man, I was so hungry for "the how of funny," I'd settle for comic actor Tony Randall with a snide bon mot about his escapades in the theater world. There's a lesson in every titter.

I'd sit within radiation distance of my '70s color TV, the cassette microphone ready to capture my favorite comics on tape. I'd replay the recordings over and over, dissecting the beats, pauses and laughs. Every joke was a project to be pulled apart and examined and rebuilt the same as I did with TVs and radios.

I used to pull junked TVs out of the dumpsters at the TV repair shops around Waterbury. I'd take them home and, with the electronics know-how I acquired from Kaynor Tech, I'd Frankenstein them together until they were in working order.

In fact, I ended up in a trade school, because academic testing showed my parents and me that I was not college material. I was advised by advisors that if I were to have a successful life, I should consider a career in fixing shit. They -- whoever "they" were -- cautioned that if I reached for anything loftier, I'd likely fail and end up a drunk, living in a rock crevice on the banks of the Naugatuck River. So I got the message.

I took the entrance exam for Warren F. Kaynor Regional Technical High School along with a few hundred others. Sitting in the gym and scribbling away at answers on the test, I was asked to figure out stuff I'd never had to deal with in my life. Like, if one gear turns one way which way does the third gear turn? If the fulcrum is 1/3rd between two unbalanced weights, what's the midpoint weight of the... well, you get the idea.

I passed the test.

Freshman year, we were assigned to our homerooms based on our exam score and our career potential in the manly world of fixing and building.

My homeroom assignment? 1-F! The gym teacher's office. The lowest of the low. Apparently my advisors' assessment of me was quite accurate.

Mr. Rice, the P.E. teacher, was also our math instructor. It was his role in between coaching intramural games in the nearby gym. We were a class of ten deficients jammed into a small room that was thick with the hearty stank of Phys Ed. teacher B.O. Most in my class chose auto repair as their major. They spent more time sniffing gas than fixing cars.

Electronics, as you guessed, was my game. As a kid, I loved watching my grandfather fix TVs and radios in his basement. He'd mostly shake and bang them around, hoping to snap it awake like you would a boxer after he drops to the canvas.

In truth, at Kaynor Tech, I didn't care so much about learning a trade. I had my life already figured out. I was going to be a hilarious, ma'fuckin' standup comic!

On the night of a very special *Tonight Show*, I warned my sisters not to wander down to my bedroom. My favorite comic was going to be on and I was going to record his set, so I didn't want any talking, laughing or noises fucking it up. This tape was going to be a keeper in the Rowe Comedy Cassette Archives.

The comic, *my guy*, was a masterful joke teller. Pure, crisp, fast and blunt. Each line was a marvel for this wide-eyed comedy nerd. I had already tape-recorded a ton of his appearances and played them over and over, burning them into my kid-brain. I'd memorize the best jokes, then serve them up with ease to friends, pretending I was off-the-cuff funny. Sure, I was a teen doing jokes about my wife and my lawyer, but who cares? A joke's a joke.

Johnny, tapping his pencil on his coffee cup, couldn't wait to bring him out. I readied my cassette recorder, "Ladies and gentlemen, a guy who gets no respect...Rodney Dangerfield." The band kicked in as Rodney nervously charged out from behind the curtain and hit the comedy-ground running.

He pulled on his tie, looked out with his bulging eyes and had at it: "Story of my life, I get no respect. No respect at all! Found out my wife was faking orgasms. Four of my friends told me. I tell ya, I'm not a good-looking guy. Halloween, kids give *me* candy. Oh was I ugly. My old man took me to the zoo. The guy at the gate thanked him for returning me."

After six minutes of rapid-fire, killer one-liners, Rodney made his way over to Johnny at the panel. Carson was still laughing. Rodney sat down and dove right back in. "I just stopped smoking, ya know? I made a deal with my wife. We only smoke after sex. I got the same pack from 1975. My wife, she's up to three packs a day!"

Johnny, in a rare moment, got Rodney to talk about his real life. He joked about his nightclub, Dangerfield's, in Manhattan and then reminisced about his early comedy career as a comedian in the Catskill resorts where he went under the name Jack Roy.

The gears in my trade school head spun and recognized an opportunity. I could send a letter directly to Rodney at Dangerfield's in New York! If I addressed it to Jack Roy, it'd definitely get his attention. This was real. I had to do it and it had to count. I came up with a plan...

I pulled out my mom's rickety manual typewriter and pecked out two pages of hard-hitting Rodney gems, "I knew my wedding wasn't going to work out. The wedding march they played taps." Okay, maybe not gems, but I mailed the jokes off to Jack Roy at Dangerfield's anyway.

Weeks went by and, of course, there was no response. I forgot I even sent them. Then, one night, our phone rang. My mom yelled from the top of the stairs, "Mike. There's a Rodney on the phone for you." Before I could even think about what was and wasn't possible, I picked up the extension and squeaked out my hello. His unmistakable voice boomed back at me, "Yeah, Michael, it's Rodney. How you doin'? You okay? You all right?" I couldn't speak or breathe. He carried on about how much he liked my jokes, "...but I can't use 'em. They're not right for me, but they're good." He kept talking, telling

```
(1) My wife had an affair with an Allstate Insurance
    man...now she knows why their the good hands people.
(2) After I made love with my wife she said..."Hurry
    and get dressed,my husband will be home.
(3) Gas is so expensive I started driving my lawnmower
    to work.
(4) I was at a singles bar,I asked a girl for a date,
    she said,.." June 6,1967!
(5) My wife found red lipstick on my collar...she thought
    I had an affair with Ronald McDonald.
(6) My wife and I made love all night long...Boy,did I
    miss her!
(7) Even at resturants I get no resepct,the Hostess had
    a sign up,It said"Please wait for a seat!" I waited
    while she set up a lawnchair in the parking lot.
(8) Some girls say I'm so ugly they should name a birth
    control device after me.
     I was at an amusement park,they had one of those
     Haunted Mansions,the fello would'nt let me in...
(9) he said I'd scare away all the customers.
(10) I was at a nude beach...Iget arrested for indecent
     exposure.
(11) I knew my marriage was'nt going to work out,
     during the wedding march they played taps.
(12) At my age it's hard to satisfy my wifes needs,so she
     bought one of those French Style Massagers,he
     would'nt pay for part of the rent so I threw him
     out
(13) My wife has a lot of class,she sits crossed-legged
     on the back of a motorcycle.
(14) I once had a jealous girl friend,we'd walk through
     Macy's and I'd look at a manaquin and she say"What
     do you want a date with one!!"
```

The first draft of my jokes for Rodney.

seventeen-year-old-me in my paneled basement bedroom to keep writing, "You're a funny kid, ya know?"

I told him I wanted to do standup and he told me about the showcase clubs, The Improv, Catch A Rising Star, Comic Strip, "...but don't come to my club; it's no good." He prepped me for the heartache that comes with chasing such a fucked-up dream. Soon after, he sent a handwritten letter, warning me again. It took him years to discover his "funny."

In essence, Rodney saw enough talent and drive in me that he was pushing me to fight the good fight. It was the encouragement I needed to go it alone.

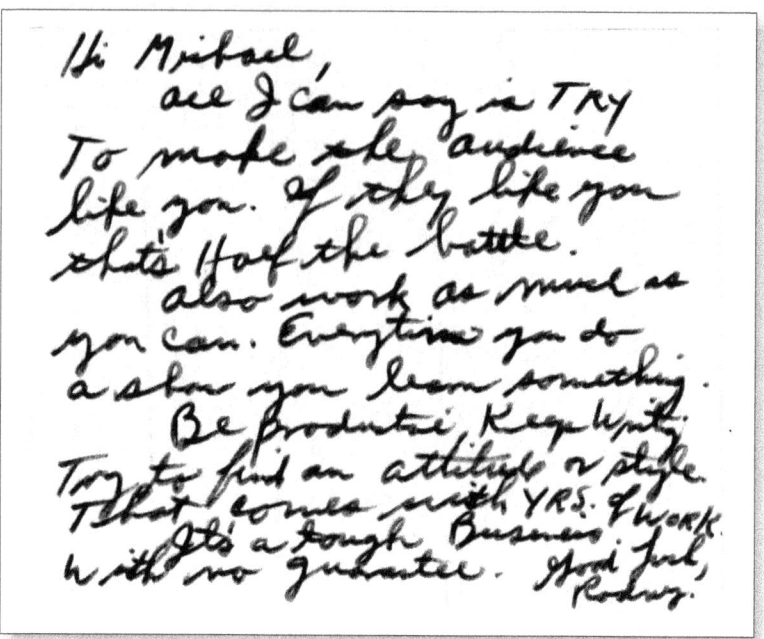

Words of inspiration from Rodney.

    I gathered the best jokes of Hollywood & Rowe and cobbled them with whatever lines my little comedy-head could think of. Some jokes I stole inadvertently. It was allowed, I thought, at those formative stages.

    Sans partner, I would wander into any and every club, bistro, bar and steakhouse in Waterbury that featured a live band. Then, I would find the manager and make a pitch for me to go onstage during the band break. I assured him or her that I had wildly funny jokes to tell. I didn't want money, no free meal, no baseball hat filled with ice cream. I just wanted to get in front of a room full of people and figure out how to be funny -- all by myself. Ninety percent of the time, they would roll the dice and let me go up and do my thing.

    These experiences were sometimes challenging and fun, but more often than not they were hell. Audiences were never mean, really. They would just glance up at me from their cocktail and think that I was a quirky employee who wandered in from the kitchen. I didn't mind. It was all just a reminder of what Rodney told me; it was going to take a long time to discover what's funny about me -- or even if, in fact, I was funny at all.

I eventually stumbled upon a tavern called Misty's. They were brave enough to feature live jazz one night a week. Who cared about jazz in a small factory town, or anywhere for that matter (except me)? This joint, I could tell, attracted people who would wholeheartedly tune in and listen to a standup comic. They liked jazz. To me that meant they were open-minded. This could be a prime place for me to learn my craft. I cornered the owner and cajoled him into giving me a shot under his blue spotlight. He told me to come back in a week, "...and we'll see what we can do for ya."

I spent the next week carefully honing my little jokes alone in my bedroom. I aimed the punchlines toward my surrogate audience -- the Marx Brothers poster on the wall. Finally, Sunday night came around and I flew to Misty's on the wings of Pegasus. Actually I drove in my rusted-out '71 Olds, but still...

I made my way into the dark, blue-lit hallway and headed towards the restaurant/showroom. The joint was more like a wedding hall with an impressively long, winding bar. I was greeted with a wave of snappy, live music flying out from the main room. Trumpets, trombone, sax, all blaring mightily.

A smiling old dude strummed cheerfully on a guitar, a middle-aged woman stared out, lost in the music as she squeezed on an accordion. The music was infectious, bouncy and undeniably Italian. The singer was not bad in that old-school, Louis Prima kinda way. The lyrics were Italian and sounded to me like he was singing the menu from a spaghetti bistro. He was, in fact, Italian. Near-middle age, no-neck, barrel-chested and wearing a white tux, he was wildly energetic, engaging and entertaining as hell.

A spotlight followed him around the room as he pulled ladies up from their tables and away from their husbands and danced them around merrily. It was a party, a celebration of life, Italian style. The singer, it turned out, was Nick Apollo Forte, the soon-to-be star of Woody Allen's movie, *Broadway Danny Rose*. In the film, he basically played himself; a kinda-talented singer who was hoping to hit the big time with the help of a misguided talent agent, played by Woody. Nick, as it turned out, was born and raised in my hometown. He was a favorite and a must-see in the local music scene. After a flash of success from Woody's movie and some self-sabotaging career decisions, he ended up back in Waterbury singing in the local clubs and gin mills.

Nick finished his set with *Agita*, a bouncy song he wrote based on his neverending battles with his digestive system. It was actually featured in Woody's movie. The club owner ran up and grabbed the mic. He stood under a blue spot above the bar, slick with confidence. It seemed like he was close, personal friends with everyone in the room. There were old, dressed-up heavyset Italian couples, some mob-looking guys in cheap suits and a few "dames" at the bar. This was not the hip jazz crowd I remembered from the week before. The owner/emcee was out of a Martin Scorsese movie. He had a tough-guy, Joe Pesci thing about him. "Awright, you jamokes ready to laugh or what?" They grumbled and heckled back. "Hope you ain't tellin' no jokes" someone yelled back, to a smattering of laughter. "We gotta Waterbury kid here for ya. Ya mighta seen him at The Ground Round. He says he's funny." He pointed me out in the back of the room, "Ya ready to make deeze goofballs laugh?" They turned around to see who he was talking to, surprised that there was an actual comic, such as I was, coming up to tell jokes. This was way before there were comedy clubs in every other building in every city. "Mike's comin' up to the bar. Get up here, Mike!"

Apparently, I was supposed to lean on the bar like it was 1969 and I'm on Hefner's *Playboy After Dark*. Okay. Fine. I'm working out with comedy weights, I reminded myself. I grabbed the mic and had at it. I did my impression of hokey bandleader Lawrence Welk as a proctologist and pretended to shove a conductor's baton up a patient's ass. We're talkin' A-plus stuff. The people laughed, though. They would chime in too, as if I were hanging out in their living room: "Oh, dat's what dat thing's for." More laughs. I talked about how setting up a hair appointment was like calling a prostitute. Pretending to be on the phone I said, "So I'd like Gina at three. And how much is a tease and a blow?" I spotted Nick Apollo laughing in the back of the room, I was finding a nice comedy groove. The ten minutes flew by and I had a blast. I thanked the audience, pushed myself away from the bar and headed off to the back of the room. These people were sweet, supportive. It felt like I just performed at a cousin's wedding.

Nick cornered me in the bar and told me he liked me and thought I was funny. He said that every once in a while he worked in New York City and told me about the comedy clubs he visited while he was there. He mentioned the same places that I talked about with Rodney, including The Improv at West 44th and 9th Ave. Nick, who'd witnessed these comics firsthand, thought that I was ready to be on the roster in those clubs.

Wow, really? And how in the hell could I possibly make that happen?

Not long after that I saw "my buddy" Freddie Prinze cohosting *The Mike Douglas Show*, a late-afternoon chat show. He told us about his hangout, The Improv, where he would do standup every night. He showed film clips of comics doing their thing in front of a shabby brick wall with a clumsily hand-painted sign hung behind them that read "*IMPROVISATION.*" "There it is!" I yelled out to no one. "That's the place!"

The Improv was the first standup comedy club ever. It started in New York City in 1963 as a late-night coffee house where Broadway actors could hang out after their shows. Soon, the actors got up and performed for each other. Comics who couldn't get stage time in the Greenwich Village rooms migrated uptown to The Improv. Robert Klein and my new pal, Rodney Dangerfield became the first regular comics to grace that stage. As the '70s rolled in, The Improv attracted a new wave of young comedians. They were energized by the influx of standup comedy that started to flood the TV screens. We were introduced to hour-long standup comedy specials on HBO, where we got to see Robin Williams, Robert Klein and George Carlin in their full glory. The fledgling *Saturday Night Live* introduced us to Steve Martin and Andy Kaufman.

On *The Mike Douglas Show*, Freddie introduced us to Alan Bursky, a friend, former roommate and a comic from the L.A. Improv. Thanks to Freddie, this was his national TV debut. At only 19 years old, Alan was poised, funny and on point. He nailed his appearance and it made Freddie proud.

"Wait," I thought. "Alan's a teenager. And if a teenager can do standup comedy on national TV with Mike Douglas and Freddie

Prinze, then why can't I?" That was it! I ran into our kitchen, cornered my mom and told her that I was moving to New York City to launch my comedy career at The Improv, and, with any luck, Freddie Prinze is gonna help me do it. I would have packed up and left home that very night, but I figured it was best that I finish high school first. My mom listened to my plan and nodded politely. She humored me, you know, as moms do when their kids tell them things like; I wanna be a cowboy or an astronaut or a ballerina. I wasn't deterred, though. I was dead set on making this comedy-thing happen.

Then reality reared its ugly head…

THE LAUNCHING PAD

Perhaps my mom was right. Striving to be a professional stand-up comic was as about as silly as saddling up to be a cowboy. My dream was like every kid-dream, except most fantasized about a life in professional sports or as a rock star. The odds were always impossible. The more I understood how the world worked, the more I realized that my dream was just the folly of youth, nothing more. Like everyone else around me, I realized that it was time for me to wake up to reality and adhere to the straight and narrow. I convinced myself that it was time to stop fantasizing about a far-fetched career in showbiz. It was time to grow up and start my real life, which meant focusing on Kaynor Tech High School.

I went into Kaynor Tech at the bottom ten percent. I tested below average even for a trade school. On paper, it looked as though, if lucky, I might land a career as a crossing guard or a parking lot attendant or, worse, a gym teacher who taught high school math at a trade school. Then everything changed. I don't know how it happened. I didn't push for it. I blindly did my schoolwork and, without much fanfare, during my sophomore year, I was put into homeroom 2-A (no subtleties in ranking system here). I jumped to the top ten percent and was assigned to the classes with other high-functioning students. In fact, during my sophomore year, I became so adept at fixing TVs, I was hired to work part-time after school at a Waterbury TV repair shop. I hadn't yet graduated high school and I somehow escaped the lowly fates that were presented to me.

Right after I graduated, in 1978, I stumbled onto a terrific career opportunity at an aeronautics plant that designed and developed digital meters for military planes. This, I thought, could be a sweet job and potentially a great place to spend my entire engineering career. This is where, after twenty years of excellent service, I would honorably receive a gold watch. A job at this company seemed like a smart idea. This was it. I was toeing the line. Ta hell with the comedy-thing.

At my job interview, I was primed and ready to impress my potential bosses. I had my neatly typed resume, a nicely ironed shirt, corduroy pants and my dad's wingtip shoes. I was walking into this with the poise of a middle-aged man. I was ready. I felt like this job was mine to lose. I talked to the head of the company about my experience in the work force and my high-school electronics education. I was charming. Well, as charming as an 18-year-old could be. My new boss-to-be was warm, engaged and, I thought, somewhat impressed. I immediately felt like a welcome member of the airplane-digital-meter family. As I looked around and considered where my office should be, the interviewer pulled out a five-page math test and a thirty-six-function calculator.

"Would you mind taking a math test for us?"

I heard screaming from inside my head: "No! No way!" First of all, my electronics specialty was more tactile; I'd repair TV and radios more like my grandfather did, by banging its insides around. I was good-but-not-great when it came to the nuts and bolts of math and electronics theory. Honestly, I took electronics class in high school to learn how to fix TVs mainly so I could watch them. I used to scavenge busted-up sets from around the shop and jerry-rig them into some sort of working order so my fellow classmates and I could watch *Happy Days* reruns in the middle of a school day. When asked, I'd tell our teacher that we were "monitoring" it to make sure it didn't spark out and implode.

But take the math test I did. It was brutal. Sweating, I found myself feverishly calculating the differences between series and parallel circuits and how they inversely react to changes in current and resistance. Then I had to find how the variance of certain capacitors affect the proportionality of the overall changes in voltage and current. I was pushing buttons wildly -- maybe randomly -- on the calculator; sine, cosine...I might even have been crying at this point. I was a fraud and I was about to be found out.

After a half-hour or so, I completed the test, handed it in and then scanned the room for an escape route. The interviewer asked me to stand by for a few minutes.

As I waited to be embarrassed by my test results, I surveyed the facilities. Workers were inspecting digital meters as they passed by on a conveyor belt, sort of like a high-tech version of Lucy in the candy factory. I noticed a small room in the back lit brightly by rows of fluorescent lighting. Two men in lab coats were calmly tinkering with odd-looking chunks of metal that were covered in circuitry. On the door was the simple logo of the Space Shuttle. I asked one of the workers about it. His reply: "That's our NASA Rocketdyne [rocket dynamics] division. They build parts for the Space Shuttle. If you're here a few years, you might get to work back there."

"*Okay,*" I thought. "*That'd be an amazing gig for me, if I'm willing to put in years of man-hours to get there.*"

The interviewer emerged from his office with my paperwork in hand, "Alright…We went through your test…Now, if you're interested, we'd like to start you in our Rocketdyne division."

I did *not* expect that. Honestly. Yet in that moment, I learned a very valuable and eye-opening lesson. I carry it with me still, and I will continue to do so for the rest of my life and career…

Never doubt yourself.

Sure, it's dumb and simple, but it's true. Most of us are so filled with self-doubt that it cripples us and prevents us from chasing our dreams. Too many lives end in regret and most of us are left wondering, what would've happened if I'd at least *tried*?

So how does one work on the Space Shuttle in the middle of Danbury, Connecticut? First of all, I never actually met the shuttle in person. The components that we built were transported to Florida or wherever the shuttle was docked. We built and wired transducers. These were chunks of high-intensity metal that registered fuel and air pressure and converted them into digital readouts. I had to put them under multiple test conditions, like in a 400-degree furnace and a minus-600-degree freezer. I recorded the data, fed it into a computer and it told me the circuit changes to make to keep it within the correct tolerances.

Mmm. Sexy-sexy stuff.

In truth, this brought me to a crossroads that most of us face in our young lives. If we're lucky, we end up in a life where we have an excellent career that we truly enjoy, or at least we think we do, or we convince ourselves that we do because, on paper, it's part of the picturesque American Dream. At this division of NASA, I was quickly becoming a fixture. I could thrive here for the rest of my life. My relationship with Suzanne was still very sweet, nice and amazingly fulfilling. Indicators suddenly started to point towards settling down, buying a house, marriage, kids...

As fantastic as all of that sounded, it didn't feel honest to me. I was trying to convince myself that I was on the right road, but I couldn't stop thinking about that evil mistress, standup comedy.

I worked closely every day with two humorless Vietnam vets in a tiny lab. They were my only audience and I constantly tried to get them to laugh. I put a sticker on a microscope and on it I scribbled in Sharpie, "Peep Show 25 Cents." They looked at me like I was Viet Cong.

The circuitry on the transducers was glued on with a special NASA-designed compound. It had to be mixed in just the right, exact proportions and with the proper viscosity in a dust-free room. It took almost a half-hour just to make a capful of this stuff and it was viable for only fifteen minutes. I'd make a batch, stick cotton-tip applicators into it, then fling them upward, hoping they'd stick to the ceiling. The vets, needless to say, did not enjoy this.

Thinking back, I realize I was subconsciously sabotaging the job. My whole being, my soul, my inner voice was rejecting my environment. I somehow knew, even at that young age, that I was heading down a path of no return and I had to make a change before it was too late. Regrets were already starting to nag at me. My idiotic, dopey dream of being a standup comic would not stop kicking at me. What do I do? Where do I go? I'd already exhausted all my comedy options in Waterbury. New York City was still beckoning me. I could no longer deny it: I had to find a route to get there before those callings grew faint.

My sister Tracy was skimming through our local newspaper, *The Waterbury Republican*. As luck or kismet or whatever would have it, she stumbled across an ad for a standup comedy competition. *Thursday Night Live* was being held at The Hartford Civic Center. First prize...first prize, oh my God! First prize was a limo to New

York City, dinner for two at a restaurant called Maxwell's Plumb and, *holy Christ*, an audition at *The Improv!*

I stared at the ad, dizzy with excitement while I read it over and over. It was just too good to be true. I was getting anxious, my brain was over-functioning, the words on the page started spinning and blurring out. Could a teen have a stroke?

Hartford heard my cries for help and answered them. This was it! This was the kick in the ass that was going to launch me into the next huge phase of my comedy career, right?

Maybe.

The *Thursday Night Live* showroom was cavernous. The ceiling was, I swear, a hundred feet high. It was a hippodrome; hardly like the intimate bars and backrooms I was used to. I was expected to be funny standing up on a ten-foot-high stage, kitty-cornered at the end of what felt like an airplane hangar. The show producers had at least tried to capture the intimacy of a cabaret. They set up a bunch of round tables with black tablecloths and decorated each with candles and uninspired flower arrangements. I was worried for a sec, thinking that maybe I was in the wrong venue and there was a cheapo wedding coming in.

My parents came to see their son do or die in front of a crowd of nearly a thousand people. I was curious about what my dad was thinking at the time. I mean, in theory, I was now potentially on the road to becoming one of the comics that he and I watched and bonded over on our TV. My mom was nervous but she was confident that I would do well. She saw me triumph at my high-school show and a few times when I was on stage alone in the local bars. Suzanne was there by my side, as she was for so many of these comedy sojourns. It wasn't until years later, after the fog of comedy-war cleared, that I was able to appreciate how she dedicated herself to helping me get on the right road to comedy success. My sister Tracy was with us as well. She was my de facto showbiz manager who found this gig for me.

This was the first comedy event where I felt like I was in big-time showbiz. Comedian David Frye was set to open the festivities. So yeah, look at me, I was sharing the bill with a master impressionist. He was a regular on TV talk shows like Merv, Mike Douglas,

Carson et al. He was especially popular during the Nixon era with his uncanny impression of the criminal-in-chief.

I was familiar with David from a short-lived TV sketch show in the '70s called *The Kopykats*. It starred all the popular impressionists of the day: Rich Little, Frank Gorshin, George Kirby, Marilyn Michaels, and our very own David Frye. Each sketch featured them impersonating other, more famous celebrities and politicians. That night, I was going to be on the same stage with -- as I saw it -- comedy royalty.

Wobbly from anxiety and dread, I had a case of the pre-show jitters. The stakes were high for me. I remember asking the wrangler-person if I could meet David Frye. I thought that shaking his hand would help ground me. She looked at me coldly: "David doesn't talk to people." I later understood what that meant when I read Phil Berger's book about standup comedy, *The Last Laugh*. He wrote about Frye's odd rituals before he got in front of an audience, including peeing in an ice bucket.

The show started, David Frye got up on stage and did a very rote, uninspired twenty minutes of his greatest hits; Nixon, Hubert Humphrey and one or all of the Kennedys. He almost didn't need to be there. They could just as easily have positioned his suit on the stage and played one of his comedy records. He was up there doing nothing more than collecting a paycheck. No doubt he had a car waiting just outside the exit so when he was done he could make a run for it. It didn't matter. I was focused on the task at hand.

I sat at a table with my posse, waiting nervously while clutching my little suitcase filled with props. Yep, I had a dalliance with comedy props. I was counting on them that night to help thrust me into super stardom. As I watched my contenders up on the stage, I couldn't help but notice that none of them were doing traditional standup. There was a woman contortionist who tangled herself into her own body. Interesting but not funny. There was a kid who juggled three balls and three hankies, and there was a guy in a full white suit impersonating Steve Martin in his *Let's Get Small* routine. It was mildly entertaining but hardly original. I started to feel a little more confident about where this might end.

I remember my dad sitting there quietly. I think he was concerned that I might be worried about disappointing him if things didn't go well. At this point, I just wasn't sure of anything except that I had to get up there and just be me, funny or not.

My intro wasn't much more than someone offstage reading my name off a list, like a maître d' alerting me that my table was ready. I bounded onstage and opened my little suitcase. My anxiety and nerves sent a low-grade ringing into my head. I had trouble breathing; I felt like I was underwater. Didn't matter, I was forging ahead. The joke list taped to the top inside of my suitcase was my guiding light, my security blanket. It had bullet points like: McDONALD'S. DOGS IN GARBAGE. HAIR SALON/BLOW DRY. GROUCHO.

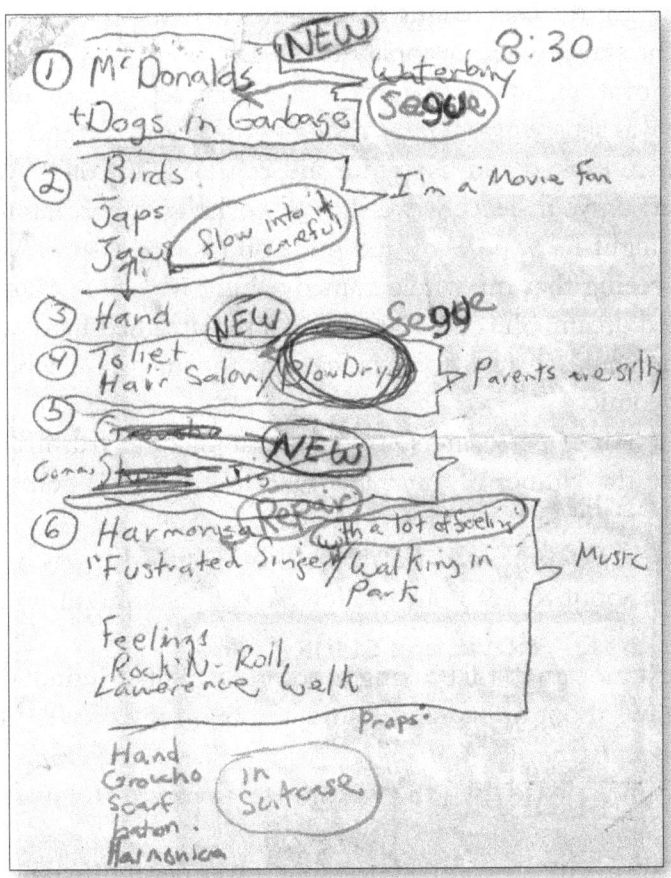

My cheat sheet (1979).

My nervousness started to subside. I was somehow able to forget that I was in a contest and I let myself believe that I was a professional doing my thing. If I wasn't a pro, I figured I'd *pretend* I was. Everything that I acquired from my standup sets in all the little bars in Waterbury came to the fore. The planets were aligning; I was letting myself enjoy this moment. I was aware enough to know that the real prize that night was me getting to do what I really loved to do. The props, though, were a crutch. I think I used them just so I'd have a suitcase to hang my cheat sheet on. I remember revealing to the audience, "My cure for acne." I pulled out an electric razor from my suitcase. That was it. That was the joke. Then I pulled out a little troll doll with a Groucho mustache, "Look, Groucho as a kid." It made no sense. Ultimately it was my tried-and-true observational jokes that got the best laughs that night. Thank God.

I left the stage to hearty applause. It wasn't a Hollywood & Rowe standing ovation, but getting a few laughs under such tremendous pressure was satisfying enough. When I got back to the table, everyone seemed excited and happy for me, especially my dad. Wearing your heart on your sleeve was a sign of weakness, according to him, but that night I saw pure joy and pride on his face. As to my mom, she was seeing that my whole comedy-thing was more than just a misguided dream. She could see that if a kid dreamed hard enough, he or she could, in reality, become an astronaut or a cowboy or a standup comic.

After ten or so performers, we hit the moment of truth. Time to announce the winner of *Thursday Night Live*. Was it going to be Steve Martin Jr. or the boneless lady or...?

"*Wait. Was that my name? I won?!*" Un-be-lievable! It was happening! I was about to head out to New York City to audition at The Improv!

The next morning, still basking in the glow of my triumphant victory, I crawled out of bed and found a note on my dresser. It read, "*You were outstanding. Keep up the good work. - Love, Dad.*" It was the first time my dad used the word "love" in regards to his feelings towards me.

It was always understood, I guess, but it was never officially documented like this.

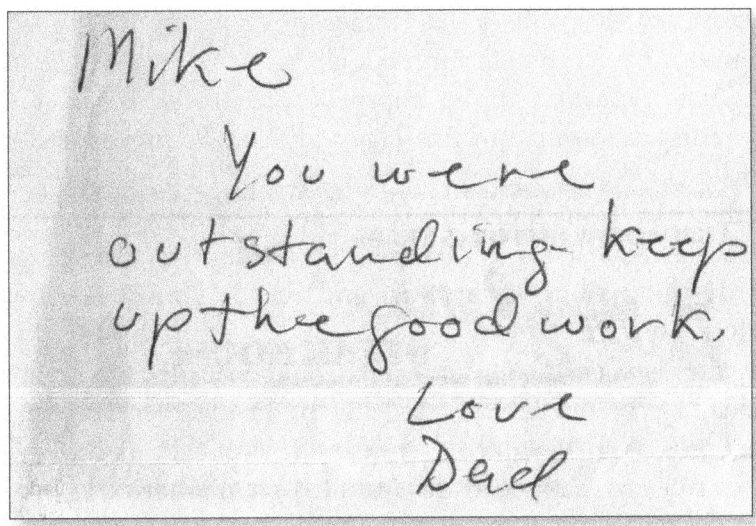

I kept the note.

I was oddly calm as Suzanne and I waited in my family living room for a limo that was coming to pick us up and take us to my New York City standup comedy debut. My parents were proud and beaming as though their son were Alan King headed off to Hollywood to do his summer TV special. Plans were set for them, my sisters and my comedy-career-devoted cousins David and Carolyn Pecka and her husband Joe, to caravan into New York City and meet us at The Improv that night.

The limo rolled up, two guys in suits poured out and came to the front door; it was my first encounter with slick showbizy types. They flashed their business cards, shook our hands, congratulated me and whisked my girlfriend and me off to the big city.

Years later I learned that Suzanne had mixed emotions about everything that was unfolding. Even at her young age, she was aware that a cosmic shift was happening. Comedy, at this point, was not just a hobby with me; she could see the gravitational pull of it drawing me in. She grew worried, wondering where and how she would ultimately fit in with all of this. If this night ended with any level of success, she knew deep down that the change in my life trajectory would be irreversible. *My* head was elsewhere. I was too focused on that night and the wave of possibilities. I didn't know it yet, but the selfishness that comes along with pursuing such a demanding career was starting to kick in.

The limo pulled up at The Improv during the peak of the show. My wranglers stormed in like Navy SEALS, as they waved their business cards about. They announced to the club manager, Steve, that they had "comedian Mike Rowe" and his party, ready and waiting. What the hell, man? This was all too crazy. I'd been doing this comedy-thing a little over a year and already I was being treated like Rod Stewart?

My family was already there in the audience, dizzy with anticipation. My parents were sharing this night together. Through the sheer force of the laughter and excitement of that night, I hoped that maybe my mom and dad would find that spark again. You know, the healing power of humor and all that good stuff...I couldn't let my head go there. I had to focus; I was going to be on stage soon.

The Improv comics were seasoned pros and I had to see how I was going to measure up with the big-boys (and a few girls). I remember future-*SNL* member and Improv regular Joe Piscopo being perplexed by my entourage as we entered the bar. He couldn't understand who I was and why I was getting the star treatment. Steve introduced me to Mark Schiff, the emcee and the person who was going to bring me onstage and introduce me to my first New York comedy audience.

Sitting in the bar, I could hear waves of laughter rolling out from the comedy showroom. It rattled me a little, for sure, but I didn't come this far to fail. I needed to do great. This was, after all, an audition and my entree into the community that I wanted and needed to be a part of. If it turned into a humiliating experience in front of these comics, it would crush me. Some, I heard, never recover from such trauma when the stakes are this high.

I tried to ingratiate myself with Mark Schiff as he joked around in a small confab of his fellow comics. He looked at me strangely, as if to say, "Slow it down, buddy." He was right, I was too anxious about fitting in. It had to be earned. *Everything* had to be earned.

Finally, I got the word from Steve to stand by; I was up next. The room was still a hot, packed house. If this blew up in my face, the only person to blame would be *me*. I clutched my suitcase for dear life as I stood on the launching pad in the back of the room. Mark Schiff was at the microphone, effortlessly wrangling the crowd as he got them stoked for this new, young, green, scared and anxious wannabe. He made a little bit fun of my entrée into the club, "He just won a contest as the funniest guy in Hartford, Connecticut, so, yeah -- you know he's funny." I went up to thunderous applause. I did have about ten relatives in the audience, so that helped.

This was it, my first time performing in an authentic comedy club, right in the heart of New York City, just blocks away from the bright lights of Broadway. I was about to get up on the very same stage where my comedian heroes started their careers. My eighteen-year-old head felt like I was stepping into a dream.

My first time on The Improv *stage.*

As I got up to the microphone, the bright stage lights started burning out my retinas. It threw me a little. I gathered myself, set up my suitcase on a stool and whipped it open. My set list -- my crutch -- was there and waiting for me with open arms. I found my focus. I let my entire being draw from everything I'd learned, studied and absorbed. I let myself be present and at ease. I knew subconsciously that this was my moment to reward myself for so many months of fighting anxiety and stress and for doing the arduous work that it took to get me on that stage. The audience sensed my confidence; they were laughing. I was finally walking the walk. At that moment, I felt that if they didn't think I was right for their club, I would get over it. I knew that I had done the best I could.

I left the stage to resounding applause, letting myself bask in it. I knew that I had accomplished something pretty awesome. I headed into the bar, unsure of what to expect. Steve made his way to me and congratulated me on my set.

I waited, but there was no mention of my standing. Was I part of this club? I mean, what more would I need to do? Just as I started getting that sinking feeling, Steve said, "Come in when you can. Hang out. We'll try to get you back up onstage."

"*Yes! I was in! Ho-lee-shit!*" I kept my cool but deep inside, all of my internal organs were melting with excitement. Just as I was taking in the warm glow of victory, however, reality hit me. I lived in Connecticut, hours away from the club. I might as well live in Brazil.

FUNNY HOW?

Now that I'd passed the auditions, I found myself driving two hours from Waterbury to New York City on Saturday afternoons to take comedy improv classes, taught on The Improv stage by Martin Harvey Friedberg. Marty was part of a comedy troupe in the mid-1960s that included Richard Pryor, J.J. Barry and Steve Landesberg (whom you might remember from the popular '70s cop-sitcom, *Barney Miller*). Marty, in his late forties, was naturally funny. He was a rubber-faced Art Carney who could incite serious laughs just by staring into the audience with his intense, dark eyes and sideways smirk. With his odd New Yorky/Chicago accent he would yell out weird non-sequiturs like, "*MEAT* comes from Chicago."

Taking Marty's comedy class was a good way for me to slowly introduce myself to New York, The Improv and the people who kept it up and running. Marty and I became close friends during my years at the club.

Al, a lovable old cuss, ran the day-to-day from behind the bar. He'd make sure there was no money being skimmed, bills were being paid, and work schedules were being built, all while chain-smoking Marlboro Reds. Then in his mid-seventies, Al was an off-Broadway actor in his youth. He was short and stout, sort of Alfred Hitchcocky, with the same hang-down, bulldog jowls. Al was the very first person to explain to me to how The Improv worked. Before the Hartford contest, I had sent a letter to the club asking how to audition as a comic. He handwrote back a long, detailed letter explaining the process, the how, when and where you audition, right down to the exact times. A small effort like that made me feel closer to my dream.

Al felt like a true ally. On those Saturdays, after my long drive into the city, I'd hang with him at the bar before class. We talked while he wrangled phone-in reservations and beer deliveries. After a few weeks of these visits, I mentioned to him that I was trying to figure out a plan to move into the city and officially start my standup career. Al told me he was living in a one-bedroom apartment right across the street and offered to let me sleep on his couch until I found my own apartment.

Yes! That's all I needed to hear. Guess what, jerks: I'm moving to New York City, 44th and 9th, right into the thick of 1979's crack-infested pit of transvestites, prostitution, muggings and murders! Hooray! What better way for a young, naive teen boy to start his adult life and comedy career?

On a hot summer's night, I moved from the comforts of my family and my paneled basement bedroom. When it was clear that my comedy destiny was undeniable, my relationship with Suzanne was inevitably doomed. As a teen, I didn't have the tools or the courage or the understanding of how to do a clean breakup. So, like with my job at NASA, I subconsciously sabotaged the relationship, pushing her to break up with me. I was devastated when it happened. We never grew apart, really. After two years of being together constantly, we still had strong feelings for each other. In the end, she was the smarter one and knew she had to send me away to start my journey. It was very hard to leave her and my family – everything – behind, but sometimes there's nothing you can do but listen to the fates.

I readied myself for the bus ride that'd take me from my hometown, Waterbury, Connecticut to my new home, big Al's apartment in midtown Manhattan. My mom was on the verge of tears as though I was headed to Nam in '69. She hugged me goodbye. I swear to you, at that moment, Judy Collins' version of *Send In the Clowns* was playing on the radio. I had five hundred bucks stashed in my pocket. That was it. I stuffed a few belongings into my one shabby suitcase. I didn't have a garment bag, just a handful of shirts on hangers that I pulled from my closet. They sat on the bed, ready for me to sling over my shoulder. I was Joe Buck in *Midnight Cowboy* heading to the big city to find success -- except for, you know, the part where I have sex with men for money. Looking back, that might've been an easier and far more sensible undertaking.

I took an evening Greyhound to the Port Authority on 42nd Street in Manhattan. The nighttime ride added to the romance of it all. I stared out at the dark sky from the front passenger seat of the bus as it hummed down the Merritt Parkway through upstate New York. I was excited and anxious and found comfort in the din of the humming motor and the clacking of the tires hitting the cracks across the highway.

It was later into the night, maybe ten o'clock, by the time the bus rolled through Harlem. For me, this was the line of demarcation; the moment where I felt like, "Here I am. I'm actually in New York City and there is no turning back."

It was 1979 and Harlem was at its worst. Every other building was abandoned, boarded up or burnt out. People were out on the streets, trying like hell to keep cool in the humid, Manhattan summer. Fire hydrants were opened and shooting out fierce jets of water into the night sky. Little kids, out late, were wading in the curbside puddles. Most people hung out on the stoops, surrendering themselves to the sweltering summer air.

It wasn't long before we hit midtown. We drove through the West Side, 9th Avenue. Every little shop and restaurant, newsstand and cigarette store was open for business. People were jammed on the sidewalks, moving, buzzing, and bustling with purpose, even at ten o'clock at night. I would soon learn it was like this twenty-four hours a day. Every block was a carnival. The storefronts and bodegas were a wild mess of neon and fluorescent lights. There were fancy, high-end restaurants and bistros butted right next to crappy smoke shops, laundromats and fruit stands, all of it enmeshed in the dirt and desperation Scorsese relied on to give us a sense of Travis Bickle's world when he drove his cab around the underbelly of Manhattan in the movie *Taxi Driver*.

There was a natural tension in the air as the bus took us deeper into the city. It felt like there was the constant threat that a fight would start up or a random gunshot would ring out. The little kid in me was worried, scared and adjusting to my new world. This intensity was the very fabric of 1970s Manhattan, woven into a quilt of crime and violence that still hangs over its skyline. It's a forever-fixture of the city's character, much like The Empire State Building, The Statue of Liberty or *Cats* on Broadway.

I felt so far from home.

Finally getting off the Greyhound, I made my way through the Port Authority and out onto 42nd street, right near Times Square. Zipping past the homeless, the junked-out junkies and the pimps, I pretended this was an everyday journey for me. I copied the game faces of the other normal people there, a natural survival technique that happens when you hit Manhattan. I was flying on the wings of hope and possibility, excited about an apartment that I'd never been to. This would be my new home, where I'd be living with an old, chain-smoking man that I hardly knew.

I slid into the back of a cab and confidently told the driver to take me to my destination. *1010 WINS News* was blasting on the AM radio. The Reuters ticker was in the background clacking away as the anchor announced, *"You give us 22 minutes...we'll give you the world."* A high claim indeed. It was the perfect soundtrack for the thick traffic at 42nd and 8th. I'm sure the cabbie could tell I was new to the city, most likely because my destination was walking distance at a mere two blocks away.

Al's apartment building was a brownstone six-floor walkup. I climbed the stairs to the fifth floor and Al greeted me at his door. A short hallway brought me into his living room. My couch was right there, off to one side. I unloaded my stuff. Al couldn't understand why I didn't have a garment bag for my clothes. I'd never used one, I explained. Such a thing was considered a luxury in my family.

We sat down and talked. He prepped me on how to behave around comics, recommending that from time to time, I tell them how funny they were. I couldn't thank him enough for letting me stay with him. I promised that when I hit superstar status, I'd buy him a car. Seriously? Damn, how old was I? Nine?

Al's place, now *my* new place, had that old New York City apartment feel that I knew from movies like *The Goodbye Girl*. The formerly white walls were lightly coated with cigarette soot and brown water stains. Built-ins and moldings were thick with probably forty years worth of paint. The whole apartment wasn't more than 700 square feet.

A four-foot stack of old *New York Times* newspapers leaned up against the side of the fridge. Apparently, Al was flirting with the idea of becoming a hoarder. The summer night was still hot and the windows were wide open. I could hear activity all around the 'hood; a random scream, the nonstop rush of cars below, and sirens…there were always sirens. Al's bedroom wasn't that much bigger than his king-size mattress. The place wasn't quite where Travis Bickle lived, but it was close, and it was home. For now. The Improv was only a half-block away and it wasn't even eleven o'clock yet. I wanted to bail out and try a test run of my new status as a club regular.

The New York Improv was a shithole. It always was, but that's a big reason why it was so successful. After all, it was a gymnasium for comics; it wasn't a Vegas show palace. As you walked in, there was a giant photo collage of comedians that covered most of the wall on the left side of the hallway that led into the showroom. I studied the black-and-white snapshots of almost every performer who graced the stage of the club since they opened their doors in 1963. I recognized a young Richard Pryor, Bette Midler, Robert Klein, even Judy Garland with her pre-teen daughter Liza. There were Leno, Carlin, Robin Williams, Freddie Prinze and Larry David next to shots of the club's founder and previous owner, Budd Friedman. There were even photos of comics who were right there, sitting at the bar. I saw up-and-coming comics Gilbert Gottfried, Rick Overton, Joe Piscopo, and Keenan Wayans, who was still working part-time at The Improv as greeter. I, of course, imagined where my photo would go on the celebrity wall and wondered what slick standup action pose the camera would snap of me while I was killing it onstage.

It took a mere five or six years, but I did finally make it up there. Embarrassingly, it was a photo of me holding my eyes back with my fingers to make the face of an Asian while I did my nutty impression of a dubbed Japanese monster movie. My words out of synch with my mouth, I was yelling a warning to the Japanese citizens that Godzilla was attacking.

It was a different time…

The showroom itself had a bevy of exposed pipes and air ducts, torn and worn red booths, wobbly tables and chairs, and, of course, the famous brick wall behind the stage. The wall was chipped,

"Oh no! Godzilla!"

crumbling in spots and dotted with random nail holes. Every comedy club since has felt that they too had to have a brick wall of their very own, but *The Improv* was the first. The whole backroom vibe of the place told the audience that the comics were going to be fast and loose and that they were in a room where any fucking thing could happen.

Al previously alerted Ari, the bartender, that I was coming by the club. I introduced myself and he looked at me curiously -- or maybe concerned, I wasn't sure, "Oh, so you're staying with Al?" A waitress overheard this, "Oh, that's you? Okay...*You're* the one." Apparently, my move to Al's apartment was the talk of the club. Everyone seemed welcoming, yet oddly curious about me.

It turned out that I had picked one of the best nights to be there. The show was vast and eclectic. I saw a very young Rick Overton tear the room apart, ending with a standing ovation. There was a seventeen-year-old Fred Stoller staring at the floor uncomfortably as he mumbled his way through a very early version of his act. "My mother tells me my brother's better than me in this, my brother's better than me in that...I don't even *have* a brother."

Steve Mittleman, with his chinless Alfred E. Newman face, had great jokes, "I went to the Virgin Islands...I got a hero's welcome." I got to see Gilbert Gottfried onstage with his eyes wide open, not yet yelling out his act. Gilly, as Overton called him, picked up the piano bench and, with the legs pointing towards the audience, held it up to his crotch and narrated a movie trailer for the thriller, *Quadra-Dick*. "*Quadra-Dick*...Starring James Mason as Quadra-Dick." Then he would go into a dead-on and intense James Mason impression: "I've got four very big, very large penises." He put down the bench and quietly picked up a stack of napkins, flipping through them like a book. "The Bible..." he intoned, and turned to the back page. "About the author...Jesus was born in Brooklyn." Then he'd flip the pages, "When you flip the pages of the Bible, in the corner you can see a fat lady with a hula-hoop. That's right. A fat lady with a hula-hoop. Yes... Yes... Yes... A. Fat. Lady."

It's odd that I wasn't intimidated by any of this. Maybe I felt like I belonged there. These were my people, we shared the same world view, I was certain of it. I somehow knew that once they got to know me, they'd offer me the right hand of good fellowship and lead me down the righteous path of funny. Or they'd hate me, and I'd be back at NASA building transducers with the two Vietnam vets.

It was a few months before Silver Saunders Friedman, Budd Friedman's ex-wife, would officially take over the club. In her divorce from Budd, she had won ownership of all rights to The Improv brand east of the Mississippi. I didn't know it then, but Budd wasn't even there that night. He had long since high-tailed it to his Hollywood Improv. Chris Albrecht, part owner of the New York club, was the one who, I'm pretty sure, was putting the lineup together.

A few years later, Chris would move to L.A. to become an agent at ICM. He handpicked his first set of clients from The Improv, performers that he felt had the potential to kick ass in Hollywood. If I remember correctly, his powerhouse list of talent included Keenan Wayans, Paul Provenza and Rick Overton. Chris soon moved up from agent to chief executive and president of HBO, where he brought in and developed, among other shows, *The Sopranos*. That night, I told him that I was new, but I was ready to go onstage whenever he needed me to. I name-dropped Al and told Chris I was staying with him until I found my own place. He shot me that same curious look.

What the hell was the whole Al thing about?

I sat in the showroom and waited and watched comic after comic go up onstage and blow the roof off the building. Marc Weiner and his crazy, original homemade puppets were hilarious. Richie Morris, an odd genius, did a fashion show wearing different clear plastic bread bags and zip locks. He strutted and posed in each of his plastic outfits as though he were on a model's catwalk. Over and over, he'd stop, look at the audience and in a vaguely French accent he'd ask, "You like?" The audience didn't.

It was getting late and the audience was dwindling. Why hadn't I been asked to go up yet? I was deemed the funniest kid in Connecticut, fer Chrissake. Did they forget I was here? Was I hated already? Did it have something to do with the whole Al thing?

On The Improv *stage, me with (left to right) Silver Saunders Friedman, Keenan Ivory Wayans, Al Armstrong.*

Over the next few weeks I learned how the hierarchy worked at The Improv and the other, more prominent comedy-showcase clubs in Manhattan. It was simple: get funnier by getting up onstage at whatever shitty-shithole bar the city had to offer. Those low-level rooms were to be used to get better, sharper and funnier. Then, hopefully, you got good enough to get a few two and three a.m. spots at the iconic showcase clubs. Over time, you would hopefully get funny enough to work your way up to the primo slots and even better, the weekend primetime slots. *Holy shit!* I had dues to pay! I couldn't just sit at the bar at a top comedy club and expect to be waltzed up on the stage during the shank of the night. Alas, the heat from my win in Hartford hadn't made me the overnight comedy celeb that I had hoped.

I did find a community of comics there who were all dealing with the same struggles. They too were new to the standup game, but around long enough to be entrenched in the bars and cabarets that were open to less seasoned performers. One of the most famous was the now defunct Ye Old Tripple Inn, directly across the street from Studio 54.

Nineteen eighty was the tail end of the disco era, but 54 was still jammed every night with an eager crowd of partiers and Tony Manero wannabes. They were all hoping against hope to get anointed by owner Steve Rubel and be escorted into those hallowed doors to party with Diana Ross or Liza or whomever else was still lingering amid the smoke machines and the flickering lights of a dying cultural craze.

Ye Old Tripple Inn took in herds of the 54 rejects. Typically, they'd sit at the cabaret tables in a haze of disappointment, wearing their shiny disco duds and perfectly coifed hair. They were couples that typically drove in from Jersey or upstate New York -- the bridge and tunnel people -- who, no doubt, had visions of showing off the new *Saturday Night Fever* dance moves they'd perfected in their parents' basements.

Ye Old was just a bar, much like my dad's when I was a kid. Christmas lights were up all year round and the walls were covered with a mish-mash of Broadway, movie and concert posters. It too had that deep, acrid smell of years of spilled beer mixed in with the varnish of the old wood bar. I felt at home there. A gallery of framed 8x10s of the famous, near-famous and never-famous who performed in the smoke-filled dank of this inn hung on the walls.

Even though it was a small, hapless gin mill, they still managed to set up a cabaret in the corner. A doughy twenty-something kid plinked out songs on an out-of-tune, upright piano as an effeminate black male host/singer flitted around, belting out melodies from *Dreamgirls* and the like. The Studio 54 rejects would sit there reevaluating their night, maybe even their lives. These were seriously unhappy couples trying desperately to get drunk on 7&7s. They weren't going back home. They made the arduous trek into Manhattan, and Ye Old was their only other option for the night. They already paid twenty-five bucks for parking; there was no way they were going to pull their Monte out of the ramp-a-rage and drive aimlessly around The Big Apple in hopes of finding another hotspot. As a hungry standup, I wasn't afraid of this audience. They were warm bodies, and that's all that mattered.

Ye Old Tripple Inn was one of a few foxholes in town that I shared with newly minted fellow comics, Billiam Coronel, Jonathan Solomon, Rita Rudner and Bill Rutkowski, to name a few. Trying to make people laugh in those dark, grim and grungy saloons created a bond of comic brotherhood that, for the most part, lives on with us to this day.

After poking at the lifeless audiences, we would gather to share and compare our experiences. We convinced ourselves that we were fighting the good fight as we assured each other that these trials-by-fire were just a stepping-stone. They were a necessary evil that we had to wade through to discover what-in-the-fuck was so funny about us.

Over time, we realized that these audiences were malleable. Once we found the skills to tame them and generate somewhat consistent laughs, we knew we were hitting a rite of passage. We were getting close to being one of those comics featured in the prime spots at any one of the three top comedy showcase clubs. That was our target, and I was focused and anxious to hit it, but I still had years of dues to pay.

Another regular spot for us Triple-A comics was the Beefsteak Charlie's cabaret on 8th Avenue at 45th Street called The Callback Lounge. It was a small but sleek Broadway showcase; bright, upbeat, new, clean and maintained by the Beefsteak Charlie's corporation. Somehow, they had managed to squeeze a baby grand piano into the long skinny bar and each night, they featured Broadway singers and us, the young, upstart standup comics. The shows were hosted by talented people who were between jobs on Broadway. Most notably was Marcy Stein at the piano and Bob Amaral as the lead vocalist.

```
I use to drive to the city from a small town in Ct.
and you know you have to be crazy to drive in thecity
Espically if you have out of state plates.I stopped
for a light.. my car was up on blocks. two guys rollin
my radials down Times Square  "What a dumb dumbesttourist

I'm nieve in the city to. You Know the fellos on the
    street corners working their way through college
         You want Opioum,Herion You want opium you want
Herion.I don't do what New Yorkers do,which is just
walk by.I walk over to them and say... no thank you
 Right away they say "From out of state,wheresyour car,
we'll take your radials "
```

Early stand up musings on my mom's typewriter.

This is where I got my education on everything Broadway. To me The Callback always felt like we were backstage at a theater on The Great White Way. It was party-like, upbeat and positive. I looked forward to doing sets in front of what was typically a satisfied audience of tourists on the heels of seeing a Broadway extravaganza. The Callback was a intimate, familial and supportive setting for my new circle of comedy friends and myself. These little stages gave us young mavericks the freedom to try anything without worry of failing.

I loved the comedy nightlife and the idea of me, barely in my twenties, staying out late in the streets of Manhattan with my new comedy brethren. My group didn't party much; we were more interested in making each other laugh. We'd sit together into the early morning hours in any one of the nearby 24-hour diners and revel in the glory of our dopiness. Back then we could be found at The Market Diner or our favorite, The Westway Diner, right around the corner from The Improv on 9th Avenue. At that point, I didn't have to get up in the morning to report to a day job. I was still living rent-free on Al Armstrong's couch and sustaining myself with the complimentary burgers and tuna melts that they fed to us comics on The Improv roster.

Once, after a long night of clubbing and diner-hopping, I ambled back to Al's around 3 a.m. The apartment was dark, lit only by the city lights streaming in through the open windows. I was tired and couldn't wait to roll onto my hard, dusty couch. So far, living with

Al had been great. In fact, I hardly saw him. By the time I got up to start my day, he was already off and working his day shift at The Improv bar. Really, the only hard part was when Al first got up in the early mornings. I'd be awakened by horrifying sounds wailing through the bathroom door, a distressing nonstop series of choking, barking and wheezing coughs that built up into a glorious and massive ejection of phlegm. Al was clearing out his nicotine-polluted lungs, one of the many punishments that come with chain-smoking Marlboro Reds. It was a ritual that I had to live with every morning; sounds that couldn't be blocked out no matter how many pillows I piled over my head. Still, it was a fair price to pay, considering the rent prices in New York at the time.

This particular night, as I was rolling out my blanket and readying myself for a cozy night's sleep on the couch, I heard Al yell from his bedroom. "Ahhh! A ghost!"

Holy smack, Al's having a fevered nightmare.

"A-a-a ghost! He's here!"

"Huh? Wha..? Where?"

He was panicked. "Right there! In front of you!"

Oh shit! Al's dying and the Holy Spirit is reaching out to take him to the Pearly Gates.

"I don't see it," I assured him.

"He's looking right at me!" Pleading, "Why?! Why is he here?!"

O.K. I was kinda getting scared. I froze, hoping the ghost might not see me in the thick dark of the apartment. Then, breathless with relief he muttered --

"He's gone...The ghost is gone..." There was an awkward silence. Was Al...dead?

Then, with comfort, he offered, "If you're scared...and you want to come in here...there's plenty of room in my bed..."

My small-town senses didn't recognize that this was his masterful ploy to get me, a naive, strapping, twenty-year-old man into bed with him.

Three years after I moved from Al's couch and into my own apartment, I was chatting it up with Judy Orbach, the Improv's talented house singer, cheerleader and shoulder for the comics to laugh on. We talked about Al. I told her the "ghost" story and she burst out laughing. What? Why? Judy, breathless from the giggles, asked, "You know Al's gay, right?"

Ohhh, okay. I got it. Yep. This explained the weird, curious looks I got during my first night at the club when everyone heard that I was "staying with" Al. At last, the mystery of the ghost was solved.

PORN: A LOVE STORY

My incident with The Gay Guy and The Ghost was a bright red, flashing light telling me that it was time to move out and get my own apartment -- which, of course, meant I had to be responsible and get a job. *Dammit!*

I found full-time work at AVCOM, an audio/visual equipment rental and repair shop on the 8th floor above what was still officially The Ed Sullivan Theater building on Broadway. This floor and my workspace later became David Letterman's offices when his late-night talk show moved into the theater in the 1990s.

I told AVCOM of my intense vocational high-school training and my last job working on the Space Shuttle. With that, they instantly hired me to fix projectors, cassette recorders, VCRs and the like. Their offices had that early 1980s grit; dirty white walls, bright white fluorescent lighting, and tall metal racks filled with used, damaged and newly repaired AV equipment, projectors, VCRs and TVs. I was stationed at a banged-up wooden workbench surrounded by shelves of mismatched tools and slipshod, outdated electronic test equipment.

I worked full-time as an audio/video technician, repairing equipment. After work I'd come home to my studio apartment and crawl into bed around 5:30, right after dinner. I'd sleep until 11 pm, then head out and wander the comedy clubs with hopes of getting my five glorious minutes in front of an audience. Finally, after a long night of comedy-club hopping, I'd crawl back into bed sometime around 3 a.m., sleep a few more hours and go back to my day job by 9 a.m. I was always tired and sleepy at work, but I desperately wanted to do my best. I needed the money. I had, by this time, my own apartment to pay for.

One morning I came in to work, tired, hung-over and frustrated with my life and comedy career (and lack thereof). I was hiding at my workbench, pretending to repair a slide projector. In truth, I was so sleep deprived, I was nodding like a 9th Avenue junkie. That's when Eliot, my department manager bolted in. "I need you to do something for me." Eliot was a ninety-five pound hippy-nerd with long greasy hair and scraggly beard. His daily food of choice was caffeine and cigarettes, and he spent most of his days copying homemade porn videos for creepy clients (back then, those sorts of "treasures" were hard to find). I'd sometimes wander into his little office in the dark back end of the building. More often than not, there'd be banks of TVs playing back whatever random perverted sex act some customer thought they needed to stash in their VHS archives and cherish for the rest of their lives.

Eliot dropped two big 16mm reels of the movie *Woodstock* on my desk. He said, "You need to telecine this movie to Beta. It's for the client's home-video library. When you're done, you need to deliver it to his apartment to make sure it looks right on his projector."

This didn't make sense to me, "Who has a video library and projector in his apartment [in 1980]?" I asked.

Through the cig dangling from his mouth, Eliot mumbled, matter-of-factly, "Martin Scorsese." It turns out that he had been a film editor on the movie *Woodstock*, and he wanted a video copy of it.

I started to hyperventilate, "What? Wait? Really? Mar—Scor-No!"

"Scorsese's a weird dude, so be cool." Eliot warned me. "If you fuck this up, I'll kill you." Which meant that I'd be fired. At least, I hope that's what he meant. It was 1980s New York City after all.

So there I was in Tribeca in Martin Scorsese's apartment building. I got to his door on the twenty-whatever floor, with the newly minted Beta video copy of *Woodstock* and my toolbox in hand. The door opened and there he was, in person, wearing bellbottom slacks, a dress shirt and vest.

"Hi, I'm Marty. You got it?"

It sounded like a drug deal, which was already pretty cool. I nodded and he let me in. We walked through a long hallway, past framed movie posters on either side of me; *Mean Streets, Boxcar Bertha, Taxi Driver*. The movie *Raging Bull* had just been out in theaters and it was the final poster before we crossed into his TV room. Marty had one of those massive clamshell-shaped video projectors that only a privileged few could afford back in 1980.

"I need you to look at it with me," he said, "make sure it's right. It needs to be right." He had that familiar stammer like the character he played in the back seat of Travis Bickel's cab when he angrily looked up at the apartment window and saw his movie-wife having an affair.

I popped in the Beta tape and he studied it like it was the video playback of a scene he'd just shot. I didn't mind; I wanted this to last. I mean, I'm hanging out with Martin Scorsese fer-fuck-sake. He shook his head; he didn't like what he was seeing. "Just bring the top down; heads are cutting off at the top." When Scorsese asks, you do it. I opened my toolbox and pulled out my trusty diddle stick (actual name for a real adjustment tool) and opened the back of the projector. I started making adjustments as Marty called the shots, "No-no, too low. Up. Bring it up. Center, too much frame left. Center it." I was being directed by Martin Scorsese! Pretty great. "Red, too much red. Can you bring it -- ?" I kept adjusting, "Stop. Nice."

During these twenty or so minutes of tweaking and adjusting I was mostly quiet and cordial. I really didn't want to "fuck it up" and say something idiotic. Then, as I was packing up to leave, I couldn't stop myself. I had to ask. "How do you have a video library?"

It was none of my business, really. I shouldn't have asked, but this was a time before things like video stores, video rentals and laser discs. I had to know. Marty grew quiet for a sec. I thought, *"Shit, I fucked up."* He smiled. "You like movies?"

"Yeah, I do." I told him how I had taken a first date to see *Taxi Driver* and how she got upset at the movie just like Betsy did when Travis took her to see porn in Times Square. He laughed, "You like movies, you're gonna like this." He took me to a room that had floor-to-ceiling shelves of movies recorded on Betamax, all with handwritten labels. I could see *Casablanca, Citizen Kane*. There was Chaplin, and foreign films that I'd yet to know. He even had Frankenstein movies. It looked like every great movie ever made was in this room. There were hundreds of tapes carefully curated and neatly arranged in custom-made shelving. It was a giant cache of bootlegs. I couldn't ask him where they came from. Again, it was none of my business. I asked anyway.

He proudly revealed a stack of *TV Guides*, all from major cities around the country. He told me he would go through them each week and find movies he wanted to see or movies he needed to have in his private library. "See, look: Fritz Lang's *'M'* is on in Pittsburgh. Channel 11 at 8:30," he said. He explained that he would call his guy in Pittsburgh and have him record it on Beta. The guy would then mail the tape directly to him in New York. Basically, he was paying people in every major city in America to build his video library.

I realized at that moment that Marty and I were kindred spirits. We were nerds who both built and carefully curated homemade archives. His library was classic movies; mine was standup comics. We both knew, instinctively, that if we immersed ourselves in what we loved, we'd find success. I decided right then that Marty and I would be lifelong buds.

I shared with him the latest news that I knew about upcoming video technology -- ya know, the way close friends do. He told me that he would be dealing with AVCOM quite a bit and from then on and he'd be sure to ask for me personally. I couldn't wait for us to hang out and talk movies over dinner. Who knows? I could probably suggest books that'd make great movies or he'd, no doubt, have me help him rewrite scripts.

Marty never did call AVCOM again. I blamed myself. I realized he was just being nice to an idiot with a diddle stick, and I guess I did overstep. I mean, I actually called him "Marty" at one point. I was worried that he might even complain about me to my boss or something. Whatever. The damage was done.

Months went by and I forgot all about it until that Christmas when the assistant at the front desk told me someone had dropped off a package for me. It was from Scorsese; a bottle of whiskey with a handwritten card that read, *"Mike, Thanks for everything. Merry Christmas -- Marty."*

That was the last time I heard from him. Who knows? Maybe one of these days, I'll run into him again at some sort of awards show. Or I'll see him on a back lot in Hollywood and I'll stop him and ask, "Hey, remember me? The guy with the diddle stick?"

Nah. See, I'd just fuck it up.

Part of my duties at AVCOM was to go to all the top ad agencies in midtown Manhattan and maintain the video equipment they used to record their commercial auditions. I'd hit six or eight big-name ad agencies once a month and at the end of the day, I'd walk off with a fat wad of cash to bring back to the office. All I did, basically, was clean the video heads and adjust and tweak a few things. I was there all of ten minutes per agency and handed a wad of cash for very minor maintenance.

Sooner or later, we'd get the same video equipment from the same agencies into the shop for repair. I'd hook them up; they'd work just fine. My big boss, who existed primarily as a voice on the intercom, instructed me to write out a fake claim and list the parts I pretended to replace and itemize the cost for the work that I didn't do. "Don't worry about it," he'd say. I later found out he had a deal with all the managers of the AV departments. My boss somehow convinced them that if they brought AVCOM five grand a year in "needed" repairs, he'd slip them a grand.

One morning the elusive boss-voice called me into his office over the intercom. I was a little worried. I thought maybe I had screwed up somehow or I accidentally let some sort of cat out of the bag. I had just fake-repaired a ton of video equipment. The name on the repair tag was "J. Colombo" who, according to my co-worker, was actually from the notorious New York crime family.

Oh, *shit!* I fucked up bad and was on a hit list! That had to be it.

I stepped into the office. My boss was on the phone and waved me in. I sat across from him while he wrapped up a call about a projection system for the pop and soul singer Tom Jones' live show in Atlantic City (I ended up supervising that project but that's a whole other story). Scratching his chin, he looked me in the eye for what felt like ten minutes, then: "Mike? Are you okay with porn?"

I wasn't sure where this was going, but since pornography was woven into the fabric of the place, I thought it best to play along, even though I really was *not* very comfortable with porn. I was aware that my boss liked me, at least what he knew of me, but more importantly, he liked my work. He told me he wanted me to be point man for his new clients and awarded me the dubious distinction of being the maintenance person for the projection equipment in the porn theaters in Times Square and 42nd Street.

Ok, wow...What did that mean exactly? I knew what it meant, but I wasn't even a year off the Greyhound and suddenly I was about to be thrust into the very underbelly of 1980s hardcore New York City smut.

The deal was, once a week, in the middle of the day, my little toolbox and I would go from porn theater to nasty porn theater and clean, tune up and adjust their crappy little 16mm movie projectors. These were the same ones that every baby boomer remembers from 9th-grade classrooms, typically used to run a warbly movie for students to warn us about the evils of uppers or the life cycles of plants.

This was a job promotion of sorts, so I wanted it to go well. My first day, I was nervous and worried, but I carried with me a sense of pride. After all, I was in charge of this new department. Such as it was. I didn't tell my parents about this, however, even if it was proof that my vocational background was paying off.

On a sunny morning I started my maiden journey to 42nd Street, the heart of the filthy theater district. Porn-show palaces had names like The Burlesque, The Gaiety, The Roxy, Show World, and Eros 1 & 2. From the 1920s and well into the 1960s, they were movie palaces and vaudeville houses. By 1980 though, they were a shell of their former selves.

This was my first time smack-dab in the middle of The Forty-Deuce, a nickname given to 42nd Street by the flotsam that hung out on its street corners, doorways and alleyways.

Twenty-five-cent peep shows and theater after theater promised the best in exotic and erotic sex. Storefronts displayed everything from cheap luggage to expensive cameras as well as a huge array of weapons: Bowie knives, Chinese stars, switchblades. An arcade was open, bright and early, clanging and ringing and pinging nonstop from rows of video and pinball games. At Tad's Steak House -- with a sign touting their steak dinner for $2.99 -- a shirtless hustler wearing a vest and a cowboy hat stood in the doorway. He flicked his cigarette butt at some homeless dude asking him for money.

Hookers, buxom and enthusiastic in brightly colored, satin short-shorts, were already in their full glory at 11 a.m. Sex in the Forty-Deuce was a 24-hour-a-day business. I made a beeline through the labyrinth of dirt, debauchery, electric sex, pimps, drug dealers and the homeless, hoping to find the first theater on my list. A crazed, wide-eyed street person cornered me, his clothes and hands covered with a month-thick coating of dirt and city grime. Holding up a dollar bill in my face he said, "Hey man, I just need a dollar more to get a bus back home to Jersey."

I would soon learn that this was one of the many street scams that kept the heart of Manhattan beating. Other such flimflammers had a little more ingenuity, like the one with a common dime wrapped in a coin collector's cardboard square. Its inflated value was carefully written in the corner in pen. "Man, this right here, a collectable. I paid two-hundred. I need me some green, my brother. Let you have it for twenty."

I was the only fresh-faced kid walking The Deuce that morning and I felt like an easy target. I needed to track down the theater and find cover. Searching through the dozen or so of them interspersed throughout the city block, I needed to find the Harmony Burlesque.

A barker shouted from a theater across the street. "Live sex. Check it out...Live sex." I looked closer. A black little person wearing a gold tux and a top hat accented with a thin layer of black street soot leaned on his pimp cane. "Yo, man, live sex. Check it out."

The theater entrance was like a carnival sideshow, covered with ads, posters and giant wooden cutouts of the tantalizing attractions inside. Horny guys were promised half-dressed hotties with wide-open legs or vixens in fishnets begging to be satisfied. A crappy TV monitor played hardcore sex-movie trailers through a dirty storefront window. The movie titles were blunt: *Taboo*, *The Ecstasy Girls*, *So Deep*, *The Voyeur*, *Face Dance* and the undoubtedly inferior sequel -- *Face Dance 2*.

Looking up at the marquee, I realized I'd found my refuge. This was it, The Harmony Burlesque -- my destination. I readied myself. I was about to go into a deep, dark, rabbit hole where I knew if I went in, I was going to come out a different man.

Taking a deep breath, I crossed to the barker. "Live sex, my brother. Check it out," he chanted. I pointed to my toolbox in an attempt to explain myself. He looked at me like I was laying out a street con so's I could see me some ladies for free.

"What in the fuck you talkin' 'bout, muthafucker?" He had that great old-school '70s pimp swagger and attitude, a little baffling when coming from a guy who barely measured up to my waist. "Wait yo-fuckin' ass right here." He swore more than he needed, like a guy who was maybe compensating for something. A few minutes later, he came back out of the theater with a middle-aged Sri Lankan dude who was nothing but angry, for no apparent reason. "What do you want, my friend?" he barked.

The famous gangster, John Gotti, had his mitts all over the New York porn district. That is, until he cut a deal with the Sri Lankan mob. The theaters were now in their hands. What Gotti knew and the Sri Lankans didn't was that the home-video market was swooping into town. If guys needed to "rub one out," they no longer had to leave their homes. Sadly, for the Sri Lankans, the porn-theater business was dropping swiftly. Gotti had conned them, so, in retrospect, I guess they had every right to be angry.

After a little back and forth, the manager-guy finally understood who I was. "Come in, my friend," he said, ushering me inside. Middle Easterners in New York City always ended their sentences with "my friend…"

He walked with me into the dark theater. I could see remnants of what it might've been during its heyday. Ornate carved-out wood framing trimmed scratched and scuffed paneled walls. Walking through the musty halls, I could hear the moans of unbridled sex echoing through the theater from the muddy-sounding 16mm projector reeling through a showing of *Sex Dungeon Wives*. He took me into the projection booth, a room with dark-red cracked walls and a light hanging from the ceiling, its metal shade hanging askew. A fat projectionist sat in a corner listening to *1010 WINS News* on a tiny AM radio that he held up to his ear. "Vlad will take care of you, my friend."

"Holy shit" I thought, *"I'm in a Scorsese movie."*

So now I was left alone with a half-conscious, mouth-breathing Middle Eastern dude who, I swear, had a gimp hand and a dead eye. This was quite a change from my rocket science coworkers at NASA.

Vlad got up and shut off the projector in mid-movie. The sound whirrrred down to a slow stop as he turned on the house lights. I looked out into the theater through the little projection window. About eight people were seated in the audience, including a Wall Street businessman in a three-piece suit, holding a briefcase on his lap. In the daytime hours, the Wall Street-type was a staple at the porn houses. A sleeping junkie huddled in the back row behind a few pimp types and some regular young Joes who, I'd bet, were curiosity seekers visiting from the outer boroughs. Vlad flipped on some '70s R&B house music and adjusted a junky little spotlight, aiming it at a small stage under the movie screen.

I tried to go to work on the projectors, but I was completely distracted by a pretty, sexy woman in a blue satin bikini strutting out from behind the curtains. She started to strip to Cheryl Lynn's disco hit, *Got To Be Real.*

I eventually got the projector open and did my best to adjust and clean it while watching what was happening on stage. The dancer's eyes were dead. She was living in another world in her head, I could see it. Gathering herself, she tried her best to tease her audience of eight. A real pro. She unhooked the strap of her bikini top, carefully and elegantly revealing her breasts a little at a time.

I'm dead, I thought. How was I going to concentrate on the task at hand? She removed her bikini top, swung it around and handed it off through the curtain behind her. Naked lady breasts before lunch? This was not the go-go dancer-type I remembered from my dad's bar. Vlad was getting worried about me. "You okay, my friend? Let's move it." Who knew that the Harmony Burlesque had such a strict schedule?

The stripper, dancing drunkenly, shimmied out of her bikini bottoms and handed them through the curtain. The junkie patron, now wide awake, stumbled to the stage and handed her some money. She continued to strut her nakedness around to the music of Earth, Wind & Fire before finally dancing her way off the stage.

A new stripper sashayed through the curtains wearing the *same bikini!* Apparently the first stripper was handing it off, piece by piece, through the curtain to her naked co-worker. I guess the policy was two strippers, one bikini. She, too, was dead in the eyes. I'm sure she was reliving a happier time in her head as she stared out blankly into the empty, stained seats of the theater advertised as "New York's Finest Sex Palace." She peeled off the community bikini, then shuffled offstage. With perfect timing, an exterminator made his way onstage and started spraying for bugs, almost as if he were part of the show. Eh. No one cared. Business as usual at The Harmony.

A young couple bounded into the projection booth. They didn't talk much; they were all business. I turned for a second to clean a lens. When I turned back, they were naked! Everything, full on, out in the open. The woman nodded at me as she slipped on a robe. I nodded back as if seeing a naked woman at lunchtime in the middle of Times Square was part of my everyday life.

Something was different about this young woman. She was beautiful. In her early twenties, she was blonde, with fresh, alabaster skin. I was convinced that deep down, she didn't want to be there. No doubt she was fresh off a Port Authority bus that came directly from her small town. She ventured to The Big Apple with pie-in-the-sky dreams of becoming a famous Broadway actress. She was kinda like me, except she had taken a bad turn somewhere along the way. I started to convince myself that maybe I could save her. You know, pull her out from under the spell of her pimp and take her under my wing.

My young, naive small-town worldview quickly started to reconsider everything when she walked on stage and rolled out a dirty and stained, gnarly mattress. Traffic's *Low Spark of High-Heeled Boys* started playing as the houselights dimmed. The spotlight hit the stage, highlighting the mattress. She slipped off her robe as her partner, completely naked, pranced up to her with clumsy ballet-like moves. Grabbing her, he kissed her deeply while fondling her whole body.

Watching this through the little projection window, I pretended to adjust the exciter lamp on the Bell and Howell. Vlad, with a filterless cig hanging from his mouth, stood behind me at a rig, rewinding a movie reel with his one good hand. The couple onstage was now groping each other's genitals. I mean, like *really* going at it. The music changed gears. *I Want Your Love* by Chic kicked in as they fell into choreographed dance moves. I remember thinking that it was like watching TV's disco dance show, *Solid Gold*. Sort of.

It was all so surreal. The guy laid down, face up, on a mattress I wouldn't touch without a HAZMAT suit. The music changed as the young woman stood over the man's face. I watched their dance for a while, fully invested in the Fred and Ginger of porn. I couldn't turn away. She squatted down and, with some elegance, dropped her "stuff" on his face as the song changed to the Spinners 70's hit *Sitting On Top Of The World*. She bounced rhythmically to the lyrics, "*Sit-ing on top on the worrr-ld...Sit-ing on top of the world.*" The innuendo was not lost on me. She lifted herself up and turned to lie on top of him, body on body. His penis was huge and erect, an impressive achievement in a roach-infested theater on a mattress that looked like it was the home to at least one murder. Suddenly, in less than a blink of an eye, there was full-on penetration.

Naked, young and vibrating intercourse in a dark theater filled with about a half-dozen onlookers was not in the least bit sexy or exciting. You'd think for a kid who was just twenty I'd be taking a snapshot in my head for future reference, but it was just too odd and weird and sexless. At least it was to me. Yet, I still felt that I could save her.

Vlad was signaling for me to hurry it up. The disco sex-dance was about to end, and he needed the projectors back up and running. All film gates and tracks were cleaned, ready to go. I clicked the lens back into place and threaded the movie. It was any one of the half-dozen or so *Emmanuelle* skin flicks. I wasn't quite sure of the difference between any of them. It's likely one movie with a bunch of different titles.

The "*Solid Gold*" dancers finished their routine, vanished from the stage and burst back into the booth, still naked. I watched them from the corner of my eye as they casually got dressed and compared notes as though they were Broadway dancers from *A Chorus Line*. I couldn't take my eyes off the woman. We shared a quick look and she nodded and smiled as she slipped back into clothes. I felt a rush. There it was, my window of opportunity, my chance to step up and take her back into the real world of dance classes, brunches, clubbing and family dinners. Nervous, I looked away and checked the focus on the movie screen. I turned back and she was gone forever, likely to sink deeper into the 1980s New York City world of pimps, drugs and sex trafficking. Of course, I knew I wasn't really going to rescue her but still...

Vlad, gimp hand and all, peeled off eighty bucks cash. There was a mirror on the floor just outside the booth that reflected out into the hallway. In it, I could see a gaggle of women in tight shorts and bikinis watching as they saw this young, pulsating kid with a toolbox get a wad of sweet cash handed over to him, money that was going back to AVCOM. Not that I was going to spend it on sexual favors from a gang of junkie whores – and I mean that in the nicest way. I was worried that, as a group, they could take me down with a few swift kicks and abscond with the dough. I tucked the green in my pocket and made a beeline for the exit. The ladies crowded me like I was a Beatle in *A Hard Day's Night*. They groped and caressed me as I zipped past them, "Hey, baby, wanna date?" "Where ya goin', baby?" Admittedly, I did feel popular for a sec, but nonetheless I hightailed my ass out of there. I stepped out into the noonday sun and stopped to take a deep breath. The little dude in the gold tux looked at me like I was just another weirdo among the low-lifes in that carnival of sex, crime and drugs.

"Fuck's up with you now, my brother?" I shook my head, assuring him I'm okay.

That was just the first of my theater visits for the day. The next stop on the list, Eros 1, was right across the street. I glanced up at it just in time to see my favorite dance couple headed in. This was an all-day thing for them, show after show, as if they were in some sort of touring vaudeville review.

My visits to the porn district continued for a year or so. I never had the chance to save the girl from her life of darkness, although I did eventually get to talk to her in one of the projection booths. Standing there naked, she told me this job was temporary and eventually she wanted to work her way up to featured dancer in a topless review in Atlantic City, "But my tits are too small," she said. "I'm saving up for bigger ones." She had a goal and she was striving to reach it. I have to say, that was rather admirable.

My time at AVCOM was coming to its natural end. I was working there 9 to 5 during the day, doing standup late into the night and still sleeping in four-hour shifts. My interest in porn-theater projector repair was waning and my bosses could see it. The job finally ended months later when the company was shuttered after my boss was arrested. His son had murdered someone in a street fight and my boss had helped his kid bury the body. It was soon discovered in a shallow grave, not too far from his house. The father and son both went to prison and I started doing standup comedy full time.

WHEN DO I GET MY SITCOM?

DURING THE LATE '70s and into the '80s, it seemed like standups were getting launched into super-stardom overnight. Usually, all it took was a flawless appearance on Johnny Carson's *Tonight Show*.

Freddie Prize, clearly an inspiration to me to from the start, was a nineteen-year-old kid from Washington Heights and a New York Improv comic when Johnny's people discovered him. Young, charming, handsome; part Puerto Rican and part Hungarian, he joked, "I'm a Hungarican." The world fell in love with Freddie during his national TV début on *The Tonight Show*. A few short days after his appearance, he was signed on to star in the TV pilot, *Chico and The Man*. It was an instant hit. Soon after, another young comedian, Jimmie Walker was discovered at The Improv. He was an instantly likable, skinny black kid who found his way out of a life with militant black activists and into a career in comedy. He was rocketed from the Bronx ghetto into a fake TV ghetto in Hollywood on a show called *Good Times*. Jimmie "J.J." Walker played the wisecracking older son in a black family living paycheck to paycheck in the projects. It ran for six seasons.

Comedian success stories like these ignited the standup comedy boom of the 1980s. When I started at The Improv in 1980, most of the comics had a simple, straight career plan. Get on *The Tonight Show*, get a sitcom, get famous. I was too young and too new to grasp the full breadth of this but, yeah, sure, I'd like to have my own sitcom. Why not? Being famous sounded like fun.

I'd never acted before, not even in a school play, but it didn't seem to matter. The word on the street was you just had to deliver a funny joke when the other actors stopped talking. It's what Jimmie "Dy-No-Mite" Walker did on *Good Times*. Florida, his mom, would weep because of the day-to-day pressures of ghetto life, like in the episode when James, the dad and breadwinner, told them he was laid off. Jimmie, fake portrait painting in the background, stepped into center stage and said, "Things'd work out if we got them *cockroaches* to pay rent." So, yeah, maybe sitcom acting's not so hard.

Michael Keaton, who had started his career as a standup, starred in the hugely successful movie comedy, *Night Shift*. Everyone fell in love with him and he became the new messiah of funny. The premise of his next movie, *Mr. Mom*, was a familiar old chestnut; the stay-at-home dad who didn't know what he was doing. The movie was wall-to-wall old-school gags. You know 'em: suds flowing out of the washing machine, vacuum cleaner blowing *out* dirt, food burning up in the oven. Keaton rose above the material and made the movie into a hit. Executives at ABC thought, "Why not make it into a sitcom?"

Keaton was a movie star now, so of course, he wasn't going to get anywhere near a sitcom, so ABC launched a national search for the TV version of Michael Keaton.

The manager of The Improv at the time was my best friend Joel Goss. His then-wife was a partner at a large New York City casting agency that was tasked to help find the small-screen Michael Keaton. That connection gave me the inside scoop on what was happening. Word was, they'd been auditioning comics and actors for over a year and were yet to find their star. Comedians Jay Leno and Bill Maher, from what I understood, had auditioned for the part. ABC was worried that Jay's chin was too frightening for the kid audience.

I felt like a big shot with my inside Hollywood news. I'd share what gossip I'd heard with my friends back in Waterbury, "Yeah, they're doing a *Mr. Mom* project, havin' trouble finding their Keaton. Crazy business." I was a gossip column idiot.

Through Joel, I found out that the casting people were coming to The Improv, hoping to strike gold from their roster of seasoned standups. I needed to be there that night. I was still somewhat new to everything, so I figured I could learn volumes just by sitting back and watching comics work under pressure. With any luck, I'd get to see one of my new comedy friends jump to superstardom!

A crew of four or five casting people, along with Joel's wife and an executive from ABC, showed up at the club, poised and ready to find their star. Everyone who went up seemed relaxed and on point. Joel was giving me audition updates, relayed to *him* from his wife. They were getting frustrated. A few hours in and they'd yet to see their TV Keaton. As the night dragged on, one of the casting executives saw me walk by their table and commented, "See, he's the look we want. Too bad that kid's not a comic."

Joel's wife perked up. She couldn't wait to spring the news. "Uh, well, it just so happens that he *is* a comic." They were all abuzz, "When is he on?" "Let's get him up there." "Great! This could be great!"

Suddenly, my twenty-whatever-year-old, inexperienced face had a network audition for a primetime ABC sitcom!

Not to brag, but in my twenties, I was mid-America handsome. A poor man's John Travolta, if you will, with my blue eyes, dimpled chin, full head of hair and chiseled cheeks. Sadly, I've since morphed into Shrek.

From the club's launching pad in the back of the room, I readied myself to be rocketed onto the stage. I had no prep time; I didn't even have time to be nervous. I was fueled on sheer will. I'd rarely been on The Improv stage during the shank of the night, but here I went. Hitting the stage, I started reeling off the jokes I'd been honing in the shitty beer joints around town.

"You been to that crappy diner on the corner? They have a lobster tank, but it has fish sticks floating around...Dogs are always comin' in my yard to eat outta my trashcans. I had to hire a maitre d'...Can for two? Right this way...Perhaps something by the hedge?"

The audience was laughing. They seemed to really like me. I suddenly felt like I was one of the primetime guys, slick and professional, as if I've been doing it for twenty years.

"My apartment's in midtown, ten thousand a month. It's two rooms -- a bathroom and a fire-escape landing. The roaches have attitude. I tried killing 'em with a Roach Motel. Not only do they *check out*, they steal the towels."

Okay, material better suited for Jimmie J.J. Walker, but it didn't matter. At that moment, I was in the zone. I even forgot that I was in the middle of a high-stakes audition. I ended with one of my dopey impressions and bounded off the stage to sweet, enthusiastic applause.

When I got back to the bar, I was crowded by the casting people. They were smiling, excited. They even seemed relieved. I was being bombarded with congratulations and handshakes as if I were THE Michael Keaton in the flesh. Business cards came flying at me. The execs were ready to set up meetings, auditions and office visits to the network. They shook my hand again and left satisfied. I don't think they even went back into the showroom to see the rest of the auditions.

What just happened? I'd been in New York City a little over a year and now I have ABC at my feet. This can't be right. It can't be!

I coordinated a meeting at a twenty-something-story high, glass walled corporate building somewhere in midtown Manhattan. Making my way up to the tenth floor, I was bleary-eyed and confused. After all, this whole thing had come down only the night before. A wrangler greeted me and told me Cody would be ready for me shortly. Cody was one of the people I had met in the bar after my set. He had cast popular TV shows back then like, *Barney Miller*, *WKRP in Cincinnati*, and *Newhart*. This was the real deal.

The wrangler-lady handed me some pages. "Here are your sides."

Sides? What the hell's she talking about? Sides are what I get with my roast beef at The Blarney Stone. These were script pages. "You'll be reading for Jack. And Caroline is your wife." Damn, a wife? I don't know anything about having a wife.

I hoped I hadn't said that out loud.

There were so many things zipping through my brain, I'm surprised I had the capacity to find the building I was in. After about ten minutes, Cody came out of his office, delighted to see me, "You got your sides?" This confirmed that the script pages were, in fact called "sides." "Let's see what you did with them."

"What?" I thought. *"What does that mean? What I did with them? I folded them."* I found out later that he was asking me how I had interpreted the sides and what my choice for the character was.

He escorted me into a little office with bare walls, a desk and not much else. My guess was that it was a temporary space and nothing like the giant, Emmy-filled office he had somewhere on a big ol' production lot in the middle of Hollywood.

He sat at his desk, his sides at the ready, "I'll be playing Caroline, your wife."

"Great" I said with a shudder. I was hoping to fall into a comfort zone, kinda like I did onstage the night before. The gruff voice of my wife asked, "How could you forget to pick up Alex? He was waiting at school for an hour."

I read from my sides, flatly, quietly, clumsily and unsure. "I, uh, I told you, uh, I had to pick up dry cleaners, uh, cleaning for [clearing my throat] We, we're, uh..."

Cody stopped me, "You okay? Relax."

I gathered myself, "I'm good, yeah."

My wife continued, "It's simple, pick up your son at school, then get the dry cleaning."

I was ready, "The cleaners were about to close, so, I uh, waited -- I wanted to shake-sure. Sorry." I corrected myself. "Uh, *make sure*. Uh, read it too fast. I thought it said...Got confused on that...part."

My chest grew cold and my head started to buzz as it got warmer. My heart punched through my chest. I was sure Cody could see me starting to melt right in front of him. He tried to help. "Just relax. You don't have to hit the words a hundred percent. Let's try again."

My wife admonished me. "The party was cancelled, I didn't need that dress. Or did you forget?"

Words were spinning on the page, "I, uh, the dress...Uh..." I was suddenly Bob Newhart when he's playing his most nervous. It's not what Cody wanted. It didn't matter; it was my natural response. "I, uh, [clears throat], I, think that, uh, [clears throat louder]..."

Cody was growing frustrated and started massaging his forehead, "Mike, just be that guy you were onstage. Loose, open, funny, in the moment."

I could do that, I thought, but it was not happening right then and there, that's for sure. I went from bad to worse. Cody's enthusiasm was waning, "I get it, don't worry." He was comforting, "You're not used to this. You usually have an audience and a comedy environment to bounce off of." I couldn't agree more, and I appreciated that he was letting me escape from this experiment with some shred of dignity.

"So, Mike, here's what I think'll help." Help? Wait, this isn't over? "I want to give you a screen test." No sense. This made no sense. "I think we'll get you in a space with lights, people will be there to laugh. It'll be more like a comedy-club feeling."

Nodding. I just did a lot of nodding. He had me take the sides with me, hoping that I would memorize them. He said he would get me on camera that weekend, "You'll do great."

I got back to my apartment, stunned, lost, confused. I kept staring at my sides. I'd pick them up, read through them. I kept doing it, picking them up, reading them. Three pages; one minute and twenty-five seconds of acting. I was freaked out. Where's Freddie Prinze when you need him? I came up with a plan. I'd record my wife's part on a tape recorder, leaving pauses for my part and then just act with myself. If nothing else, it was a clever idea. I fumbled through it, but the plan wasn't working. There was nothing natural about it. It was Friday afternoon and my screen test was set for Sunday morning. I still had to suffer through two days of this.

I had a standup gig that Friday and Saturday night at The Cork 'n' Board, or some dumb comedy shithole like that. It was all the way out in Long Island, I think. All I remember was that I had to get on a train at Penn Station and schlep out to who-the-fuck knows where. *Christ*, just let me stay home. Don't they understand I have 90 seconds of script to learn? And if I didn't, America was going to miss out on TV's Michael Keaton. *Ahh, shit*! I was having a breakdown.

I took my sides with me on the train, read them aloud, pretending to talk into my tape recorder. Which was, again, kinda clever of me. I don't remember a thing about the gig or that whole weekend; I just kept studying the script. Reading it really, I didn't know what else to do with it... except fold it. Finally, Saturday night, I'm done with the gig, I roll back into Penn Station and...

I can't find the sides.

"Where are the sides? Are you shitting me? Gone! The sides are fucking gone!"

They weren't in my pockets, not on the seat or the floor. It was time to get off the train. *"Dead. I'm dead!"*

Now, this was years before the Internet, email and texting. I still had a rotary phone *fer-fucksake*! There was no way anyone could get new pages to me.

Saturday night, I'm spinning in my apartment. I can't go to this audition. I need the comfort of those pages in my hand. Wait! My tape recorder. I recorded myself doing my wife's part. That would cue me for my part. I played it back. It worked. It helped me remember my lines. It should have; I went through the fucking script one thousand times. I scribbled out the script, then typed it up.

Sunday morning and I was fantastic, young–boy adorable and as ready as I was gonna be. I headed out to ABC Studios in the upper West 70s and into the small castle-looking production studio. Cody greeted me and escorted me into a full-on TV soundstage. Rows of hot white lights hanging high up on a grid pointed down onto a fake TV bedroom, the set from one of their popular soap operas. Cameras were everywhere, along with a full production crew; cameramen, lighting people and sound guys holding boom mics. Folks with headsets and clipboards were circling and pointing randomly.

I was never ever on a real TV production set before and was trying hard to keep it together. They introduced me to my wife. Uh, wait, wife…? I was doing this with a real actress? She was a cute, perky, and smiling redhead. I was not comfortable chatting it up with random pretty women as it was and now I'm married to one?? Cody instructed me to crawl into bed with her for this scene.

I had questions --

"PLACES EVERYONE." Oh well. Forget that.

I realized I still had my sides in my hand. What the fuck was my plan with those? I squished them into my pocket and got into bed with my wife. I was expected to get all cozy with her. I stared out at the crew staring back at me. I could tell that the schlubby guy holding the boom mic hated his life and hated it more because he was working on a Sunday. *And* it was all *my* fault. A bell sounded and someone yelled, *"ACTION!"*

Wife: "Jack, did you pick up my dress for my San Diego conference?"

Mike as Jack: "Ahbaa, did you...I, uh...[GOING BLANK] Yeah?"
Wife [FORGING AHEAD]: "No? Really. Jack?"
Mike as Jack: "I, uh, I was going to but, uh. Uhhh —- [EVEN MORE BLANK]."

The schlubby boom-guy rolled his eyes. Cody, frustrated, rubbed his forehead as he paced. At this point I was staring out, my eyes dead, like I had just gotten biffed in the noggin' with a 1-by-8.

"*CUT!*"

A loud bell rang and then things got quiet. Cody stepped over to me and quietly told me to relax. "That's all you need to do."

Yeah, right. All I *really* needed to do was study three years at the Academy of Dramatic Arts. My only other acting experience was when Waterbury had a pageant in the local stadium to celebrate its 300-year history and I was a Chickasaw warrior dressed in buckskin and a feathered war bonnet. I was supposed to chase a Confederate soldier across a football field, and I slipped on a pile of horseshit and fell on the back of my head. So far, my *Mr. Mom* audition was about as humiliating.

Cody, clearly exasperated, could tell I was collapsing just like I did in his office a few days earlier, "Mike, just make up the words. Say whatever you want to say. Play." My wife nodded in agreement. Little did she know a divorce was imminent.

"*PLACES.*"

I crawled back into bed with my wife. She was comforting, as a wife should be when her husband is in trouble. The bell rang again. "We're rollin'."

Wife: "Jack, did you pick up my dress for the San Diego conference?"
Mike as Jack: "Heeey, yeah. I was going to, but then I didn't...do...it."
Wife: "No? Really. Jack?"

I actually got a line out -- sort of. I felt confident enough to turn to her. I was still wearing my shoes and my feet got tangled in the bed sheets. I felt like a fish caught in a tuna net. My body was contorted as I tried my best to continue.

Mike as Jack: [*NOTHING... I HAD NOTHING*]

The anxiety of it all won, and won big. My mind was one hundred percent blank. I saw Cody sink, "Okay, that's a cut! Take five everyone."

With that, the crew slinked out. My wife didn't even say goodbye to me. I tried to untangle myself from the bed sheets. Cody, disappointed that his experiment didn't work, thanked me for trying. It was all he could do.

I remember walking twenty or so blocks back to my apartment. Through the din of the thick Upper Westside traffic, I was trying like hell to make sense of the whole experience. It was obvious that I didn't have any natural acting ability. If I did, this memoir would likely be about my battle with drugs during my *Mr. Mom* days in Hollywood.

This moment of reflection reminded me how much I liked writing. I could focus on that, I thought, and with any luck I'd become successful enough to write myself into my own projects. It was youthful innocence talking, but it still made some sense. I found comfort with this plan.

The acting bug never took hold. As for *Mr. Mom*, ABC made the pilot with Dick Van Dyke's son, Barry, as the new Michael Keaton. That one episode aired later that year on ABC's *Summer Playhouse* -- better known to the industry back then as "the TV pilot graveyard."

As I reached my corner on West 54th and 9th Avenue, I felt the crumpled-up sides in my pocket. I fished them out, looked at them, thought about what just happened to me and echoed, "What have I done with them? Here's what I've done with them..." I ripped them to shreds and, in celebration, tossed them like confetti. The Korean lady at the corner store yelled at me for messing up her sidewalk.

NEW YORK IS WHERE I'D RATHER STAY

During the mid-1980s, if you owned or operated anything resembling a pool hall, piano bar or car wash, chances are you converted it into a comedy club. At the crest of the comedy boom, I was hitting countless one-nighters in every bar, closet and cubbyhole in New Jersey, Long Island, Connecticut, and upstate New York. I was raking in fifty-five buckeroos a show at such prestigious establishments as Mermaids Landing, The Penny Arcade, Chester Drawers and The Cinnamon Tree. In Manhattan, I'd take in a few hundred more on weekends at the primo clubs like The Improv, Catch A Rising Star or The Comedy Cellar. At my New York standup peak, I was looking at thirty large a year. That was a lot of cash for me, especially since I was single and paying just three fifty a month for a fourth-floor walkup studio apartment in midtown. Yep. I was finally living alone, far away from Al's couch and his pesky ghosts.

During those days, comics were flying around the country working week-long gigs in converted barns, truck stops and bowling alleys and making some serious bank. I finally signed on for a three-week run in Atlanta and Savannah, Georgia. They handed over a handsome three hundred and fifty smackers a week for me to do my twenty hilarious minutes a night, twice a night, three nights a week.

One club owner, thinking drugs were currency, kept trying to pay me in cocaine. This was the same guy who drove me to the gig from the airport, and for the hour-long ride, he bragged about the star-studded, big-time wedding he had the previous weekend. Comics, bookers and club owners flew in from around the country to witness his nuptials.

That first night after the show, I was road-weary and anxious to get back to the hotel and hit the hay, but I had to wait for the newlywed club owner to finish his club-owner business. He was my ride back to The Red Roof Inn. After a half-hour, I finally got his attention, "Uh, hey, I need to get back to the hotel. I'm tired."

He was so disappointed, "Aw, man. Really? I thought you and I were gonna hang out and pick up some skank."

I called a cab.

This was not the grand comedy tour I had imagined. In Savannah, I had to share a condo with a female comic who farted nonstop. In Atlanta, I had my own room in an amazing historic hotel. The closing act, a prop guy, showed up in my room, desperate. He needed money badly, so he lied to the club owner and told him that he wasn't staying at the hotel. Then he convinced him to pay him the money he's not spending on the room and told me that now he didn't have a place to stay. He'd live in his car if he had to, but he hoped I'd let him stay on my couch. I agreed. A few minutes later, he walked in with his wife and kid. He assured me they wouldn't get in the way.

I came home to New York broke, puffy-faced from drinking, and bright red from some sort of bedbug back rash from the comedians' condo. Clearly, "the road" was not my thing. I needed the energy of the wild-eyed crack heads, wandering hobos and teams of prostitutes of NYC to keep my comedy fire burning.

Every crevice and corner of Manhattan had its charm -- like the homeless dude that slept in my doorway. His pants, soaked in pee and soot and filth, were ripped open at the crotch. His jacket was torn in shreds like he'd just had a tussle with a bobcat. He was sniveling, unshaven, and he had missing teeth. His knit hat read, "I'd Rather Be Skiing."

The Blarney Stone Pub in my 'hood was the place to be to see real life play out. One night, while sitting there assessing the health risks of my roast beef -- if you slapped down five bucks, they'd let you eat like a king at their tasty steam table -- a crazy drunk guy started screaming at a sleepy-eyed old lady slumped over the bar. She likely had a few too many Midoris. The drunk started wailing on her. I mean, he's throwin' full-on haymakers at her head. Luckily, another guy swooped in to save the day. The bartender, calmly wiping a glass, stopped this hero in progress to tell him, "It's okay. Dat's his mother."

New York always had that undeniable energy where I felt that something surprising or special or weird or dangerous or life changing could happen at any moment.

Almost every Friday night, right after the Broadway shows ended, my friend Joel Goss and I, along with other comedy friends, Broadway actors, singers and the like would meet up at Barrymore's, a now-defunct bar just blocks from the warm lights of Broadway. You would find us gathered at a huge round table (identified by staff as Big B) where we'd all tell rousing showbiz stories, old jokes and whatever else would make us laugh (or "larf," as Joel would say) like idiots. We also drank. On some nights, we would imbibe with the gusto of John Barrymore himself. More often than not, a Broadway star would join us. They'd be fresh off the stage, still with hints of greasepaint on their faces.

Joel was well known and liked in Broadway circles. Affable and charming, he loved it when he could connect people together and get them laughing and having a spiritedly good time.

I had met Joel some time before at The Improv. He would stop by the club from time to time to chat it up with his comedian friends. They respected his sharp eye for comedy and his thoughts on how they could better their standup sets. Silver Friedman recognized his ability and it wasn't long before he was manager of The Improv and assembling the nightly shows.

Joel was friends with the captain of Big B, Broadway legend, George Hearn. I was too disconnected and ignorant of anything to do with Broadway to understand who I was fortunate enough to get drunk with on these Fridays. George wasn't afraid to sip a few Rob Roys and command the table with his booming Broadway voice. I always appreciated the joke he'd retell whenever a new celeb would join us. I remember, at different times, watching Chita Rivera, Fred Gywnn and Sally Struthers laughing hysterically at George's punchline that I think had something to do with a bull moose fucking a tree. George, at the time, was starring in the hit Broadway musical, *La Cage Aux Folles*. *La Cage* also had a co-star slot designed to rotate high-profile actors into the mix.

One Friday, our surprise mystery guest and *La Cage* co-star was 1940s movie icon Van Johnson. He was surprisingly tall and quite dapper in his classic, black and sleek, yet slightly ill-fitting tux. My guess: it was a rental. Barrymore's was funky and laid back, an odd place to wear a tux. He still looked like the same fighter pilot I saw in the old black-and-white war movies. I watched them as a kid with my dad on Sunday afternoons while my mom wrestled pots and pans in the kitchen, readying up our Sunday pot roast.

Looking closer at Van, I couldn't help but notice that he was wearing bright blue eye shadow. I'm talkin' something buxom comic actress Renee Taylor would paint on her lids to match her blouse. I thought, *"Was he in such a hurry to get here that he couldn't find the nine seconds to spit on a towel and wipe the* La Cage *off him?"*

He sat next to me.

Drinks were flowing, stories of the old studio system were retold. George got to tell the bull moose fucking a tree joke. We laughed at it yet again. Eventually, Van talked to me directly, face-to-face; mostly small talk, but the whole time I thought, *"I can't wait to tell my parents that I was talking to the real deal World War II ace fighter-pilot, the MGM machine gunner who, throughout his movie career, killed thousands of Krauts, Japs and still found time to kick Gig Young's ass and romance June Allyson."* Casual yet with an off-putting sense of confidence, he asked me if I lived nearby.

"Yeah" I answered, thinking maybe he was considering buying up some property on the West Side.

"So, uh, is it walking distance?"

"Yeah" I said. "I walked here tonight." He leaned in, not much but, you know, just enough. He stared at me with his robin-egg-blue-shaded eyelids and asked me, "You want to go for a walk?"

Wow...! Wow! Van Johnson was hitting on me!

My knee-jerk reaction was to go into Bill Daily mode. You know, the guy from *I Dream Of Jeannie* and the pilot neighbor from *The Bob Newhart Show*. Like him, I started to repeatedly yet lightly slap my open palms on my chest while gasping for air and words, "I uhh...wow, uh...hmm...woo." Through desperation and misguided instincts, I actually did the finger tap to the face of my watch and placed it to my ear to check if it was still ticking. This was to create the illusion that I was supposed to be somewhere of import, and I was seriously late due to my crappy watch.

I politely told him that I couldn't walk anywhere. I mean, I could *walk*. I was able. My legs worked, but not at that moment, because I was thrown off-balance. I told him, unconvincingly, that I had to leave so I could get across town to start my night of standup...comedy...shows. Yeah. That seemed like a viable thing to say.

He gave me a nod that let me know that he fully understood the subtext of my response. He knew that any sort of hand-in-hand romantic walk through the drug-dealer-filled 9th Avenue to my studio apartment was not likely. I was rejecting him. It was a feeling I was all too familiar with. Many's the time I'd ask a woman if she'd like to "go for a walk." More often than not, I'd get that same panicked, wide-eyed reaction, clumsy lie, and then their mad dash for the nearest exit.

I really was flattered, to be honest. Unfortunately for Van, I had a different romantic preference, although if his favorite costar, June Allyson, wanted to go for a walk, well, I'd take that walk.

I thought about that moment and considered for a second what might've happened if things, you know, went a different way. I laughed thinking about my parents (especially my dad) and what that phone call would be like the next morning, "Dad, I've got some good news and some, uh, interesting news..." He never would've understood. All I told him was that I had drinks that night with one of his fighter-pilot buddies, and left it at that.

This was New York City. If I were working shithole gigs out on the road, I wouldn't have had these experiences. Like the time I ran into a true comedy-hero. I was dining at a mid-town deli, and Carl Reiner, yes, *THE* Carl Reiner, came in alone. Carl started as a writer/performer on one of the very first TV sketch shows, the legendary *Your Show of Shows*. He later went on to create one of the best sitcoms ever, *The Dick Van Dyke Show*. Carl inspected a table near me. Finding it suitable, he slipped off his coat, folded it and carefully laid it out over the back of the seat. He took off his walker snap-brim hat and placed it elegantly on a shelf high up behind him and sat down to study the menu. I stole looks at him, hoping that I could conjure up some sort of moment that would connect us. I mean, I was a friggin' standup comic for almost two whole years at that point. Carl and I were peers, we were brethren of funny, so why shouldn't I talk to him?

He finished his triple-decker corned-beef sandwich and alas, there was still no connection, no knowing nod, no idiotic thumbs-up from me to him. He got up and gathered himself while still sucking meat trapped betwixt his teeth. It was my final window of opportunity, but there was no way I was going to gather the courage to make my presence known. I just nibbled at my chicken sandwich, resigned to the notion that I could at least someday tell my kids that I saw him, Alan Brady, Rob Petrie's boss, right there, two tables away.

He slipped his coat on and reached up and grabbed his hat up off the shelf. Flypaper was stuck to the bottom of it. He tried flicking it off. No dice. He pulled on the corner of it. Half of it tore off and stuck to his fingers. He studied it in disbelief before desperately trying to flick the gluey paper from his fingers. *Holy smack,* suddenly I was in a real live *Your Show of Shows* sketch!

He caught me smiling at him. Seeing that he had an audience, he started playing up the comedy of it all. He tried again to pull it off with a napkin, only to make a bigger, sticky, papery mess. He inexplicably whacked it on the table. Then he stared it down like it was an animal ready to pounce. He shook his head in defeat and presented the compromised fedora to me and asked, "Wanna hat?" I smiled as I tried to figure out if he was serious or not. He shrugged and walked off with the hat, likely to fight it again, head-to-head in a more private moment.

I CONSIDER TRANSITIONING

From 1980 to 1990, The Improv became my home away from home. If I didn't get onstage, I'd at least get to hang out with my comedy brothers and sisters. Those long nights guaranteed laughs, great stories, idiocy, camaraderie and free tuna melts. I was living my comedy dream.

In 1981, Andy Kaufman got back to his comedy-club roots and started hanging out with us at The Improv. This was right around the time he "hurt" his neck wrestling. He stayed committed to his character and proudly wore his neck brace 24/7.

I did get to spend some time with Andy during those days. He was a soft, gentle, childlike soul. Over time, he got to like me and trust me. One night, he took me aside and asked if I'd referee a wrestling match on The Improv stage. Yes. Of course, I would!

I had no idea what I was in for. He didn't give me any instructions or anything. He just told me he was going to get a real woman from the audience to volunteer. All I had to do was make sure I'd "call it" when he pinned her to the floor.

Neck brace and all, Andy got onstage and strutted, as wrestlers do, and mocked women. He mimed the indignity of household chores, barking out that they should stay at home and "Do the cookin' and cleanin' and ironin'." He was no longer that little kid I just talked to, he was an asshole, on point to provoke every woman within earshot. I was standing alongside him, feeling the wave of anger build as women started to crowd the stage. He made his offer. "One thousand dollars to any of you little ladies who thinks she can take me down!"

Andy, of course, picked the smallest woman from the audience. She jumped onstage like a bobcat, ready to pounce. Andy's provocations had her white hot with anger. They went right at each other. I circled them as I'd seen refs do on TV, not really sure of what else was expected of me. More women gathered from the audience and formed a human wall at the edge of the stage. They whooped and screamed and cheered on their scrappy soul sister as Andy flipped her around like a sack of laundry. I was worried -- someone could get seriously hurt.

He thumped his chest as he circled her, "Women are nothing! You are weak!" Things started to get tense, I could feel it. One wrong move and this could take a bad turn.

As ref, I did have some power up there. When Andy dropped her on her back, I called it. I had to. I wasn't sure if it was the right call, but I had to stop the match. Those ladies were heated and poised to attack like a pack of wolverines. Someone could've ended up dead. In the end, Andy got to keep his 1K and his bragging rights.

On another night, Andy had me play the drums for his famous Elvis impression. (I'll explain about my drumming a little later.) "I do dee Elvis de-Prezly," he told the audience in a Middle-Eastern, childlike voice. He turned his back to the audience. After a quick, dramatic slick-back combing of his hair, he slowly turned back to the audience. He curled up his lip as he morphed into a confident and powerful 1950s Elvis. He shook and shimmied around as he sang *Hound Dog* exactly like The King. I clanked away at the drums as I tried to remember whatever skills I had from my garage-band

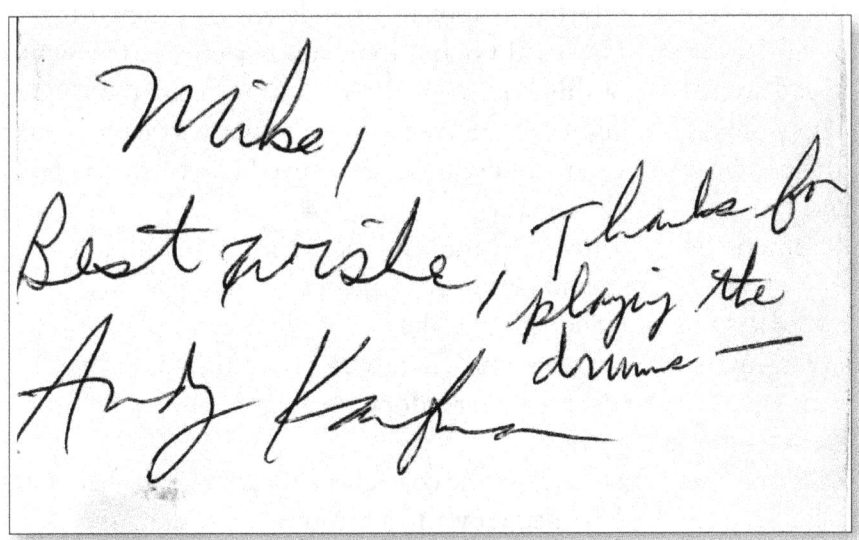

A treasured moment.

days. Andy danced in front of me. I saw only his silhouette through the bright spotlight. At song's end, he took a few Elvis-type curtsies and then strutted off the stage. "Ladies and gentleman, Elvis has left the building!"

My short time with Andy was inspirational. Unknowingly, he helped reignite my writer's brain. It motivated me to use the entire Improv in weird and experimental ways. One night during my set, I stepped offstage with mic in hand and exited the building. Invisible to the audience, I changed up my voice and pretended to be random passers-by like a scary, hardcore dealer selling muffins. "Yo. I got loose blueberry-ass ma'fuckin' muffins! Check 'em out." It became a regular part of my act.

One night when I was emcee, I set up Ray Romano, then unknown, in the back of the audience. I told everyone that we had an up-and-coming Broadway star with us. I made up the name of a stupid musical and gave Ray a dopey stage name. The spotlight swung over to him and the audience applauded as Ray stood up and took a few bows. They just assumed he was legit. Later in the night, I sat Ray in another section of the audience and told everyone that we had a famous sitcom star with us. Again, I made up a name of a stupid sitcom and gave him a new actorly-sounding moniker. The spotlight swung around to him, this time to the other side of the club. The audience started to applaud, then laughed as they realized it was Ray again. He stood up and took another precious showbiz bow. I went for it a third time. Why not? I introduced the star of a new movie. The light swung over to yet another part of the club. The people knew what was coming. Ray bowed his "celebrity" bow and everyone laughed again.

Sometimes I'd just wander into the room during the middle of a show, holding a pen and clipboard. I'd carefully and quietly inspect the pipes and air conditioning, then scribble down notes while I shook my head with concern. There was no point, no ending, no punchline. It was just me being a dope, stealing focus from whomever was onstage.

I found a set of golf clubs in the coat-check room. Pulling them out, I slid out a club and handed it over to a fellow comic. I slung the clubs on my back, and then we stepped into the room, interrupting the show. With me as the caddy, we pretended to be playing through. The comic onstage, Mark Cohen (my close friend for much of my time in New York) waited patiently as he tossed out hilarious puns about balls and a hole-in-one. We eventually exited out the door onto 44th Street.

Around this time, I was learning more about who I was and what I wanted out of my career. It turns out that Rodney Dangerfield was right: it does take a long time to discover your true comedy voice. I was a bunch of years in and started thinking that maybe I didn't have that fire in me to get to a level where I'd have the same impact as my heroes, Robert Klein, Steve Martin and George Carlin. My years of give-and-take with every kind of audience in so many different situations made me feel like I'd already discovered everything I needed to discover about myself as a standup. Maybe it was because by the mid-1980s, during the comedy boom, standup was becoming oversaturated. To me, it didn't seem as cool and special as an art form like when I first started. Even in Manhattan, the comedy spaces started to become slipshod and uninspired.

Maybe I just needed to be more discerning with my choices.

There was a mob-owned strip club in the East 50s in Manhattan. The owner, Donny, a little weasely thug with that New Yawk "Wha-da-fuck?" attitude, concluded that patrons would be more excited about standup comics than naked lady breasts. He haphazardly renovated this shithole into a comedy club and called it Rags to Riches. Leaving the stripper poles and a scuffed up, mirrored stage, he didn't even bother to steam out the steeped-in smells of horny businessmen and topless lady perfume from the worn-out carpeting.

After seeing me perform at The Improv, Donny wanted me there for their grand reopening. I was hesitant; my home clubs were all on the West Side. The trek in a cab through Central Park to the East Side and then all the way back to the West Side could easily topple my carefully curated comedy-club plan.

On my best nights, I'd set up a straight shot down 9th Avenue into Greenwich Village, hitting every funny hut along the way. I'd start at Standup New York in the upper 70s, then hit The Improv at 44th and 9th, then Caroline's when it was on 8th and 23rd. Next,

The Comedy Cellar in the Village, along with The Village Gate, and The Boston Comedy Club. On some nights, I'd open for the headliner at The Bottom Line along the way. One Saturday night, I think I broke the record, coming in at eleven ma'fuckin' shows in one swoop!

Donny heard the hesitation in my voice when he offered me the opening 9 o'clock spot for the next Saturday night. He quickly turned into an angry mob guy, "What? You don't wanna do my club? Sometin' wrong with my fuckin' club? Fuck's wrong with you?"

I was in a cab heading across town.

I arrived ten minutes early and there wasn't an audience member in sight. Donny was pacing as he grumbled to Joe, some bad-hairpiece-wearing business partner, "Jesus, Joey where in-da-fuck is ev-ra-boddy?"

The strippers were replaced on stage by two life-sized stuffed clowns wearing full-on bright, puffy clown suits, red-and-white slap shoes and clowny face makeup. Each was on a motorized spinner that slowly twirled it round and round like souvlaki in a Times Square food stand. In the din of the vacant room, all I could hear was their little motors chugging and whirring mightily. These smiling cotton-filled bozos were, I'd bet, refugees from a Chuck E. Cheese who'd taken a bad turn in their careers. It sadly landed them in Manhattan strip palace.

A rumpled and round middle-aged guy wearing a fat black mustache and serial-killer aviation glasses stepped in. He looked around, then instantly backed out. My guess was that he didn't get the mailer that noted the change of venue. Or maybe the clowns understandably scared him off. Not sure.

It crept towards fifteen minutes past show time and still no signs of an audience. A few waitresses stood at the ready, trays in hand. The clowns little motors somehow sounded louder. I think Donny took this failure personally, as if people weren't showing up was a "fuck you" to him. I started to get anxious. As predicted, this gig was going to throw off my whole West Side comedy schedule. I had no choice, though; there was a decent chance Donny woulda put a hit out on me if I didn't show up.

As the clock hit 9:30, Donny scanned the empty room, then shook his head in disbelief. Defeated, he muttered, "Joey...Shut off da clowns."

My desire to get a room full of strangers to like me was waning. The standup-comedy fire in me was flickering. It was hard to admit this to myself. After all, standup had been all that mattered to me since I was fourteen. I hoped this feeling was just a phase and I figured that if I just kept hitting the stage, I'd find my way again.

My instincts told me to try writing jokes again for Rodney. I called him at his club and he jumped on the phone when he heard I was a joke writer. I didn't bother to tell him of our past; there was no way he'd remember. I did lie though and told him I had an armload of killer jokes at the ready. He couldn't wait. "Stop by the club. Lemme see what ya got."

Holy shit! I had nothing. Cornered and panicked, I whipped out a legal pad and spent the next week in my apartment scribbling out comedy gold.

"I went out with a woman. Ooh, she was ugly. After we had sex, I got arrested for bestiality."

Okay, maybe not gold, more like copper. It didn't matter; I was making inroads into what turned out to be the next phase of my career.

With notepad under my arm, I headed across town to Dangerfield's.

Rodney, wearing his blousy, worn-out blue robe, paced, nonstop in his dank, windowless dressing room. I was nervously pitching my clunky one-liners and it wasn't going great. Finally, after one of my jokes, he stopped pacing. Did I finally land one? He turned, opened his robe and started peeing into the sink, "They don't gimme a toilet down here. I gotta piss in the sink, ya know?"

And there was my first big-time professional showbiz lesson: While you're pouring your heart out, they're pissing in the sink.

I WAS HAVING AN AFFAIR

It's eleven at night and I was alone on a train platform in the middle of Newark, New Jersey. I was too young and dumb to know that the only reason to venture anywhere near there was to buy crack or get shot. It was 1980, thirteen years after devastating race riots tore through that city, and it had not yet healed. The burned-down buildings were vacant lots that the homeless converted into trailer parks fashioned from abandoned cars and torn pup tents. Most of the tenement buildings that survived were abandoned and boarded up. The few signs of life came from the flickering lights on the corner liquor store and check-cashing depot. If you were living there at that time (if you call that living) you were, no doubt, working professionally as either a thief, a crack dealer, a serial mugger or a hobo -- or all of the above. And there I was, a dopey Connecticut boy, standing in the dark quiet of the ravaged platform waiting for the PATH train to shuttle me back into Manhattan.

I was risking my life in a post-apocalyptic shithole, all in the name of comedy.

I was also growing more concerned about what I had to offer as a standup. I was trying to ignore my feelings for comedy writing, because standup was my lady and I wasn't ready to give her up. There was some flirting with writing, yes, but no betrayal. Okay, well, I found myself sneaking around and helping comics with their sets, adding and editing thoughts and ideas and pitching jokes that'd better suit them than me. It was satisfying to see another comic squeeze out a few extra laughs due to my help.

I was also spending more time with comics who were considering a comedy-writing career. Kevin Rooney was one of the smartest and most eloquent standup comics in my circle of funny friends. Any one of his standup sets could've easily been a piece from *The New Yorker* or *The Harvard Lampoon*. He was a great source for me.

When I was twenty years old, I admitted to him that I hadn't read all that much and wanted to start cracking open some books.

"Mark Twain," he told me without missing a beat. "Start there." *A Tramp Abroad* was his favorite. It soon became one of mine.

Another writer/standup, Barry "Berry" Douglas was a hilarious joke machine. His standup was an unrelenting fireworks display of brilliant one-liners. Quick-hit comedians like Rodney Dangerfield and Redd Foxx courted him for his gags. Barry had already made some headway into the scripted TV world. I wanted to know what he knew. We quickly became good friends and many's the time we'd find ourselves in a 24-hour diner, jabber-jawing into the early morning hours about the best and worst TV sitcoms. We'd nerd-out and break apart episodes and explore their plots, hoping to find clues on how and why they did or didn't work. We'd share and read and reread sitcom and sketch-writing books and, like a book club, we'd discuss their merits.

I still loved standup though. (If standup asks, you and I never spoke.) It's just that comedy writing kept nagging at me. I figured I needed to make good use of the eleven extra hours a day I spent waiting for the comedy-club doors to open. I was drawn to scriptwriting, so, I figured, why not teach myself to write during the day, then tell jokes to the bridge-and-tunnelers at night?

The first thing I learned about the writing process is that before you put pen to paper, there were many more important things that needed to get done first and foremost, like, you know, polishing the fridge door, arranging the coffee cups in the cupboard, cleaning out a drawer. Also, Manhattan Cable had eighty-whatever channels that required careful investigation.

There were no cable-streaming restrictions in 1980. I stumbled onto a phone-in show where you could talk to strippers live and suggest which article of clothing needed to come off next. There was a nude talk show. Yep, fat, middle-aged nude folks, hanging out and chatting away about city ordinances as well as the new porn flick the guest star shot that afternoon. Local hero and smut newspaper publisher Al Goldstein hosted *Midnight Blue*. It was a raunchy, slipshod and dirty talk, review and entertainment show that ran porn movie clips -- carefully obstructing all the hardcore goodness with a floating blue ball -- pun intended, I think. Goldstein would review bad eateries around the city while shoving their shitty food into his face. With his greasy mouth, he'd happily bark out his review, ending with a giant *"FUCK YOU!"* as he angrily threw his middle finger at the camera.

There was infamous videographer Ugly George (an accurate moniker) who skulked the city streets wearing his trademark tight silver-lamé jumpsuit with short shorts. Carrying a video camera and a giant recorder on his back, he would document his exploitation of women. His goal was to coerce an average, everyday New York City lady to duck into the nearest bathroom or alley and take her shirt off for his camera. He was surprisingly successful at this more often than any of us would've guessed. These were weird times.

Then I discovered a show that connected directly to my comedy sensibility. On its surface, it was an old-school TV kiddie show with its congenial and earnest host sporting a colorful porkpie hat and loud jacket. I tuned in just as he was trying -- and failing -- to send out birthday wishes to his fans. His cast and crew mocked him and each other off-camera as they laughed their asses off.

Throughout the show, unwanted and weird characters wearing homemade wrinkled and worn costumes wandered in, one at a time, demanding the host's attention. This led to a fierce back and forth of godawful puns. One of the cast, as Springsteen, warbled through a *Born To Run* song parody. There were corn-ball sketches, pratfalls, pies were thrown, sets collapsed and klieg lights fell as puppets danced to old-timey songs masterfully jangled out on the piano by the host. This was a 1960s TV kiddie show after a deep hit from a 1980s crack pipe.

Live on tape from Newark, New Jersey, it's *The Uncle Floyd Show!*

Uncle Floyd hit all of the sweet spots of my little boyhood days spent in front of our black-and-white TV watching kids shows starring Soupy Sales and Chuck McCann. Floyd was sped-up vaudeville for everyone from kids to stoners (especially stoners). Like Soupy, it had that welcoming clubhouse feel. You felt like you were part of the privileged few who were invited to be a member.

Uncle Floyd -- New Jersey's own Floyd Vivino -- was twenty-five years old at the time, but carried himself as if he were a forty-something knockabout comic from a bygone era. He idolized distant showbiz stars like George Jessel, Al Jolson, Charlie Chaplin and, of course, Soupy and Chuck McCann.

The Uncle Floyd Show became appointment television for me. Since there were no VCRs in 1980, I couldn't record it, so I had to be in front of a TV every night, 6 o'clock to 7, five nights a week. If I missed an episode, it'd be gone forever into the ethers.

Floyd would anchor *Fan Club News;* basically, a commercial for their upcoming live events. Or he'd review actual crayon and pencil-drawn fan art for his *Pictures On The Wall* segment. He'd transform into any one of his dozens of characters like Ricardo Romatico, a pencil-thin-mustachioed Latin lothario. He elegantly puffed his cigarette from a long holder and looked into the camera as he enticed his next lover with all of the romantic Jersey hot spots they'd hit on their date, "Then it's off to Clifton, New Jersey to the Tick Tock diner where'll we watch hobos move into the bathrooms."

Floyd was Eddie Slobbo, a gruff, blue-collar slob who reveled in finding the sloppiest ways to eat the messiest foods. Among many other characters, Floyd also played a possessed preacher, a silent comic and a befuddled Julia Child. He was also the perfect straight man not only for his puppets like Oogie, Mr. Bones and Boxy, but to any one of the dozens of walk-on stooges played by his cast of regulars.

There was Charlie, a great mimic who'd stumble in with his version of Rocky Balboa, odd ball singer Tiny Tim, Rodney Dangerfield or any one of his original off-beat characters like Sven Sweep the janitor or Mr. Mumbles, to name a couple. Netto, who resembled a *Fabulous Furry Freak Brother*, was the bemused resident Dead Head. He was celebrated by fellow cast members if he made it through a sketch without fucking up (because he may or may not have been high on something). Mugsy bridged old school into the new(er) with his parodies of classic rock stars like Springsteen, Dylan, and Neil Young. Scott Gordon was the heavy-set, round, put-upon simp who worked best in tandem with one of Floyd's crazier characters. He was the Oliver Hardy to Floyd's Stan Laurel. Looney Skip Rooney, with his tattered top hat, oversized bowtie and clowny sport coat, was a super-hyped-up Soupy Sales, and he had the font of terrible puns to prove it. Floyd ordered egg-drop soup, Skip got up on a ladder and dropped eggs into a bowl from above. "That's the bit!?" was Floyd's declaration of disappointment after most of Skip's routines.

When a sketch was dying, the real chaos would ensue. Firecrackers were thrown, sets were pushed over, or Africa chanting and sirens were played loud enough to drown out the performer. In truth, the show really worked because of the relationships of its cast. Accidentally or on purpose, each member was a piece to a perfectly fitting puzzle of relationships, the way Hollywood builds out a cast in a sitcom. There was the boss, the stoner, the clown, the bully and the sad sack. More importantly, they were friends, tried and true. It was comedy through camaraderie, like what I witnessed as a kid with the softball players in my dad's bar.

I became obsessed with *The Uncle Floyd Show* and decided that I had to write for it. I'd barely scripted out anything at that point, but I knew this show would be the perfect place to start. I tracked Floyd down through the Channel 68 studios. I got him on the phone and told him I was a standup, I was funny and I was a huge fan. I lied, like I did with Rodney and said I wrote sketches for the show and I'd like to send them over. (The lies were to corner myself into writing.) He was happy to look at them, but warned me that there was no budget for writers. He said that the cast came up with most of what they did on the show. I didn't care about the money. My payment was an education on how to write scripted "funny." Or at least what I thought was funny.

Floyd invited me to a taping to meet up with guys. This was a rinky-dink no–budget show produced in the Channel 68 studios in the middle of where else but downtown Newark? The facilities were surprisingly sleek, modern and sophisticated. I was impressed with it all as I was escorted down the halls into the studio. I bumped into Floyd just as he was unloading boxes from his car. Oogie's puppet head was peering out of the top box, anxious, no doubt, to get out and get on camera. Floyd was harried but happy to meet me. He explained that the boxes of puppets, props and costumes were that night's episode. No scripts, really, just whatever improv, tap dance, messin' around it took to get to the waiting gag or punch line. The show was an hour a night. Some nights they would produce up to three shows.

He took me into the studio. The whole gang was excited I was there. Free bits and gags from a New York City standup, what's not to like? Mugsy was jerry-rigging props together with duct tape, Scott Gordon was carefully trying on different little hats, Looney Skip Rooney was latching on his giant bowtie. Floyd set up his boxes behind his desk as he explained how it all comes together. I felt like a kid in Santa's secret workshop watching the elves gear up for the holidays.

At that moment, Mugsy decided he could use me in one of his bits. That's how things went; pretty much make it up as you go. I was honored to partake. He and Netto were going to race around the Channel 68 studios on little kid pedal-vehicles. Skip called the race as they tooled around, head-to-head, Mugsy on a fire truck, Netto on a racecar. After getting lost and tangled up in bathrooms and offices and production rooms, they passed me at a desk writing for the show, stealing directly from a joke book. I instantly felt like one of the gang and I loved it!

Over the next few days, I wrote up and sent a handful of scripts over to the studio. I watched the show every day, anxious and hoping. Nothing. No sign of my brilliant puppet sketches. I wrote and sent a few more scripts. Days went by, then weeks; no Mike Rowe sketches. Looks like I'd hit the first phase of my comedy-writing education -- rejection. I thought I had a handle on the show. I'd ingested five hours a week of their shenanigans. I mean, I was accepted by the guys with open arms, so you'd think something of mine would've landed over there.

One night, while watching the show and wallowing in self-pity, Oogie, Floyd's ventriloquist puppet, started talking about his weekend with Netto. He was starting my bit.

OOGIE: We went to a baseball game and I caught a foul ball.

FLOYD: Wow. That's great, Oogie.

OOGIE: Then we went to a football game and the quarterback threw the ball and it came flying into the stands, right into my lap.

FLOYD: Wow, those are nice souvenirs. You're very lucky.

OOGIE: Yeah, well, I think my luck's about to run out.

FLOYD: Wha'd ya mean, Oogie?
OOGIE: This weekend Netto's taking me to the Indy 500.

I don't remember what the reaction was, but it didn't matter. What mattered was that it happened. My very first scripted comedy pages were performed on TV. Okay, it wasn't a classy sketch show like *SNL* or *SCTV,* but I wanted to get a sketch on *that* show and I had gotten what I wanted.

Over the next year or so, I ended up writing over three hours of bits, jokes and sketches for *The Uncle Floyd Show*. During that time, I was all too happy to take the PATH train to Newark in the middle of the night, if it meant I got to be a part of a wonderfully crazy show that made me laugh really hard. I couldn't help but think, *"This comedy-writing thing is a blast."*

HOW YA LIKE ME NOW, MOTHERFUCKERS?

MANY STANDUP COMICS in the early stages of our career will take on the Herculean task of opening for rock bands and big-timey singers, or we'd wrangle audiences as a warm-up comic for TV-show tapings. The opening act or the warm-up person is expected to entertain a group of hundreds or sometimes thousands of people, all the while recognizing that he or she is the absolute last person in the entire universe that the audience wants to see -- much like me at my family reunions (anyway gang).

Somewhere around 1981, Keenan Wayans was opening for Prince at The Bottom Line music club in the Village and he asked me to come along. At the time, I had no idea who Prince was. In fact, most of America had yet to discover him. More importantly, through Keenan, I was hoping to learn a little something about how to open the show for a music act.

For a brief time, Keenan and I had worked the door at The Improv, and we had become close work pals. He was quickly rising through the comedy ranks and, as expected, greeting people at the door of a comedy club was not his lifelong ambition. He and his brothers went on to create the hip and controversial 1990s sketch show, *In Living Color*.

The Bottom Line was packed that night. There was a vibe happening; everyone was buzzing. They could sense that the massive Prince-wave was about to crest. Keenan got up in front of the audience and quickly took command. He knew, right away, to stay strong and own the stage. Keenan was fairly new to standup, yet he somehow knew exactly what to do.

My big lesson from that night: If you're going to successfully open for a superstar music act, be Keenan Wayans. I also learned that some people are naturals. They don't have to work as hard or as long to figure out how to be effective. I'd already determined at that point that I was not a natural and I had a shit-ton of work ahead of me before I'd become an outstanding comic.

The lights fell as the announcer built up Prince's entrance. The audience let out a mighty, collective roar. It shook the building. The spotlight kicked on and Prince strutted onto the stage, wearing some sort of bikini, garters and other girly stuff.

"That's cool!" I thought. I was experiencing the decadent Greenwich Village underground scene that I'd heard so much about.

Oddly, the audience's energy dropped as Prince came up to the microphone. They started to murmur as he stood there, silently glaring at them. I asked Keenan if something was up. He had some knowledge of Prince and said this was one of his first big, live performances. People knew what Prince looked like from his album cover, but he figured they were probably thrown by how short he was. Even Keenan was surprised by his Lilliputian stature. Prince was, in fact, five feet three inches "tall."

Prince tilted his head and rolled his eyes dismissively. Then – BAM! The music exploded! His hardcore funky-ass sound tore the room apart. People were screaming like he was the Second Coming, visiting us mere mortals from the heavens to bless us and kiss each and every one of our souls. I mean, c'mon, it's Prince. His first song ended with a slamming stop. In the half-second before the audience could applaud, Prince, now mighty, yelled out, "How ya like me now, motherfuckers?!" The audience erupted!

Opening for a music act brought with it a tremendous amount of anxiety. Every show, for me, was basically the same: The room would go dark and a hush would fall as anticipation built. I'd peer through the curtains at the audience as they readied themselves for the time of their lives. A booming voice over the PA would announce, "Ladies and gentleman..." The crowd would start to lose their shit. They'd think, holy fuck, The Fugs or Lone Justice or whatever band they paid to see, was about to jump onstage and blow the room apart! "Please welcome..." Clapping would start. Sometimes I'd even hear screams. "...The comedy of Mike Rowe!"

Instantly, the room would go quiet. Then, I swear I'd hear a collective gasp of disappointment. The venue, to me, was suddenly like a giant elevator in a free fall -- and I hadn't even hit the stage yet.

What in the hell happened in my childhood that made me want to get up and do this?

Deep down, I understood that every impossible challenge like this was an exercise. I was working out, bulking up my comedy muscles to better fight the mighty battle to stardom. Shows like this, in these situations, were ultimately a helpful and educational experience for me -- as long as I didn't shit myself onstage.

I also liked opening for shows so I could party with the band. Ya know, kick back, be all cool and shit, "Hey, Al Stewart, how's the new album coming? All good with the wife?" You know, pretending I'm all rock star and whatever. I especially wanted to hang with the bands that, as a teen, I drummed along with on their records.

My parents bought my first drum kit for me when I was nine. We lived on the second floor of a three-story apartment building. The second I started pounding away on the skins, old lady Inglass from downstairs would start banging on her ceiling with the stick end of a broom. I'd feel it under me, and I'd answer rhythmically, using her pounding as the backbeat. To me, though, there was nothing better than playing along to percussion-driven records by Led Zep, Chicago, Tower of Power and the like.

By 1986, I became the house opener for most of the bands that came through The Bottom Line.

Me jamming to Led Zep.

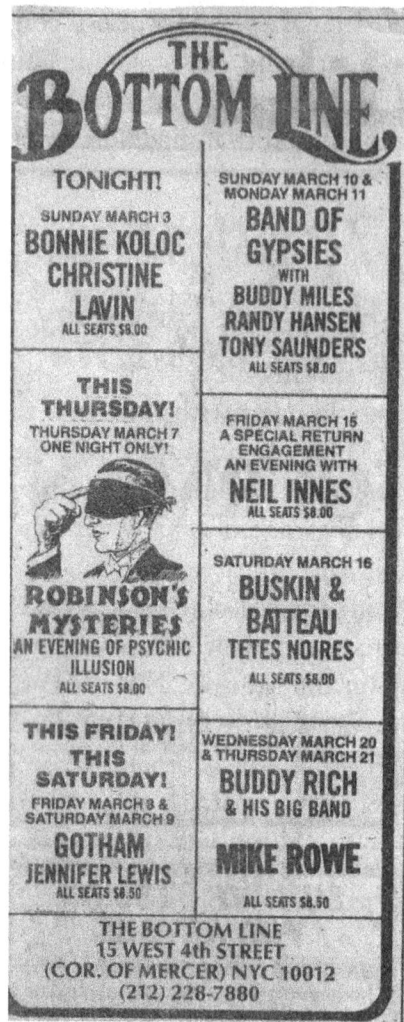

Sharing the bill with my hero.

It wasn't all that long ago I was the wide-eyed kid, thinking I wasn't worthy of that stage. A few years later, I was *their* guy. The co-owner, Alan Pepper, called me one night, "Are you available this weekend?" ...*to open the show for my hero*, was how I heard the rest of his ask. Yes, of course I was available (although I cancelled two gigs to do it)! Anyone who's ever sat behind a drum kit revered this artist. He was the Willie Mays of the Slingerlands.

I got to the club early that Friday night and paced backstage, waiting for him like a stalker. I heard he could be volatile. Do I say hi? Ask for an autograph? Shake his hand? I was so lost with concern that he slinked right by me and vanished into his dressing room.

Fuck!

This wasn't over. It was my duty as a professional entertainer to let him know that I was his audience warm-up guy and that we were both part of the brotherhood of the drum. I took a deep breath and carefully tapped on his door.

"Yeah? Come in."

My chest tightened as I slowly opened the door and peered in. There he was: *BUDDY...FUCKING...RICH!*

He was alone in the big, stark dressing room, sitting cross-legged in his white fluffy robe. No pants, just spindly white legs and black slippers. He was crunching on his contractually obligated veggie plate, happy and smiling. I introduced myself and let him know that I was his very capable opening act for the weekend. He seemed genuinely happy to meet me and curious about who I was and where I came from. We hit it off and talked, drummer to drummer (yeah, that's right), about music, Johnny Carson, comedy, and drums. Buddy, though, spoke in old-school jazz scat, "Yeah, *daddy-o*. I'm *hip*. That *cat was wild*." The lingo threw me a little, but it didn't matter. Buddy and I were buds. It was nuts, really, a *daddy-o* like me, hanging with Buddy Rich. That *cat* played *the skins* for Charlie Parker fer-fuck sake.

Directly backstage, through the curtains, I got up close to watch Buddy play. He was older by then, mid-60s maybe, but he still kicked ass. He reinspired me. After not playing the drums for years, I bought some sticks, (5As were my sticks of choice). In my apartment, I fashioned a drum kit from a metal ashtray and some pots and pans. Thanks to Buddy, I was a drummer yet again. Sort of.

Buddy did have a reputation as a uh, well...a hardcore asshole. Don't go by me; dig around online and find *The Buddy Rich Bus Tapes*. You'll find multiple rants where he's reaming out his band members. He threatens to throw them out of the band and even off the bus because of stuff like hitting a few bad notes (*clams*, as he calls them) or because they let their sideburns grow out too long. Each tirade is masterful and poetic.

When I was with him, his big band consisted of twenty-something-year-old kids just out of music school. All were competent, but I saw them, firsthand, fall victim to Buddy's assholery. Each musician had a few-hundred-page stack of sheet music on his stand and each sheet had a number on it. The band *never* knew what song Buddy wanted to play next. "I just go with the flow, man." At the end of each song the band would lean in and wait for him to announce the number for the next song. Buddy, staying true to his reputation, would whisper or mumble it: "Forty-seven," and then he'd immediately start playing.

The band would look to each other, panicked, as they asked each other, "What'd he say?" "What is it?" "Forty-what?" Buddy would continue to barrel through as band members would frantically flip through the stacks of sheet music. They'd try desperately to find the correct pages and catch up to Buddy. He would roll his eyes in anger and disbelief for a problem that he instigated.

Look, that was his *bag*, man. It's *cool, daddy-o*. I still *dig the cat*.

Around this time, I opened for smooth jazz saxophonist Kenny G for two nights, also at The Bottom Line. Hearing him play in that small venue was amazing. This was during a small window of time before he hit big and played much more honest, pure and soulful music. Every night, in fact, jazz musicians of note showed up just to watch him play.

The dressing rooms in the club were huge -- like, New York City apartment huge. They even had a full bathroom. The second night, between shows, I was sitting in there alone, picking through my veggie plate. I glanced down the hall and noticed that Kenny, my new buddy, had a kick-ass party going on in his dressing room. It was jam-packed with partiers, celebs, hangers-on, all drinkin' and smoking the Mary Jane (or whatever those cats smoke). He even had it catered. I swear there were steam tables of noodles in there.

So, wait. What about me?

Watching from my doorway, sad-eyed and lonely, I felt like Woody Allen in *Stardust Memories*. Like him, I was an outcast on a train that was parked directly across from a party train full of revelers. In my head, I even imagined Sharon Stone, like in the movie, taunting me to join her in the festivities. So, yeah, I was disappointed. I mean, I thought Kenny G liked me.

I stood in my dressing room doorway, hoping to get his attention. I figured he'd see me there, all somber and in dire need to party and smoke some doobage (not that I even smoked pot) with the swingin' Kenny G celebs. I was steadfast; he had to acknowledge me at some point. Finally, like lovers, our eyes connected. He smiled as he, no doubt, realized the error of his exclusion. He trotted over to me at my doorway. Embarrassed and apologetic, he was all like, "Uh, Mike, hey man, sorry – I gotta a big party happening in my dressing room." He pointed into my room, "Is it okay if I take a shit in here?"

My next opening gig was, no doubt, going to be a bit more elegant, classy and sophisticated. It had to be.

I was booked to open for Andy Williams in Westport, Connecticut.

From the late 1950s through the '60s and '70s, Andy Williams was an easy-listening pop artist and a fan favorite to audiences of all ages, especially the boomer parents. He was the real deal. When I was a kid, his hits, especially *Moon River* and *The Days of Wine and Roses* played constantly in our home. The gig in Westport was just a few miles from my hometown. "*This is perfect,*" I thought, "*I can invite my mom to the show and she can see her son share the stage with the legendary Andy Williams.*"

Sometimes I would jump too quickly at these opportunities and bypass the fine print when booking them. The contract demanded that I wear a tux. Well, there goes a hundred bucks of my not-so-great fee. Fine, I'll manage. This was Andy Williams, fer Chrissake. It wasn't until I got there that I realized it was an outdoor arena that seated over three *thousand* people. Ah, hm, uh, wow...Three thou -- Okay, but you know what? I gotta do it.

It was a full house and a spectacular Connecticut evening. The setting sun painted the clouds a fiery orange and there was a warm breeze; all was calm. Three thousand Andy fans were sitting out there waiting to *not* see me. I vowed not to let all of these dynamics throw me. I was backstage, strutting around in my rented tux, gearing up to introduce myself and then my mom to my new friend-to-be, Andy Williams. Who knows, if all went swimmingly, he might even invite me to be on his next TV Christmas special!

My mom and I searched for Andy. I felt like I needed to throw him a perfunctory thumbs-up to let him know that I'd have his audience primed and ready for his glorious night. I even thought for a second that he and mom could hang backstage together where they could watch me and my tux do my thing.

A full orchestra beckoned me; it was time to get out there and literally face the music. I told mom if she ran into Andy backstage while I was onstage, she'd need to behave herself and just wait till the after-party before she got all flirty.

Surprisingly, the orchestra rocketed into a tribute to Andy's top hits. Not good. It was telling the audience that a spectacular Andy moment was coming, like, he was going to emerge from under the stage like Elvis on a towering pillar, surrounded by fountains of white-shooting fireworks. I mean, what was gonna happen when they realized that instead, they were getting a dopey kid with diner jokes and a ninety-dollar tux? Didn't matter. I couldn't let Andy down.

As the last notes of *Moon River* faded, the announcer jumped in. "Ladies and gentlemen..." Happy place. I went to my happy place. "Welcome the comedy of Mike Rowe!"

They applauded. There was no wave of disappointment. What? Really? They were genuinely excited to have a comic open the show. I stepped out, center stage. All three thousand of these Nutmeggers were quiet, ready to hear what I had to say. I quickly found an intimacy in the vast sea of Andy devotees. There was a connection, a rapport that made my cornball comedy observations all the funnier...

"Hard to believe the song, *Get Down on It*, is now a wedding standard. [singing] *Get Down on It! Bride and the groom! Get Down on It! Mom and dad!*"

They loved Mike Rowe. I was picturing Andy in the wings, laughing and slapping his knee with delight, then winking to my mom for producing such a perfect son. I wrapped up my adorable set, took a bow and skipped offstage like they came that night just to see me. Andy was, you know, an added attraction. I couldn't wait to run into him, standing there ready to greet me with open arms.

Backstage, Andy was nowhere to be found. His intro music started to build, the audience swooned as spotlights swirled around and filled the night sky. Timpani drums rolled. But where was Andy? I wanted to at least throw him a brotherly fist bump as he made his way to the stage.

Suddenly, a limo pulled up to the back of the audience. The door swung open and Andy, sitting in the backseat, was readying himself to jump out. He was handed a microphone and he started singing *Moon River* before he even got all the way out of the car. He made his way through the crowd towards the stage, half-heartedly engaged as he greeted his excited fans.

Well, I'm guessing Andy wasn't around to see my stupendous comedy performance. I'm betting his wranglers saw me kill it though. Maybe at the after-party, they'd tell him how hilarious I was that night.

Checking his watch periodically, Andy managed his way through the fan favorites, *Born Free, The Hawaiian Love Song, Dear Heart,* then, of course, *The Impossible Dream*. After just under a half-hour, Andy crooned his way off the stage and back into the audience of adoring fifty-something-year-old housewives. He reached out to shake hands as the women stole kisses. Out of nowhere, the limo zipped up to the back of the arena. The passenger door swung open. Before he even finished the last note of the song, Andy all but tossed the microphone, jumped into the car, and hightailed it outta there as if he were taking cover from sniper fire.

What-in-the-fuck?! That was it? I mean, was the gig on his list of things to do on his way home? Pick up milk, drop off dry cleaning, do concert in Westport, buy socks. I was standing beside my mom, frozen and quiet. We shared a look. All I could squeak out was, "Busy guy."

That night, my mom, my then girlfriend, my sister and I (still in my tux) went to the nearby Howard Johnson's and quietly stuffed our faces with grilled cheese sandwiches. That was our after-party.

A FLUFFER'S JOURNEY

IN THE MID-'80s, I was the audience warm-up guy for the TV series *Kate and Allie,* starring Jane Curtin and Susan Saint James. It was about two single moms in Manhattan. An audience warm-up guy is just that; I'm hired to keep TV show audiences entertained, engaged, and excited before the show and during breaks in the taping.

There were so many reasons for me to love this gig. I'd be hanging out with some real-deal stars and getting paid a nice amount of money. More importantly, this was a chance to work in the legendary Ed Sullivan Theater on the stage where The Beatles made their American TV debut!

Zig-zagging through cameras and cables that zipped by me as they reset the scenes, I was having the time of my life. As I kept the audience filled in on the story of that episode, I'd drop in some of the choice jokes from my standup. I'd also have everyone write down questions on index cards before the show and then I'd pretend to answer them in that moment. Of course, I spent time before the show scribbling down joke answers or writing fake questions with joke answers. Sometimes I'd reread cards that got strong laughs from previous weeks. I had my own little weekly show within a show; it was, ya know, *Mike Rowe Live* from the historic Ed Sullivan Theater! Kid's gotta dream, right?

One time, an audience member spotted one of the crew kicking around a hacky sack (Google it) and asked if he'd come out to center stage and hacky for the audience. I liked this idea."I'll bring him out" I announced to the audience, "but I'm going to stand where Ed Sullivan stood and I'll introduce him the way Ed introduced the acts on his show. But every time I say The Beatles you have to scream your asses off."

"The Mike Rowe Show" in The Ed Sullivan Theater.

"All riii" I said in my lamest Ed Sullivan voice, "before we bring out The Beatles..."

The audience screamed; it was a shocking, guttural, primal roar that shook the building so violently, it woke the very spirit of the '64 Beatles! This was a powerful recreation of what it was like on that historic night. I felt a chill rush through me and my knees buckled a little. Even the audience was shocked as they felt the same rush that I felt.

...Or maybe they were just excited about my splendid Sullivan impression? Not sure.

The theater, because of its showbiz history, was designated by the city as a national landmark. There was even a curator on the premises. He was a weird dude who had a kind of *Phantom of The Opera* thing about him. I was sure he lived up in the balcony or somewhere in the crevices of the building.

After a taping one night, he leaned in towards me. Looking to make sure no one was listening, he said, "I'll show you something that no one knows about." Uh, okay. He walked me across the dark stage, opened a hatch to a secret tunnel and led me inside. It was a cold, dark catacomb with just a few dim, naked bulbs on a wire. Where was I going? What was happening? As we got deeper into the tunnel, past the point of no return, I started asking tons of questions. He was enigmatic: "Just wait. You'll see."

Great. I was about to be murdered in a tunnel deep under the streets of Manhattan.

He stopped me and then proudly pointed out a shrine in honor of Garry Moore, a popular variety and game-show host from the early days of television. Laced with Christmas lights, it was a wildly ornate, framed oil portrait of Garry, sitting there smoking a cig. It was odd and a little bit eerie. I mean, what was I looking at? Did game show fans wearing hoods and carrying torches climb in here in the middle of the night and pray to the mighty host of *I've Got A Secret*? I was getting the willies.

"Almost there," he assured me.

Wait, we're going in deeper? Yep, definitely getting murdered. We eventually hit a doorway. Putting his hand on it, he was ready to push it open. Dead bodies were in there, I was sure of it. "You know Jackie Gleason, right?" he asked mischievously.

Aw shit, this was his grave. He was going to show me Gleason's body in a glass case, like some sort of comedy Tutankhamun. That had to be it. How in the fuck did I end up in an underground graveyard?! I was getting panicky! The dirt walls felt as if they were closing in on me.

"Well, in the '50s" he continued, "Jackie Gleason starred in a variety show in this theater..." Dead body's coming, I know it. "He wielded so much power back then that he demanded that the network dig this tunnel..."

I was confused. "What? Why?"

He pushed the door open. I braced myself.

I found myself looking into the back room of the corner bar. The curator explained that Gleason had gotten the TV network to dig a half-block-long tunnel under The Ed Sullivan Theater so he could make clandestine trips to the Cordial Bar. All this was just so he could sneak out between scenes and toss back a few shots of scotch. Wow. *"How sweet it is"* indeed.

Being an audience warm-up guy brought with it huge responsibilities. Like the night I saved Eric Clapton's life.

Broadway Video, Lorne Michaels' production company, produced a weekly music show called *Night Music,* hosted by jazz horn player David Sanborn. On set, Sanborn would walk the TV audience through a semi-circle of a wildly eclectic mix of classic rock stars, jazz artists, new artists, international musicians as well as a crazy array of interesting musical talent. With quick, intimate interviews, he'd tell the audience of the musician's history or, in some cases, he'd jump in and jam with them. The show was fantastic!

Broadway Video called me out of the blue. There was an emergency; *Night Music* needed an audience warm-up guy *that very night*. It was 1988 and at this point, I had built a rep as a capable audience wrangler. Before I could even tell them whether or not I could do the gig, the producer prattled on about my call time, monies, and how long I'd need to perform. Then she listed the guests for that night. All I heard was "...*Eric Clapton* and *Robert Cray*." What? Yes! I'm in!

This was not long after my encounter with Buddy Rich, so I was still banging around on the drums. In fact, I'd graduated from pots and pans to jamming on a *real* kit on a regular basis with my comedian friends Mark Cohen and Jon Manfrellotti, in different Manhattan rehearsal spaces. We called ourselves MegaHax. Over and over, we'd play the songs from Robert Cray's new *Strong Persuader* CD. That is, when we weren't playing any one of the hundreds of Clapton hits.

So yeah; I'm doing this gig.

I was ushered into the studio. The producer greeted me and took me backstage to meet David Sanborn. He was easygoing, sweet, and happy that I was there to corral his audience for him. David warned me that it was usually a tough crowd.

You know what? It didn't matter. That night, I was about to share a stage with Eric Clapton.

I'd worked with so many impressive and iconic people, heroes and legendary figures and I'd yet to ask any of them for their autograph. But Clapton is...well, Clapton is *God*. I had to have his autograph.

Megahax (left to right) Mark Cohen, Me, Joe Mulligan, Marty Rackham, Jon Manfrellotti.

I circled though the green room and spotted Clapton lost in conversation with Robert Cray. If I remember correctly, Dan Hicks and His Hot Licks, a Theremin player, and a South African choral group were also in the mix. As I considered a way to get to Eric, a crew guy yanked me out of there and into the studio to do a sound check. After a few "check-check, 123s" he vanished.

Clapton and Robert Cray wandered in, smirking and excited (and maybe high). They strapped on their guitars, plugged in and stared each other down. Then, they effortlessly and magically began trading fat, hardcore, ma-fuckin' down-home blues.

It was just them and me. That was it. I sat on the piano stool and lost myself in the intimacy of this private, up close and personal concert from what were arguably two of the world's most famous blues artists in recent history. They were at arm's length and it felt like they were jamming just for me.

Clapton started singing Ray Charles' song *Hard Times*. It was thick and soulful. His guitar gently wept. Cray traded licks with him in the break. I might've been crying at this point, I'm not sure. After about fifteen minutes, they got a nod from the producer: The audience was coming in. They stopped mid-song and ran for cover. *Fuck!* It was over and, oh yeah, I had that warm-up thing to do.

The audience filed in and readied themselves for a fantastic night. I hit the stage, ready to do my thing. I tried to get a fix on what was ahead of me. The people in those seats were like a thousand feet away; I couldn't see anyone in the dark theater. It didn't matter. They were in no way interested in what I had to say anyway. I think they figured I was just a crew guy checking the mics.

I got through my ten minutes of yuck-'em-ups with my dignity somewhat intact and wandered back into the green room, hoping Clapton had seen none of it. I found him sitting there, staring at the TV monitor. This was my chance!

I mustered up some courage and introduced myself. His fingers felt odd as I shook his hand. They were skinny and long; his gifts, I thought, like Jimi Hendrix. It helped him swiftly manipulate his way around the frets. He recognized me as the smily guy who was sitting in the studio watching him play. I let him know I worked on the show as the audience warm-up guy. This, no doubt, put us on equal footing -- entertainer to entertainer.

I blurted out, "Sorry, but could I have your autograph?" Yep I did it, and he was happy to comply. As I leaned in, my pen at the ready, some Nazi from the show barked at me.

"I'm sorry. He will *not* be signing any autographs today."

Another member of her army pulled me out of the room and into the hallway. Getting up in my face, she waved her finger at me and explained the rules: "*Staff does not talk to guests!*" Clapton, out of the corner of his eye, watched this go down. For a second, I thought he might jump to my defense and take a swing at one of these KGB jerks.

It looked like I was leaving *Night Music* sans autograph.

The audience long gone, the crew was breaking down the equipment in the studio. Clapton and his entourage entered at the far end and stopped to thank some people. In the middle of his conversation he happened to see me and abruptly ended his goodbyes. He made a beeline towards me. "Hey, man. Got that pen and paper?" he asked. Surprised and in shock, I was about to comply when we heard an explosion. It sounded like a plane plowed through the roof of the studio. A gigantic audio monitor had crashed to the floor like an anvil, and it was hanging *directly above* where Clapton was just standing. Seriously. Right-where-he-was-standing! He stepped away just in time from that spot to get to me.

Clapton looked calmly at the shattered monitor on the floor, looked at me, shrugged and said, "Well, that was close, wasn't it?"

"Wow," I joked, "Looks like I just saved your life."

He chuckled and pulled the sheet music for *Hard Times* from under his arm. With a flourish of his long, lanky fingers he signed it and handed it to me.

It read: *"You saved my life. Thanks. Eric Clapton."*

WRITING A SITCOM IS EASY, RIGHT?

I WAS ABOUT TO HIT my mid-twenties and I was still whoring around the Manhattan comedy-club scene, waiting and hoping to hit the next level of my career -- whatever that might be.

If I was not going to take the comedy world by storm, what was going to happen when I hit my fifties? Do I and *can* I soldier on and travel the country to every shithole town and joke it up at comedy barns like Sir Laff-A-Lots or Uncle Funny's? Or worse, spend weeks at a time in the Pacific confined on a Cathy Lee cruise ship headed to Turkey or Mumbai? These options weren't appealing to me while in my twenties, so how happy would I be onstage fending off drunks thirty years down the line?

I actually do have comic friends well past their fifties who enjoy joking it up on the road or onboard big ol' cruise lines. They're making people all over the world laugh while raking in decent money along the way. I wish I had that in me, but I don't.

I knew deep down that I wanted to be a sitcom writer, but I was fighting it. In truth, I was scared. Even for an excellent and highly educated writer, it's still an extremely difficult road. Seriously, how was I going to do it with hardly any knowledge of the basics like grammar or sentence structure? I didn't go to college. I spent two of my high school years in the electronics shop watching *Happy Days* on busted TVs. I read my first book, cover to cover, when I was eighteen years old. It was a novelization of a *Get Smart* episode. At least, finally, in New York, I actually started to read.

In the early 1980s, New York City had a ton of used bookstores. The best ones were hidden in the nooks and crannies of Manhattan. My friend Joel took me into an old three-floor walk-up right off Times Square. The store was a labyrinth of three connected rooms with floor-to-ceiling shelves of used books, scripts, first-issue collectables, movie stills and posters. There was that perfect, acidy smell of old, rotting books and magazines in the air. We were in one of Joel's favorite bookstores; it quickly became one of mine, too.

Joel is a practitioner of what is truly funny. He helped me discover the humorists of the early 20th century. I fell in love with the works of Ring Lardner, Robert Benchley and, of course, S.J. Perelman, a major contributor to the Marx Brothers' movies.

It was in this bookstore that I found my first actual TV sitcom script for a short-lived Witt-Thomas series called, *You're A Big Girl Now*. The show didn't matter. What mattered was that I had a real Hollywood TV sitcom script in my hand. It was dog-eared, wrinkled and scribbled-on. I felt like Indiana Jones after uncovering some sort of ancient scripture. To me, it contained all the clues I needed to help figure out how a sitcom is built. It was a roadmap showing me the format, the correct number of pages, how many jokes per-page, and where the act breaks should land. For me, just seeing how sitcom dialogue looked written out on the white page spoke volumes.

After reading the script cover to cover multiple times, I felt that writing my own script was finally manageable. These crinkled yet majestic three-holed pages demystified it all for me.

My first plan of action was to write what is called in Hollywood a "spec script"; "spec" as in "speculative," because you write it with the hope that'll generate some money, or at least some interest. Ideally, big-shot producers would read your spec and love it so much that they'd shower you with untold riches and entrée to work on the sitcom of your choice. For me, that was highly unlikely. That'd have to wait until, ya know, I wrote my second, more seasoned script.

There were two TV shows I loved back then: Bob Newhart's sitcom, *Newhart*, which took place in an old inn in Vermont, and Garry Shandling's meta sitcom, *It's Garry Shandling's Show*. Garry would, from time to time, stop the show and address the camera or the audience directly and share whatever crisis or concern that irked him at that moment. The whole show, at its core, was a commentary on Hollywood and TV sitcom tropes. It was the first series that was a comedy about comedy, and it brilliantly highlighted the fun in Garry's neuroticism.

I studied these two shows. I recorded them on VHS (*fuck* I'm old), but even better, I recorded them on my Walkman (*really* old). I felt that just listening to them over and over was a better way to let the rhythm and sounds of the characters soak into my noggin. I was so absorbed with transferring these comedy voices into my system that I found myself, uh, st-stuttering and, st-stammering like Bob Newhart for the rest of that winter. After weeks of osmotically injecting sitcom funny into my core, I started to scribble down a few story notions. Happy and satisfied with my undeniably brilliant ideas, I went to work on a *Newhart* episode.

There were no word processors or home computers back then. Well, at least nothing that I could afford. I wrote everything out on yellow legal pads, and when I felt the words and comedy were white hot, I'd go to press. I'd drag out the old manual typewriter that my mom bequeathed to me and, with a bottle of Wite-Out and a bottle of scotch at the ready, I'd hunt and peck my way through forty Emmy-worthy pages of sitcom funny. It was an arduous and tedious task to build a script so primitively back then. The excitement of seeing it unfold on the white typed pages and resembling a genuine Hollywood script kept me forging ahead with the glee of a young Norman Lear.

My *Newhart* spec idea was somewhat viable; Bob's onscreen character Dick Louden, wrote how-to books. In the story, we find he's struggling desperately with writer's block. His handyman, George, played by Tom Poston, kept a small notebook of how he repaired things around the old inn. Dick's publisher keeps nudging him; his next how-to book is past due. With no other way out, he makes a deal to write George's Handy Man book for him, based on his handful of scribblings, which he would give to his publisher to fulfill his contractual obligation. As Dick ghostwrote the book for George, he found inspiration and got carried away with George's few notes and ended up writing his best book ever. George, the de-facto author, ends up with all the credit, attention and glory for the success of the tome. Dick's friends and family praise "George's" book and assure Dick that he too could someday write one just as powerful. The script did start to get some attention, which encouraged me to write a spec script for *It's Garry Shandling's Show*.

Back then, my friend and fellow standup, the late Ken Ober, hosted a popular show on MTV called *Remote Control*. It was a goofy 1980s game show for baby boomers that presumably took place in Ken's basement. He knew of my dedication to writing and hired me to write bits for that show. Among the cast of funny dopes were Colin Quinn, Dennis Leary and Adam Sandler. From there, I was hired as a staff writer at the launch of Comedy Central, known then as The Comedy Channel. I was in charge of a wraparound comedy clip show hosted by Tommy Sledge, a standup comic who played a 1940s detective. I was expected to write over thirty-five wraparound segments a day and they all had to connect to a story arc. The dialogue needed to be written in 1940s *noir* slang. I didn't know it at the time, but it meant I was basically required to write a full sitcom episode every twenty-four hours, five days a week, by myself. No one at The Comedy Channel, including me, knew that it was an impossible task that typically takes a team of people to handle such a humungous challenge. It was harder in this case, because Tommy was not well versed in improvisation. He needed every word to be scripted. Comedian Allan Havey, on the other hand, had a wraparound show on the channel as well, but he could pick up a paper clip and, on the spot, find four minutes of on-camera funny with it.

I was able to keep up the Tommy Sledge grind for a few months before I collapsed under the pressure. The final straw was when the executives called me into the office and complained that the quality of the latest shows was lacking. I quit right then and immediately ran out of the building, jumped into a cab and took it cross town to HA!, the competing comedy channel. HA! hired me on the spot. They put me on an animated series that required a mere half-hour script per week.

Those formative days, where I churned out a script a day, wired my brain to write in bulk and at a very fast pace. If only it reconfigured it to make me a funnier writer.

I was still writing gags for Dangerfield, but I wasn't making a lot of headway. I reached out to a few other famous and semi-famous standup comics, like prop comic Rip Taylor:

"I'm reading a good book, 'The History of Crazy Glue.' I can't put it down...Hello!"

Fifty big ones for that sucker. I found myself in a world where I could, pretty much, pay most of my bills by writing comedy. It felt like I had a license to print money. I'd type out stuff, hand it over to an unwitting participant, and they'd give me money. It was analogous to the sex trade and almost as exciting, just not as messy (in most cases).

THE UGLY TRUTH ABOUT STAR SEARCH

Star Search was a nationally syndicated weekly show that, in the '80s, was as popular as the current reality/talent shows like *The Voice*, and *American's Got Talent*. Hosted by *The Tonight Show*'s sidekick Ed McMahon, *Star Search* ran the full gamut of undiscovered talent: singers, models, actors, rockers, dancers and, of course, standup comics.

In early 1986, I got a call from Claudia McMahon, Ed's daughter and talent coordinator for the show. She wanted me to audition for *Star Search* on-camera at Catch a Rising Star. Why not? A shot on national TV could be a blast. At that time *Star Search* didn't really register to me as a serious showbiz launching pad, although it did help bring Sinbad and Rosie O'Donnell to the fore.

If they picked me to appear on the show, I'd get my first round-trip ticket to Los Angeles. More importantly, if my young face showed up on *Star Search*, my friends and family would feel like I'd officially arrived. They'd forever consider me a Hollywood big shot.

The night of the audition, the audience at "Catch" was packed and white hot. My comic friends were all nervous and anxious as they paced the bar, waiting to audition for their shot at *Star Search* stardom.

I felt like I had the advantage that night. I was the only comic wearing a skinny tie, pleated dress pants and a mismatched sport coat with pushed-up sleeves. The look was the iconic '80s standup look, popularized by Jay Leno, a comic's comic at that time. We figured Jay's look was a major accoutrement for success, much like the way jazz guys of the '50s shot up junk, thinking that it'd convert them into Charlie Parker.

That night, my skinny tie and pushed-up sleeves won Claudia's and the producer's hearts. I was set for my first-ever trip to Hollywood for an appearance on national TV alongside Ed McMahon!

Sadly, this was as close as I ever got to appearing on *The Tonight Show*.

Around the same time, I was booked for my very first national TV spot on a syndicated TV standup comedy show out of New York, Bill Boggs' *Comedy Tonight*, hosted, astonishingly, by local TV host, Bill Boggs.

Comedy Tonight was set up for me to tape on the day before I was to fly out to L.A. for *Star Search*. Suddenly, I'm like, ya know, George Carlin, bouncing from TV show to TV show.

The producers remarked that when they saw me at The Improv, they really liked my impression of David Brenner. Brenner had appeared on *The Tonight Show* literally hundreds of times and was known for his funny, family-friendly observations. Most jokes started with, "Ya ever notice…?" or "You wanna hear sometin' weird…?"

From David's first *Tonight Show* appearance in 1971:

"Did you ever notice you go into a gas station, the attendant's directions always start the same way: 'Now look buddy, you pull out of the station --' No, I wanna drive around the pumps for nine hours…"

I did a dumbed-down impression of David. "Ya ever notice ya run outta toilet paper when you need it most?" I'd end with, "Ya ever notice I'm not funny?" This impression was more to make the comics in the back of the room laugh. I never intended to do it on TV.

Bill Boggs and the producers wanted me to open their show with the impression. It'd be the first thing that viewers would see before the opening titles. I told them I couldn't do it. It was my first time on national TV and I didn't want to kick things off by making fun of a comedy icon. They were disappointed and begged me to do it. I finally agreed, but I had a plan…

They readied the audience, a camera rolled up to my face, "Action." I dove in, "Ya ever notice dogs are weird?…Ya ever notice airplanes are weird. Right? They're so weird." No punchlines. I was doing just the voice. I figured that'd be enough to quell those dopes. I ended it with, "Ya ever notice this routine's not funny?" I heard, "Cut. Cut it!" The producer made his way over to me, "Mike, do it the way we saw you do it the club." I refused.

It became a standoff. In truth, I was worried. Who was I to make fun of David Brenner on national TV? My biggest claim to comedy fame at that time was…well, it was that very show.

I was holding up production. It started to get tense. The producer finally made up something about how I was breaking my contract. I felt cornered. I did the impression with the original punchline that they wanted. Yeah, great, a young comic, Mike Rowe, basically told David Brenner on national TV that he sucks. There were going to be repercussions, I was sure of it.

The late Richard Jeni appeared on the same *Comedy Tonight* episode as me. That night I found out that I was competing against him on *Star Search*.

Rich was one of the sharpest, smartest, cutting-edge standup of the '80s and '90s. He was highly respected by all the comics of that generation. He and I knew each other pretty well; we had played a ton of clubs together in Manhattan and Jersey. We were flying out to L.A. together the next day. We were even staying at the same hotel. Great. I was happy to have the companionship. Sitting together on the plane on our sojourn to Hollywood, I told him about my concerns with the whole Brenner-thing.

Comics have trouble handling anything with personal or emotional weight to it. Heartfelt discussions will quickly devolve into a volley of insults and mom jokes. At one point, Rich and I spent close to an hour trading a Walkman back and forth, making up a joke about it on the spot, "Look, Billy Barty's casket." We laughed like idiots, but I still couldn't get the Brenner incident out of my head. Rich's way of helping was to talk like Brenner. We immediately slipped into dueling Brenners, and it went on for hours, "Ya ever notice they give you a vomit bag but they don't give you a shit bag." It wouldn't stop. "Ya ever notice planes go up, then they come down again? Isn't that weird?"

Even after we got into Hollywood and were sitting at dinner together, we traded Brennerisms. "Ya ever notice waiters make you wait? Isn't that weird?" Laughing about the idiocy of it all eventually helped me get over my Brenner concerns. Maybe the comic's way of handling emotional quandaries isn't so dumb after all.

We were scheduled to show up at our first *Star Search* production meeting early the next morning. The meeting is where the contestants from all the competing categories got to meet each other. Kenny James, the reigning champ in the Male Lead Vocal category for twelve weeks running was also from my hometown. Kenny had that slick, '80s soulful Peabo Bryson kind of voice. He was quintessential 1980s, cool black dude with his Jheri-curled hair, Cosby sweater and black leather pants. I introduced myself and jokingly said, "Looks like we're going to put Waterbury back on the map." He shot back, "I already did, my brother." He sipped his tea for effect and slinked off like a jaguar.

Each week, *Star Search* dragged in whatever celebrity was available to help introduce the contestants. The producer read from his notes as he announced, "On tomorrow's show, the comedians will be introduced by...David Brenner."

Rich and I shared a long look and exploded with laughter. We were so flabbergasted that we literally curled up into a ball, dropped off our seats and rolled onto the floor in hysterics. The producers were lost; they needed to know what was happening. We wouldn't get into it and waved it off.

Eventually, we all had to, one at a time, get up to the microphone in the middle of the room and introduce ourselves. As a comic, I also had to give a few sample jokes from my first set. The producers were distracted; they had to know why Rich and I were laughing so hard.

I couldn't tell them the real story. I just rambled, "Rich Jeni and I like David Brenner so much, uh, and we were both doing this impression of him for the last two days and, uh, now...he's here. So, it's just...funny. To us." I even mumbled some of the impression. They looked at me quietly, wondering if perhaps I had some issues with my faculties.

Contestants were stationed at The Hyatt on Sunset, known since the 1960s as a Hollywood party hotel. I didn't see all that much partying. I just remember hanging out in my hotel room with New York comedy friends, Max Alexander, Mario Cantone and Paul

Provenza. At one point, I stood on the hotel balcony and stared out at the smoggy land of opportunity, uncertainty, high stakes, and dream fulfillment. I knew right then that sooner or later this town would be my home.

Rich Jeni understood that I was serious competition for him. For good reason. I had an arsenal of high-octane vocal impressions that killed with most audiences. That could be a blessing and a curse, however. If I was bombing onstage, I could pull myself out of it with any one of my trusty vocal oddities. I imitated a siren, a beatbox or the classic Chicago hit, *25 Or 6 To 4*. This impression, from my face, included the drums, bass and horns all at the same time. Okay, my noises were blunt and dumb, but they paid my rent for ten years. They also launched my career during my early days, as you may remember, at The Ground Round in Waterbury.

On show day we had to get to the theater on Hollywood and Sunset at 9 a.m. and we weren't allowed to leave the building until after the show was taped at 9 p.m. There was not a lot to do while trapped in the theater for twelve hours, so I decided to spend my valuable time hitting on the spokesmodel. C'mon, I was in my early twenties, it was my first time in Hollywood, and I was about to make America laugh on national TV. I was a walking aphrodisiac, am I right, ladies? (Wait; where're you going?)

I'd already chatted it up with one of the spokesmodels at the run-through and we seemed to hit it off. She was smart, sweet and adorable. She was from New York City, where she worked regularly as a model, and she also understood that this show wasn't necessarily a career breaker or maker. It was just a fun adventure. No matter what happened to her that night, she knew she had a modeling career ahead of her.

Rich was intrigued by my newfound girlfriend and he wanted updates throughout the day. He could see my excitement, "Maybe this could be a thing. She lives in my neighborhood, she laughs a lot. She's really cool." Rich was my outside eyes and helped guide me through this. He was fighting for something to happen with the model and me.

Once the show actually started, things got exciting very quickly. I instantly got caught up in the pageantry of it all. The studio was a cacophony of everything Hollywood; spotlights swirling around, the crowd cheering as the band blasted out the *Star Search* theme. Excited contestants in full dance gear, suits, high hair and layers of makeup, readied themselves for camera. The judges, all show-biz industry giants, sat at a panel in the back of the room, poised and ready to discover Hollywood's next superstar. The audience was jam-packed with screaming tourists and *Star Search* fans. At that point, all I could do was have the time of my life.

Rich and I paced backstage as we occasionally glanced at the monitor to watch the show in progress. Spokesmodels, singers, actors, each had their turns. They were quickly burning through the show. As I paced, my stomach tightened. Everything started to feel different. Suddenly, *Star Search* wasn't just a fun gig. This was the real deal. Right then, I decided I had to do great!

I kept mumbling my three minutes of funny to myself, trying to burn my set into my brain. If I went blank, I could just throw myself into autopilot and safely land this sucker in front of twenty million TV viewers. The pressure was on.

Rich and I watched our new friends lose in their categories and get summarily tossed into oblivion. My new girlfriend-to-be was on camera billboarding the exciting things that were coming up after the commercial. Sadly, it did not look good for my New York cutie. She was considerably shorter and less engaging than the reigning champ. Her competition was a majestic, striking, camera-ready blonde straight out of every convention-center car show. Statuesque is going to win out over short and adorable every time. My girl (all imagined, by the way) would need some comforting later on.

I looked at the monitor. Ed was introducing David Brenner. Our category was next. *"Deeeeep breaths. What's the worst that could happen?"* Ed excitedly told David on camera, right then and there, "You're going to like tonight's comics because...they both do an impression of you."

Rich and I both stopped in our tracks and then our heads snapped up like you do when you hear a horrendous car crash. Our mouths agape, we looked at each other, wide eyed and frozen. Apparently, the producers thought that because we both did our Brenner impressions in rehearsal, it was a part of our act.

I let out a loud, *"Oh-my-God!"* as my knees buckled.

I thought about running out there to shut down the show so I could clarify the fuck up. Instead, I paced like a caged animal. Rich was about to be launched out on that stage in the next twenty seconds. He was lost in his panic, "What do we do?" he begged. I had no response. Shock and fear shut me down. Ed started Rich's intro. We shared a look of horror as he backed away from me like an Apollo astronaut exiting the capsule to drop into an uncharted world.

Rich grabbed the mic and did his thing. He was well received but you could feel the constraints on his time limitations. We had all of two and a half minutes. He was a long-distance runner, not a short-burst comedy performer. The good news was there was no mention from anyone about the Brenner thing. That cleared the gates for me. If he didn't have to do it, I certainly didn't have to do it.

I went out and did basically the highlight reel of all my big, loud, weird and dumb sound effects. There was my Chicago impression, sirens, gunshots. I was a freak show, but the crowd went crazy. Their response was thunderous. It's typically how these audiences reacted to the *Star Search* singer right when they hit that enormous, dramatic, bendy and overblown crescendo. So I, for all intents and purposes, was a *Star Search* singer that night.

I moved over to the judges' box and stood alongside Rich. He knew what was coming. He shifted back and forth, waiting to take his beating. With a mighty drum roll, Ed announced Rich's 2.5 stars. Then, me, the challenger, Mike Rowe -- *4.0 stars!* That's a perfect ma'fuckin' *Star Search* score right there, people! As Rich was jettisoned offstage, I made my way over to the winner's circle with Ed and...Oh wait, in the glory of my win, I forgot all about the Brenner thing. Ed acknowledged that I was the first of that season to get a perfect score. Good. This distracted him from the Brenner impression. "Mike, before you go..."

Ew boy, here it comes.

"Before you go, I want you to do a little of your impression of David Brenner." Brenner shot a look. He hated the idea from the get-go. I was in a panic. Even after eighteen straight hours of dueling David Brenners with Rich, I couldn't gather my wits. I mumbled some odd David Brenner sounds. *Help!* I couldn't find an appropriate joke. Finally I gave him a, "Ya ever notice, heh, heh. Ya ever notice planes go up...Then they come down again?" David looked at me blankly, his mouth hung open. He didn't even fake laugh. I, at least, had enough showbiz savvy to pretend it went great. With my painted smile, I waved to the audience with aplomb as I walked off to applause. Earlier, I had been instructed to leave when Ed threw it to a commercial. I left too early and screwed up the ending of the segment. But *fuck it!* I'm Mike-4.0-Perfect-Score-Rowe.

Drunk on my powerful win, I figured it was time to make my move and officially ask my New York spokesmodel girlfriend out to dinner. She did, in fact, lose in her category that night, so there was no doubt she was gonna need a shoulder to cry on. I found her backstage as she was gathering her things and told her I felt bad for her loss. She shrugged it off and congratulated me. I told her that I originally auditioned for *Star Search* as a spokesmodel. It made her laugh. That was all the opening I needed. "Hey, I hope you're not doing anything tonight. How 'bout we go to dinner?"

"Good idea. Rich just asked me. You can come with us."

What? Wait. No. Oh-no. What in the fuck happened? No way! I excused myself and quickly tracked down Rich. I cornered him. "What the fuck are you doin', man?!"

He felt no guilt. "What? You won the show. You want the girl, too?"

"Yes! That's how it works!"

I was fuming. I could not believe his flagrant disregard. Sure, this was silly, twenty-something-year-old man nonsense but regardless, there's a code. You don't usurp a woman from a man when you know there's a shared interest and rapport and a magical connection happening (well, not quite that, but the night was young?). To me, this was serious stuff. "You need to go to her right now and tell her that you can't make it. You can't go to dinner with her!" He saw the anger on my face. On some level, it was less about the woman and more about the principle of the whole thing.

Rich gave in. Defeated, he sheepishly went back to her and told her that he wouldn't be able to make it to dinner. That was it; all was settled. It was going to be just the cute New York model and me, going off alone together to one of the hippest restaurants in Hollywood. Check me out, I'm Mike-4.0-ma'fuckin'-Rowe.

What I didn't know was that Rich and a few of our fellow comic friends that were in the audience that night, Paul Provenza, Max Alexander and Robert Schimmel (my challenger in the next show) had piled into a car and followed us to the restaurant. They all sat at the next table and heckled me for the bulk of the date. Hardly the romantic dinner I had hoped for.

In the end, my spokesmodel girlfriend thanked me for a nice time, then called the *Star Search* town car. She vanished into the night and out of my life forever. So, in the end, Rich ultimately won the night, even though he lost the show.

Making my way back to the Hyatt, I figured I'd go to my room and wallow somewhere in the grey space of winning and losing. As I headed through the hotel lobby, I spotted the woman singer from the band that lost that night. She was sweet, Southern and actually quite upset that her *Star Search* days were over. I sat down with her and gave her a shoulder to cry on. She pulled out a flask and asked me to join her in a drink. Things got silly and fun, and we ended up getting drunk and laughing in the lobby throughout the night and into the bright early morning.

Robert Schimmel, my new contender, was known for his filthy yet hilarious standup act. He never told a clean joke ever. I couldn't, for the life of me, figure out how he was on *Star Search*, America's favorite family show. I have to say, he too must have felt that I was heavy competition. He spent the whole ten-hour show day, while trapped in the studio, trying to psych me out. He would conjure up tears as he showed me a photo of his nine-month-old child in a hospital bed, "I hope I win tonight. My kid is sick, man. Any money coming in is really gonna help him." Wow. He was exploiting his sick kid to take me down. This was his game. I knew it for sure when, years later, I heard him admit to it on Howard Stern's radio show. Bob had to do what he had to do. He'd never worked clean in his life and was about to go head-to-head with a noisemaking, 4.0 *Star Search* champ!

That night the comics were to be introduced by Sherman Hemsley from the 70's sitcom *The Jeffersons*. I caught him backstage talking to Schimmel. "What the fuck you doin' here, man? You ain't got no clean jokes, motherfucker." Schimmel seemed defeated, "Yeah, man. I don't know what's gonna happen."

As champ, I came out first. I wore my dad's sky-blue Mister Rogers-looking sweater. I didn't have any nice clothes in those days. The suit from the week before came from a storefront on 14th Street in New York that sold clothes, household cleaning products, and alarm clocks.

That night, I wore the sweater in honor of my dad. It was the type of thing he'd tell me to wear, thinking it'd be a good look for me. The sweater was my first mistake. I also strutted around, feeling a little too confident. I did so well the first time, I figured I already had a handle on the *Star Search* audience.

When I got out there and my first joke didn't kill like it did the prior week, I felt my brain freeze. It was only a nanosecond, but it felt like fifteen minutes. It threw off everything. I suddenly had no confidence. I was working through it though, and doing okay, but in the end, I knew it didn't go great. I figured my only chance of winning this sucker was if Schimmel tanked it, and there could be a strong chance of that happening. He was a filthy comic, what was he going to do, say *frig* instead of *fuck*?

He went out and did great. He hit all the prime mid-America standup comedy tropes; jokes about the game show *The Price Is Right*, getting pulled over by a cop, airplane jokes. Where did he get this stuff? It all sounded oddly familiar. He ended with rousing applause. We lined up in the judges' box, me in my dad's sweater. My score tanked at like a 2.0. Schimmel won with a resounding 2.75. I hightailed it off the stage, slightly dazed as I tried to figure out what in-the-hell just happened? Did Schimmel in fact psych me out?

When you first get to the *Star Search* campus, there are teams of people at the ready to press your suit, style your hair, or get you whatever you desire. The second you lose, no one even looks at you. Backstage, I felt like I was trespassing and that at any second, security was going to swiftly bum rush me out into the street and into oncoming traffic.

I went to Schimmel to congratulate him on his win and wished his family well. The comics from the night before, Paul Provenza, Max Alexander and Mario Cantone, surrounded Schimmel and greeted him with glee as they commented on the jokes that killed. I quickly learned that they each gave him jokes from their act to help him beat me. I shook my head and laughed because apparently, if you are going up against Mike-4.0-Rowe on TV's *Star Search*, you are going to need a big fucking team of people to take me down!

WHEN COMEDY WAS KING

AFTER MONTHS OF WRITING and rewriting my Garry Shandling and Bob Newhart spec scripts, I got a call from Jim, a writer friend who was in a mid-town office working on a network TV pilot. He wanted me to get my ass over there ASAP.

I found myself in a giant office building on Central Park South high up on the 25th floor. I walked into an enormous office with couches and wide, plush chairs. I felt like I was a guest in someone's Park Avenue living room. There was a meeting in progress. Writers and producers were sitting around, going over story cards up on a big board. Standing at the board and shuffling the cards around was a corpulent, older, bearded man in a suit. He was holding his cig deep down between his two middle fingers, in an old-school Vegas sort of way. He pointed it at us for effect as he barked out his thoughts like a Catskill comic. Upon closer examination, I saw that he was THE Alan King. Alan, too, was one of the many comics that showed up on the TV screen during those shared comedy experiences I had with my dad.

I should've recognized Alan at first glance; his moves were the same as I remembered from TV. He had his thumb carefully resting in his vest pocket, as he'd stiffly turn his arched back and shoulders to and fro. Watching him comment on the story cards on the board in that old-school comedy way was almost exactly like his signature routine from his primetime TV specials. He'd stand in front of a board that listed the new shows from fall TV lineups and he'd angrily comment on each and explain how and why it would fail. Then he'd rip it off the board and chuck it across the TV studio.

This was his project, his baby, a show he was producing, not performing in. The premise was about what goes on behind the scenes in the bar at a comedy club on a night when the comics are auditioning for their big break. A viable idea (and very relatable to me), yet oddly, we were not going to see any of the actual standup in this show.

So what was happening? Why was I there?

My friend Jim introduced me to everyone in the room. They acknowledged me politely. Alan pointed at me, "Jim says you know how to write scripts." Fresh off writing four hundred hours of Sledge's show at the Comedy Channel, I guess you could say that. "Yeah. Sure. I do."

"Good" Alan said. "Then sit down!"

Okay. Wow. Just like that, I'm writing a CBS primetime network sitcom.

I had to play catch-up and sound like I knew what I was doing. Instinctively, I knew not to jump in unless I had something of value to add to the story. I looked around and recognized a bunch of writer friends I'd worked with in the recent past. None of them had any real long-form scriptwriting experience. This gave me a sense of confidence. I mean, I'd spent a whole eight months figuring out how sitcom stories worked. I was an old pro, for chrissakes. After taking it all in, I had a few suggestions for Mr. King. Some maybe made sense, I think, but nonetheless, I was confident enough to go "wrong and strong."

By the end of the day, the cards were aligned on the board to where everyone felt the story made sense. We were to reconvene the next afternoon. I jotted down the layout of the cards, went home and typed up a very rough draft of the episode -- remember, I was quite fast due to my Comedy Channel days. My actions were driven by hunger, naiveté, youthful innocence (or ignorance) but whatever; I had this blind drive to succeed (or fail). I felt like this was a great opportunity for me. Fuck it, I was going to swing for the fence.

I don't remember how it happened, but the next day when I showed up at Alan King's office, none of the other writers were there. It was just "the King and I" sitting in his gigantic office overlooking Central Park South. He was at his huge wooden desk, looking off, lost in thought. Concerned, he asked me if I thought the show was actually going to work. He wanted to know if this was a viable premise.

Maybe he recognized that I had some knowledge of actual scriptwriting and some storytelling ability. I wasn't sure, but I pulled out a script from an envelope and gingerly handed it over like it was the top-secret *Pentagon Papers*. I told him that I spent the night laying out the story beats into script form. I explained that it was a very rough draft, but it should give us a sense of whether we're on the right track or not.

Alan reached for the script, "Great. Let me see it."

Aw, man...I was sitting across from Alan King and he's going to read, in front of me, a script that I shit out the night before. I *had* to write it, though. I didn't know why, really. I was just following my instincts.

Alan was flipping pages. I heard a few grunts and a few other low guttural noises as he skimmed through it. This was torture. He read it, top to bottom, tossed it on his desk, then paused. "It's good."

Relieved I said, "Yeah, this could get us started; it's basically a frame. We can build out from it, punch it up and --"

He stopped me: "No. This is good. This'll work."

I was new to the writing game, but I had enough wherewithal to know that this script needed a ton of rewriting. I pushed: "We should get together with the writers and the comics in the show, sit down, let them fill out their parts, let the story build out and --" He stopped me again: "Yeah, we can put some jokes it." His confidence in my pages was unwavering: "I'll get a rehearsal started today. Let's get going on this."

Okay, look: At this point, I was thinking, *"This is Alan King. He's been in the comedy game for at least forty years, so he must know something that I don't know."* I did let myself think that maybe I'm just a comedy genius. Maybe everything I type is comedy gold. That was a fun thought. For a brief second.

I don't really remember too many more meetings with the other writers after that. Alan would call me to come to his office to punch up and adjust and rewrite the script with him. It was crazy, but I was flattered. Sitting together in his glass-walled office, with his thumbs deeply pushed into his vest pockets, he'd pace the room while considering my pitches. He'd repeatedly call his assistant to come in and make drinks. She'd pull out a full bar from a hidden compartment in the bookshelves and carefully mix fresh martinis.

During all this, he'd jump on and off the phone with his lawyers. Knee-deep in a lawsuit with Neil Simon, it turned out Alan was friends with Smith & Dale, the vaudeville comedy team that Simon's *The Sunshine Boys* was based on. From what I was hearing, I gleaned that while Neil was writing the movie, he kept calling Alan to get stories about Smith & Dale. This went on for months. Alan saw the movie and realized that most of his stories were up on the screen! This prompted the lawsuit. From what I understand, Alan did win some sort of settlement.

As the martinis poured, it became more and more difficult to wrangle Alan and get him to focus on the rewrite. I'd push him and start picking out spots in the script to work on: "Let's raise the stakes in the second act and --"

He'd interrupt: "1962. The Copa. I'm opening for Judy Garland. Henny Youngman's in the audience..."

Suddenly, I'm caught in a yarn from his old nightclub days. I liked them, but there was a ton of work to do. The more his assistant made martins, the deeper we'd fall into the rabbit hole of his glorious showbiz past.

The comics slated to star in this TV extravaganza, called *Nothing Upstairs*, were Judy Tenuta, Bob Nelson, Paul Provenza (Why is Provenza in all my stories?) and the late Dennis Wolfberg. It was ultimately a hybrid, variety-sitcom-standup special. There were broad pre-fab comedy set pieces laid out throughout the show. For instance, we had a comedy team planted at the bar as customers who got into a weak argument that somehow led to a silent challenge to see which one could devour the most saltine crackers. Things kept building until they ended up spitting fountains of wet cracker crumbs into each other's faces. That was it. That was the bit.

There were flashbacks rolled in for our star comedians, each designed as their own separate and personalized short film. At one point, Alan King's favorite old Catskill comic friend, Gene Baylos, wandered into the bar. With paper cup in hand, he asked the owner for spare change. Gene was portraying a once-famous standup comic who was down on his luck. This let him segue into his actual act, so he could show the young upstarts how it was done back when comedy was king. He ripped through a barrage of one-liners like, "I got a nice apartment. It's in midtown, overlooking -- the rent!" When he was done, he turned to the studio audience and took a bow. I didn't know what the fuck was happening, but the audience was laughing their asses off. I mean, it was like something you'd hear if you looked at old kinescopes of the *Milton Berle Show* or Sid Caesar's *Your Show of Shows*.

By the end of it all, I couldn't tell you if the show was good, bad or great. Perhaps CBS' decision to air it at 2 a.m. on a Sunday morning might be a clue to how much they adored it. That said, *People,* the all-showbiz-knowing magazine of the day, gave it a glowing review and graded it with an A-. Welp, as screenplay writer William Goldman says of Hollywood, "Nobody knows anything."

SNL, MY UNREQUITED LOVE

IN THE MID-1970s, I was still wedded to the old-school comedians; Berle, Jack Benny, Groucho, as well as the new young standups of the day like Leno, Elayne Boosler and Letterman. *Saturday Night Live*, though, was the first hip, young, culturally relevant, hard-hitting comedy inspiration of my generation -- especially in its first seasons where Richard Pryor, George Carlin, Lily Tomlin and Steve Martin hosted during the days of cast members Belushi, Chevy, Gilda, et al. *SNL* was late Saturday-night appointment television and remains so to this day, at least for me.

I was just starting to play around with standup comedy during *SNL*'s early seasons, back around that time I won that comedy contest in Hartford, Connecticut. With that summer-long comedy experience under my belt, I figured I could just type up a letter and send it off the offices of *SNL* and ask them if I could be a cast member. That's how it works, right? You just ask, they send a car to your door, drive you off to 30 Rock on show night and toss you into a sketch on live TV. Okay, maybe a misguided notion at the time, but who knows what an innocent letter from a hungry wannabe funny person could bring? After all, at seventeen I sent jokes to Rodney Dangerfield and it prompted him to call me at home to encourage me to get my ass to NYC and get onstage in the comedy clubs. So, yeah, I did send a letter to Lorne Michaels at *SNL*.

I don't remember exactly what I wrote but it was no doubt hilarious. I think I sent a cash bribe of a quarter to help me secure a position as a *Not Ready For Prime Time Player*. Look, as a teen you're allowed to do such idiotic things. I encourage my young sons to do the same. I think the problem is that as we get older, most of us let our ego or maturity or common sense get in our way and keep us from taking impossible and bold chances. Showbiz or not, I've learned that you have to keep looking at the world with wide-eyed innocence, curiosity and a sense of adventure. It's the philosophy I live by and it might be one of the reasons I continue to work as a writer in Hollywood. It's the reason I wrote this, the world's best book ever about what happens behind the brick wall of comedy!

Anyway, I did get a response from *SNL*, basically a form letter telling me that "We currently do not have any needs in our cast, however, your letter will be kept on file should the situation change." Aykroyd left. Belushi quit. I never got a call. There have been hundreds of cast changes over their 40-whatever years. My phone has yet to ring. There's been no text, no email. Oh well, showbiz, right? In truth, as a kid, it was exciting to get an official rejection letter

NBC   National Broadcasting Company, Inc   Thirty Rockefeller Plaza
New York, N.Y. 10020   212-664-4444

11/6/79

Dear Mr. Rowe,

    Thank you for your letter. Unfortunately, there are no job openings at present on the staff of Saturday Night Live. Nor is it likely that during the remainder of this production season any additional hiring will take place in the administrative, production, writing or casting areas.

    However, your letter will be kept on file should the situation change.

    Again, thank you for your interest in Saturday Night Live. Best wishes to you and Good Luck!

Sincerely,

Cristina McGinniss
Secretary to
Lorne Michaels

Rejected! Saturday Night Live.

from Lorne Michaels during that early season of *Saturday Night Live*.

Somewhere around 1987, during my later standup days at the New York Improv, I met Bob Odenkirk (as of this writing, Bob is Saul on *Better Call Saul*). He moved to New York from Chicago, where he was a member of Chicago's Second City Theater. Bob was the newest member of The Improv and his standup act was different from the type I'd become used to seeing. It was meta, crazy-weird, smart and subtle, yet somehow bigger than life. He was truly funny. I'd seen so much standup at that point that it was hard for me to get excited about watching anyone on the comedy stage, but Bob's act grabbed my attention. After his set, I cornered him in The Improv bar and just started asking a barrage of questions. I wanted to know about his background, his heroes and his journey into Manhattan.

Like me, Bob was inspired by Steve Martin. The *Let's Get Small* record had become part of our DNA. When he told me he had moved to New York to write for *Saturday Night Live*, I perked up. Now I *really* had to know everything: "How does one get to do that? What's it like? Is it as fun and great and everything you've hoped it would be?" Again, I was like a child, wide-eyed and excited. Bob was patient with me. He invited me to visit the *SNL* offices.

The next afternoon, I wandered into the hallowed Art Deco halls of 30 Rock. This was a huge thrill, especially for me, the nerdiest of comedy nerds. Riding up to the 17th floor, the elevator doors opened into that familiar hallway that I had seen so many times on *SNL*. That hall where Lorne had stopped George Harrison, hoping against hope that he had brought the other Beatles with him. That same spot where Paul Simon had gotten angry at Lorne for forcing him to wear the embarrassing turkey suit for the opening of the Thanksgiving show.

Bob greeted me and took me into the writers' bullpen, a conference room at one side with a bunch of small writers' offices on the other. The whole floor was buzzing with writers and cast members. I was trying to take everything in while pretending to be cool and collected. I spotted Tom Davis looking high and happy. His former partner, Al Franken, was dealing with scripts at the conference table. Bob introduced me to everyone, including his close writer friends Conan O'Brien and Greg Daniels. They were kids, not that long out of college. Conan, I think, did well for himself. As for Greg Daniels, not sure. I think he did some sort of *Office* TV show...

Suddenly, Dan Aykroyd showed up to visit his old stomping grounds. I was living in some sort of weird dream. This was all pretty great. He seemed jolly and everyone was excited to see him, especially Franken and Davis. The scene was casual and relaxed, even though there was a show happening that night. Bob told me that I should come by and see it. What? Yes, for sure. That's exactly what I was going to do!

That night, I thought I was going to be sitting by myself in a nice, prime seat as an audience member in the middle of studio 8H. Instead, he brought me into the conference room on the 18th floor just outside of Lorne's office, where the writers typically hung out. The cast and a few writers were zipping in and out, preoccupied, worried, but energized. It was that window of time between dress rehearsal and air, when Lorne would squeeze everyone into his office to lay out what sketches had been cut, which would survive, and in what spot they would land in the show. All hoped their sketch landed in the prime of the show, any time before *Weekend Update*.

Tom Hanks popped out of Lorne's office, nodded and tossed out a friendly hello. Oh, right. He was the host.

Whenever Bob would invite me, I would always show up. Eventually I was comfortable enough to wander backstage, or into Lorne's office or the director's booth while the show was live, on the air. I'd see glimpses of the cast doing quick costume and makeup changes or going through last-minute cue-card updates. These were the days of Dana Carvey, Phil Hartman, John Lovitz and Dennis Miller. I was taking in every morsel of the goings-on, because I just knew this was the environment where I would be spending my career. I needed to absorb all aspects of how it worked.

I might've become too comfortable there, because at one point, I found myself helping Dana Carvey write promos and eventually, I started contributing to Dennis Miller's *Weekend Update*. I'd submit jokes by Saturday afternoon, in time for the *Weekend Update* brunch where the writers cobbled Dennis' jokes together.

Once, Alan Zweibel stopped by one of these brunches. He had been a writer for the show during its first few seasons and I knew exactly who he was. I had to introduce myself. As nonchalantly as possible, I let him know that I was starting a career as a writer. He didn't know me, yet he seemed genuinely happy to hear that.

Alan wrote most of the jokes for Chevy's *Weekend Update*, and he cowrote most of what Gilda did from behind the news desk. He was, before that, a comic at The Improv. He also loved the standup comics that performed at the Catskill resorts back in their heyday of the '50s and '60s. As a teen, he wrote gags and one-liners for most of them. He told me that he was hired by *SNL* based on his two-hundred-page book of Catskill-comic jokes. It seemed Alan and I were kindred spirits, because, to this day I'm still impressed with the old-school comedians. There's an infectious musicality to their snappy timing and silly long takes after a punchline.

One night, as I was walking through Times Square and heading back to my apartment on 54th Street, someone walked past me and blurted out, "Nice shirt." I was wearing a *Saturday Night Live* sweatshirt. I'm not sure why. I likely fancied myself a real writer for the show, because I had some jokes on *Weekend Update*. It was Alan Zweibel headed to his office in the famous Brill Building. He stopped me to ask how my writing was going. I told him I had just written two *It's Garry Shandling's Show* spec scripts. By this time, Alan happened to be the executive producer, co-creator and showrunner of that show. Talk about kismet. Without hesitation he told me to get the best one of the two scripts to him. He promised he'd read it, but couldn't promise anything would come of it; just some feedback.

I heard from him a few days later. He liked the script and thought it could get some attention for me out in the real world. He set up a meeting with me and a manager friend, Barry Secunda, who managed all the original writers of *Saturday Night Live* and was still, in 1987, representing Rosie Shuster, Michael O'Donoghue and Franken and Davis. He took in all the writers on that first season of *SNL*, and legendary manager, Bernie Brillstein took the original cast.

So now I had a literary manager. It's crazy how things fall into place like that.

My first order of business with Barry was obvious: "We have a direct line to Shandling's show; let's make our move." Barry was already on it, but said Alan had a new show that he thought I'd be perfect for; a sitcom called *The Boys* about the Friars Club and the dynamics of the old-time comics that hung out there. "*Holy smack*, of course I'm perfect for that!"

Now, if this writing job were to actually happen, it meant that there'd be a big change in my life. I would have to move from the comforts of my studio apartment in midtown Manhattan and away from my "family" at The Improv and out of reach of my family back in Connecticut. But this job would fulfill my vision and the promise that I made to myself. I was not going to move to Hollywood unless I had a writing job waiting for me. Barry knew this was how I wanted things to work out.

After weeks of waiting for *The Boys* to get a pickup, I finally got an official job offer from Alan. I was asked to come out to Hollywood and work on the show as a staff writer, the lowest rung on the writer's ladder. Barry told me that, unfortunately, the show could only offer me a thousand dollars a week. Wait, are you kidding me? One K a week to a struggling standup comic was a hugely grotesque amount of money. I was doing one-nighters in Jersey and Staten Island, upstate N.Y. or wherever for fifty or sixty bucks a show. So that, along with weekend gigs in Manhattan, I was maybe making two hundred bucks a week. But now, a thousand a week? *Damn!* It was happening! I was on track for my ten-room house in the Hollywood Hills.

A HOLLYWOOD VIRGIN

THE IMPROV WAS A FANTASTIC experience for me. I cultivated friendships there that I cherish to this day. New York City in the 1980s was an exciting time to be part of the comedy scene. The Improv was my college and my campus was midtown Manhattan. It was also my home away from home. I spent countless nights there laughing, learning and struggling with a group of amazing, supportive and talented people.

Mark Cohen's apartment during a more innocent time (1984) (left to right) Louis CK, Dave Atell, Sarah Silverman and Me.

To this day, I thank Silver Friedman for her support and guidance during those very important formative years, not only comedy-wise but life-wise. She pushed me through the ranks of The Improv, but only when she felt I was ready and able and funny enough. It wasn't until years later that I fully recognized and understood the impact she's had on my career and my life.

"Follow your truth," she'd remind me.

News had trickled down into the standup community that my big 'ol comedy-writing job was forthcoming and I'd be moving away to Hollywood. That news came by way of me. This prompted my comedy compadres to throw a going-away party that best suited me -- an old-school comedy roast. Comedians Michael Patrick King and Ned Rice were at the helm of this extravaganza. Held in the banquet room of a 10th Avenue hotel that was typically set aside for business meetings and quickie wedding ceremonies, the "Mike Roast" was a night of tuxes, cigars, drinks, a crappy buffet and a dais of comics who were out for blood.

My blood.

My first time as emcee at The Improv. *The lineup included Jon Katz (Dr. Katz) with Robert Klein and ending with Robert Altman (Uncle Dirty).*

The night was glorious. I reveled in the old-timey jokes, insults and heckles. In addition to Michael and Ned, the dais was packed with my close comedy friends; Mark Cohen, Marty Rackham, Susie Soro, Jon Manfrellotti, Steve Skrovan, Ken Ober, Mike Ivy, Bill Grundfest, Joe Mulligan, Eliot Cameron, and Chris Blitman.

Special guests came up and roasted me in character; Barry Mitchell hilariously and accurately played Woody Allen, Mark Vaselli was a dead-on Red Buttons. Cheryl Bricker as '70s Latin singer/sex kitten Charo was so lost in her oversexed character that she basically #MeToo-ed me right there at the podium.

The room was packed shoulder-to-shoulder with such comedy peers as Larry David, Barry Berry, Billiam Coronel, Jonathan Solomon, Mike "The WID" Baldwin, Sue Kolinsky and Martin Harvey Friedberg, to name a few. David Derickson videotaped the evening. My manager, Barry Secunda, was on hand, keeping a close eye on me, his new comedy investment.

My mom and my sister Tracy drove in from Connecticut to be there that night. My sister was always supportive of my comedy journey and had some show-biz aspirations of her own. She too made the trek to Hollywood in the early 1990s, where she found some success in stage management and set building, painting and design.

Silver Friedman was in the audience as well. She somehow thought this night was a ploy so I could publicly announce to her and my comedy family that I was engaged to her daughter, Zoe. I was close friends with Zoe, but we never dated. It was never clear to me where that notion came from.

My comedy roast was, in truth, a ceremony for the graduating class of my generation of New York comedians. We were all on the verge of making the move to Hollywood or at least on the precipice of making that leap to our next level of success, and you could feel the significance of it in the room that night.

The next morning, I was on a plane to Los Angeles, ready, willing and -- I hoped -- able to take on my very first writing job in Hollywood.

I proudly drove onto the Sunset Gower lot in a sputtering, banged-up 1977 Ford LeBaron rent-a-wreck. As I found my way to the production offices, I was, of course, a little nervous. Alan Zweibel was at the helm and I wanted to prove to him that I was worthy of a seat at his writers' table. I really had no clue how a TV sitcom was put together, especially from the ground up, so it was hard for me to be fully prepared.

Alan's assistant showed me around the offices. As she entered the writers' conference room she told me, "This is the only room that really matters. You'll be spending most of your time in here with the other writers."

This struck me as odd. Most shows I'd worked on, albeit cable comedy shows, we wrote alone in our offices. I was soon to understand that legitimate, grown-up TV sitcom writers live in the writers' room for hours at a time. In some cases, we'd be in there from 10 a.m. until as late as 2 a.m.

The assistant showed me my office, a room about the size of my wallet. Apparently, the week before, it had been the Xerox room. I spotted a lowly copier sitting in the hall outside my door. I could feel its resentment; I'd kicked it out of its home. If it could, it would have thrown the finger at me. That didn't matter though; I was a staff writer with a desk in a room that, I soon discovered, was also the conduit to the bathrooms and showers. Still, it was all good.

These offices were, it turned out, the same offices where they wrote and produced Shandling's show. There were a few times where a sweaty Garry would walk through my office after his workout and jump into the shower room.

On the first day, Alan came into my office. He made me comfortable and basically laid out how he hoped to best expedite the making of *The Boys*. He introduced me to the writing team of Tom Gammill and Max Pross. Their relaxed, nonchalant, confident style was calming and comforting. Gammill and Pross had come from Lorne Michaels' camp in New York where they worked on *SNL* and other Broadway Video projects. They were also writers on Shandling's show, but for the time being, they were helping Alan out on *The Boys* until Garry's show got picked up for the next season.

Alan was a fun spirit in the room; just what I needed to stay as calm and funny as possible. I was so uncertain and green that I thought for sure it was only a matter of time before everyone discovered that I was a fraud and hiring me was some sort of horrible mistake. After a hundred years of writing and producing comedy, that feeling still chases after me from job to job.

The legendary writing team of Bob Schiller and Bob Weiskopf joined the writing staff of *The Boys*. These guys wrote for, among other things, the legendary *I Love Lucy*. Alan felt they would be perfect for his show. In their mid-seventies, he figured that Bob and Bob would have a great perspective on that generation of old, funny codgers.

When I learned of "The Bobs'" writing pedigree, I became a pest to them. I'd corner them in their office for hours at a time and ask about those early days. Lucy, they told me, would quickly flip through the first draft of their script and acknowledge if there was enough "black stuff." This meant that she skimmed the pages looking for the blocks of comedy action lines. These were typed in bold, uppercase letters, hence, the "black stuff." To Lucy, it represented the volume of physical comedy she had in that week's episode. The more there was, the better for her. William Frawley didn't want any lines, they told me. The fewer lines he had, the happier he was.

It was hard for me, at first, to figure out the dynamics of a comedy writing room. I was used to sharing funny thoughts and ideas with friends and comics in social circles, but suddenly I was in a space where I was expected to be funny in a very specific way and in a style that suited the show as well as the temperament and personality of the room. I had to learn to navigate all of this and still generate laughs for the script. In truth, after all these years and over fifty writing staffs later, I've yet to master all of that, although I've become better at pretending that I have. I think most comedy writers would tell you the same.

The Boys was also the first place where I experienced a table read. This is when the stars gather to do a read-through for the writers, producers and the network. The cast for *The Boys* at our first read were:

Norm Crosby, an actual Friar and a hilarious, old-school standup who was the master of the malaprop: "Or is that a pigment of my ejaculation?"

Norman Fell, who we all know from, among other things, *Three's Company*.

Jackie Gayle, an old-school standup and actor for at least forty years, fresh from a co-starring role in the movie *Tin Men*.

We had character-actor Alan Garfield, who had been a part of every smart, hip project that came out of Hollywood, starting with the movie *Putney Swope* to Woody Allen's *Bananas* to *Serpico*.

Lionel Stander was known to TV audiences at the time from the show *Hart to Hart*, but I knew him as a seriously legitimate comic actor. He played alongside such comedy legends as Fatty Arbuckle, Harold Lloyd and Bob Hope. He was 86 years old at the time, yet he had the stamina to withstand the pressures of a weekly sitcom.

Jane Carroll played the first woman ever allowed to join the Friars club. You'd recognize her as Tom Cruise's mom in the movie, *Risky Business*.

These were the people who were about to utter my first words in a script, what few there were. Everyone settled in and sat side-by-side at the long table in the cavernous conference room. Opening their scripts, they focused and gathered themselves as they prepared to launch another great comedy series and then...

The building started to wobble! What was --? Was it an anxiety attack? Was I --?

EARTHQUAKE!

People scrambled for the exits. I was lost and confused. If you hadn't guessed, there weren't a lot of earthquakes in Manhattan. I was panicking and zig-zagging around the room, unsure of what-in-the-fuck to do before the building came down on me. Lionel Stander just sat at the table, unflinching, as if to say, "Fuck it! Buncha pussies!" The man's seen some shit in his life.

I followed the people as they rushed the door to the outside. Huddling with everyone out on a balcony, I was unsure why a third-floor balcony was considered a safe place for cover. We held still as the building danced for all of ten or fifteen seconds. To me, it felt like an hour. Once the city stopped rattling, the team, frayed nerves and all, sat back down at the table and geared back up to read a happy-happy comedy script as though nothing had happened. Welcome to California.

After weeks of pitching jokes and ideas, struggling and trying desperately to figure out the process that would help the scripts get better and funnier, I was starting to lose confidence. I was getting jokes in, sure, but things were getting cloudy for me. I wasn't clear on what was landing or if Alan or anyone else in the room liked me. In Hollywood, people like to keep things close to the vest. I wasn't used to this. It was hard for me to get a bead on where I was in the heads of everyone on this show, especially Alan.

After six or so months, we finished the seven-episode order for the first season. It was a grueling process for me as I dealt with the daily fog of uncertainty. In the end, Alan called Barry, my manager in New York, and told him that he liked me and if the show got picked up for another season, he hoped I would come back as a writer.

When Barry called me to relay this news, I was so excited that I did an involuntary dance around my little office/Xerox room.

Alas, the show was not picked up, but I survived my virginal comedy-writing job with flying colors. In my "baby writer" mind I was a hugely successful Hollywood sitcom writer. In reality, I was seriously unemployed.

THE LOVE LIFE OF A HAPLESS COMEDY WRITER

I WAS STILL NEW TO Los Angeles and segueing into my illustrious career as the World's Greatest Hollywood Comedy Writer. This was around the time I started my second job as a low-level staff writer on a failing sitcom. Back in the days of my latter youth, I was in decent shape with my kinda chiseled cheekbones, a boyish round face, bright blue eyes, and a mostly full head of hair. At the time, I could be found in the local bars waving my big-shot Hollywood comedy writer card around. It was mostly to help me feel better about my impending hair loss.

During this time, I was close friends with comedy writers and producers Sally and Maxine, who happened to be sisters. Maxine was a fellow standup with me at the New York Improv early in my career. She was a hot shot sitcom producer and helped me get a prime-time, network sitcom-writing job with Ed. Weinberger, the cocreator of *The Mary Tyler Moore Show* and *Taxi*. This was not a bad early entry into the TV sitcom-writing game... I thought.

The show was called *Baby Talk*, starring George Clooney, Julia Duffy from *Newhart* and a baby who talked and sounded remarkably like Tony Danza -- mostly because it was, in fact, Tony Danza. The show was, well, not great. Let's just say, if you're working on a sitcom with a talking Tony Danza-baby, there's a strong chance you're not clearing a shelf for an Emmy.

I ran into George Clooney in recent years and we re-bonded with *Baby Talk* stories. With absolute confidence, he said that show was the worst experience of his entire career. He was telling me this even after his epic fistfight with director David O. Russell on the set of the movie, *Three Kings*. If nothing else, I have the distinction of working on George Clooney's most-hated project. A lot of it was due to the mismanagement and stubbornness of the mercurial Ed(period) Weinberger. Anyway, the single guy story…

Maxine and I were pretty close back then, we spent a lot of time together. Through her, I met her producer friend, whom we'll call Emma. Emma was my type. She had that young Valerie Bertinelli thing that many guys of my generation were cowed by. Also, Emma was smart, compassionate, sweet; all those great things that typically, for me, laid the groundwork for massive heartbreak.

I made my interest in Emma known to Maxine. I figured I'd employ her as my wing-person, and in the meantime, I'd do my best to charm her. I'm not even sure what tools I had in my tool belt that'd knock the ladies off their feet back then (okay, ever). They were likely not the sharpest because, as usual, I was getting nowhere with young Emma.

Eventually I found myself in that place where many of us hapless young fools end up; alone with a sweet, cute woman going on dinner dates, to the movies, long walks in the night. All under the guise of "friends." I was relentless though. Emma became a summer-long project for me. Now, considering her as a "project" might tell you that I hardly oozed the charm and class to woo her.

I mentioned to her that I was planning a weeklong visit back to New York City. I had been living in L.A. for a few months, yet Manhattan still felt like home to me. She suggested that while I was there, I should meet up with her friend Jen. "She's done some comedy acting. You'll like her; she's funny. You guys will get along." Ugh. There it was. The final nail in the coffin of possibility. The inevitable line of relationship demarcation was set.

Most adult men know that once a woman sets you up with a friend, there is nary a chance that you and your sweetums-to-be will be skipping hand-in-hand through a field of lilies and grasshoppers.

Jen was kind of an afterthought during my adventures back in the Big Apple. I visited a bunch of standup friends, I got back onstage a few times, I went to some of my old favorite restaurants. I later found a crumpled-up piece of paper in my jacket pocket. It was Jen's phone number. Emma had scribbled it out for me. *Okay, all right. Jen. I get it!*

I called her up. She sounded happy to hear from me and she said that Emma couldn't stop talking about what a great guy I was. If I'm so great then...Ugh, never mind.

Jen sounded pleasant enough on the phone. We figured out a time to meet up the next day. I trekked across town to her apartment somewhere on the Upper West Side. We had no specific plans; hang out, see a movie, lunch, whatever. It was still morning, so the day was our oyster. My concern was, what if this is bad? How could I bail out of it ASAP? Well, I had committed myself to this day. So be it.

Jen lived in a fabulous apartment building. It was a giant, clean and bright townhouse with the sun beaming down on a fluffy flower garden out and around a frontyard. A frontyard in New York City? Damn. Back then, living under a stairwell for five hundred a month was considered a sweet deal, so who was this person who gets to live here in the Garden of Allah?

I made my way into the building and through a long hallway. The ceilings, I swear, were seventy-feet high. The halls were lined with old, carved wood, likely all original from the early 1920s. I was finally going to meet Jen and, who knows, she's close friends with Emma, so I thought, *"Maybe she'll have some pointers on how I can maneuver my way into her heart and..."* Damn. I was such a dope.

I rang the bell. The door was oddly huge. It might've been pulled from a castle or a cathedral or some such thing. Jen swung it open: "Hi. Mike?"

Wait. Jen...Wow! Jen was adorable. She was small with a cute, round, bright face and piercing icy-grey eyes. Her smile sent a wave of energy that conked me full on in my face. Man! I was in trouble!

Jen, as it turned out, was Jennifer Aniston.

My mind was racing. What do I do? How do I handle this? I had to stay calm and collected. With confidence, I said, "Ahhhba, jabahh haa, ba maaa." At least that's what it sounded like in my head. Nonetheless, I stayed strong and positive as we headed out into the streets.

Jen was not a quite a celebrity at this point. She was still a few years away from starting her run on *Friends*. Since she was a working actress, she wanted to know everything I knew about how the system worked out there in La-La Land. I shared what I could. I thought for a second that maybe she thought that I was some sort of Hollywood big-shot jerk who could help jump her career up to the next level. I didn't deny that.

We had a fun day as we walked and talked through Manhattan and around Central Park. The day was very pleasant. We ended up going to see the movie *Green Card*, a romantic comedy because, you know, maybe it could help ignite some sort of...yeah, nah, what am I saying?

At the end of the day, she said, "I'm going to move to L.A. soon. Can I call you?" Uh, yes, of course, Jennifer Aniston, you can call me when you move to L.A. She jotted down my number.

Many months went by and Jennifer Aniston didn't call; not that I really expected her to. I did stay in touch with Emma, though. At one point, she called me to say that Jen had moved to L.A. and wanted us to meet up with her to see a play at a small theater in Hollywood. Of course. I'm there. Yes!

Jenifer Aniston greeted me at the theater as if we'd been friends forever. There I was, in a quaint little theater, sitting in-between two women that I had a silly boy-crush on. I didn't even know what the play was; it never occurred to me to ask. Like it mattered. The lights dimmed. I was doing what I could to keep my cool.

Where was I? What was happening?

Soon it was clear that this play was a one-man, over-acted, spirited Shakespearian comedy from 1593 and it would not end! I convinced myself that sitting through the torture of this meant there was some sort of payback in the end. That was the only thing that kept me from jumping on the stage and taking the rusted-out dagger and shoving it into my chest.

So after the show, we gathered in the lobby. I was steadfast as I praised the show I hated. Good thing too, because right then, the one-man in the one-man show stepped in and...hugged and kissed Jen -- his girlfriend. Of course, he did. You saw this coming. I didn't because, you know, that was who I was. Anyway, all was good. She introduced me to her actor/boyfriend as her comedy writer/friend. I corrected her and introduced myself as "the guy who has moved on from his Jennifer Aniston fantasy/friend."

The next time I saw Jen was at an all-you-can eat salad bar, the Souplantation on La Cienega Boulevard in Hollywood. It's, ya know, a big Hollywood hang. It was about a year or so later and she greeted me with a warm hug. Her career was going great; she was on a primetime sketch show on Fox. My guy friends at the table fell in love with her on sight (men are dopes) and they wanted to know everything about her. My story was long; I was going to need reinforcements. I went up to the soft-serve yogurt machine, oozed out a hearty bowl of vanilla, sat back at the table and told the tale of my day with Jennifer Aniston.

Not long after that, Jen's life changed when she landed on the TV series *Friends*.

I hadn't seen Jen until many years after her explosion into celebrity stratosphere. It was a Sunday and I was headed into Victor's restaurant in Hollywood, where I had a standing weekly brunch with my comedy-writer friends that lasted 25 years. Jennifer was standing out front. As I got closer, I looked at her straight in the eyes and I could tell she did not recognize me. She looked at me as if I were considering some sort of bodily attack. I was about to say something to remind her who I was and how we knew each other, you know, there was our lovely walk through Manhattan, the romantic movie, the Souplantation and -- I stopped myself as she turned to hug and kiss Brad Pitt.

WRITING THE WRONGS

BY THE EARLY '90s, I was landing some sweet work on network sitcoms. While writing on *The Nanny*, a family series starring Fran Drescher, I was asked by a producer friend if I'd spend a weekend helping to write a TV special for the Lifetime Network. I'm sure all of you remember that extravaganza; there's the moon landing, The Beatles on *Sullivan* and Lifetime's *Free to Laugh: A Comedy and Music Special for Amnesty International*. It was a night of singing, comedy, and testimonials, all in the name of women suffering around the world. It sounded like fun.

They needed writers to assemble some filler and patter for the hosts. It was a star-studded night, with Jackson Browne, Susan Sarandon, David Crosby, Robin Williams and the like. The night was hosted by the lovebird couple and sitcom stars of the '90s, Tom and Roseanne Arnold.

A few days before the event, I got together with a handful of comedy writers and we started to piece the show together: Quips, segues, intros; everything Tom and Roseanne would need to make it a smooth night of songs, laughter and harrowing stories of women who were tortured around the globe. As we went through the lineup, we saw that Roseanne was assigned to read a moving speech about a brave woman who ran for president in her country. And she won. So of course, her government put her under house arrest for four years. It was heartbreaking and poignant and an important moment for women. Being a comedy writer idiot who needed attention in a room full of other comedy writers I yelled out, "She couldn't leave her house for four years? That's almost as bad as waiting for the cable guy." The room laughed. Typically, comedy writers laugh hardest when stupid, dark and unusable jokes are tossed into the mire.

On the night of the big show, Hollywood showed up in all its glory. The Wiltern Theater was packed; people were dressed in their

Sunday best. Seats were selling as high as eight hundred dollars, all marked as donations in the name of *Amnesty International*. I was sitting third-row center and felt the buzz in the air. Cameras were circling, notables were sitting all around me, celebrities were wandering around the theater, glad-handing donors. I brought a date, and how could she not be impressed? I was, after all, a big-time writer for this star-studded gala. The curtains parted, Tom and Roseanne came out to huge applause. They kicked off the night with the happy, adorable patter that came via our hard work. They introduced David Crosby and Jackson Browne. They performed a moving and heartfelt duet as slides of brave women throughout history were projected behind them. It was a great way to start the night and it built from there. Robin Williams made a surprise appearance. Lily Tomlin made a powerful speech about the treatment of women.

Eventually, Roseanne read the speech about the woman who ran for president in her small country. Her interpretation was very moving. She connected to the story; it resonated with her and the audience felt it. Eleven hundred people in that theater fell in love with Roseanne all over again -- especially when she revealed the part about how that same woman was placed under house arrest for four years by her own government. The entire Wiltern was quiet as they tried to absorb the tragic events of this woman's life.

That's when Tom, over Roseanne's shoulder, barked into the microphone: "Can't leave your house for four years? That's worse than waiting for the cable guy!"

"Wait. That wasn't...How did...? The joke got in...? No! Oh. My. Sweet. God!"

No one laughed. It got very quiet. A rumbling broke the silence. It started from the back of the theater and built, like a tsunami, towards the stage. The rumblings turned into boos. Tom, who seemed shocked and surprised by this response, was thrown back on his heels. He tried saving it as only he knows how.

"Fuck you!" he shouted out.

This turned the booing into retaliate shouting. I tried my best to sink down into my seat and slide under the seat in front of me. Tom started screaming into the mic, "Fuck you! Fuuuuck you!! I didn't write that joke...Some *writer* wrote it!" I looked for the fire exits; they were my only means of escape. The screaming became unbearable; it's now WWF night at the Wiltern. Tom and Roseanne finally bolted. They just up and left the stage. There was still over an hour of show left; cameras were rolling. The stage was empty, the crowd was still yelling. No one was up there -- what-in-the-fuck was happening?

Ten minutes go by, then twenty minutes. The producers tried to quell the chaos by sending the staff into the audience with free wine. After almost an hour, we heard a lone, unconvincing voice on the sound system bellow out from offstage:

"Uh, Tom and Roseanne have to get to the airport...to catch a flight...They have a time constraint, so right now they're going to record all of their segments and then they will be leaving the theater."

The audience grumbled as Tom and Roseanne begrudgingly stepped out to center stage and in about ten minutes, one right after the other, rolled out intros for the rest of the people on the show, "Ladies and gentlemen, Marlo Thomas... Please welcome, Color Me Badd... The comedy of Pam Stone," etc. When they finished, they stomped offstage and headed straight for the exit. This tangled up everything; the flow, the technical orchestrations of setting up bands and comic performances. Sinbad ambled out to centerstage and did his "milkshake make your head hurt" routine while a crew banged around drums and tuned up guitars as they set the stage for Bonnie Raitt.

After we hit hour four of what was supposed to be a ninety-minute special, I went backstage and found everyone still circling in a rage. I even heard Marlee Matlin carrying on angrily as her interpreter signed her words, "Tom-Fucking-Arnold..." I'm pretty sure Woody Harrelson was trying to rally the stars into a lynch mob. I might be misremembering, but I think Marlo Thomas called him a cocksucker. I basked in the warm glow of the chaos that was created by my ad-lib. I considered its power. My one single joke had capsized a titanic, star-filled Hollywood gala in one fell swoop.

Man, showbiz can be so fucking cool.

A FAREWELL TO STANDUP

I WAS QUICKLY LEARNING that writing a half-hour sitcom was all consuming. Still relatively new to the comedy-writing room, I felt I had to prove myself to everyone, every day. It was, to me, an uphill climb. At times I was worried that focusing less on my standup and going for a career as a writer had been a huge mistake. So what if I had to bop around comedy clubs for the rest of my life? It was a few hours of work each night. I was my own boss. The only person I had to please was me.

I was feeling lost, alone and worried in Hollywood, but nonetheless, I was "following my truth," as Silver Friedman put it.

Emotionally, I took the job home with me, worried that I wasn't helping enough with the scripts. I was also trying to adjust my perspective from *standup comedy* to *closeup comedy* in the intimacy of a writers' room. As a standup, you tell a joke and you get a genuine, visceral, hardcore laugh (or not) from a room full of people. At that moment, you know where you stand. In a comedy-writing room, things were a little different. An effective joke pitch or idea was typically met with a happy little chuckle or a comment like, "That's good; let's do that." It was hardly the satisfying cacophony of rolling laughs that come from a live comedy-club audience. The writing game was taking up my life *and* affecting my standup career, such as it was. I was happy to continue doing standup, even though I was out of my New York Improv comfort zone. Standup was a place I could find my comedy confidence. If I could still provoke a room full of strangers to laugh, it would remind me that I was, indeed, funny.

My relationship with the New York Improv helped with my standing at the L.A. Improv. Budd Friedman, who was still at the helm at the Melrose Avenue club, was putting me onstage somewhere between ten and eleven at night. These were nice primetime slots, and I used the room the same way I used the New York stage, as a comedy gymnasium -- a place to work out some bits while I fueled my comedy soul.

What I didn't know about the L.A. comedy scene at the time was that when you go onstage, you are supposed to hit the ground running with your A-plus material. The unspoken rule was, each time you are up there, you were to perform as if you were on *The Tonight Show* and Carson was waiting to invite you to sit with him on his panel. I didn't do that. It was not why I wanted and needed the stage time. As a result, my spots gradually fell later into the night. I didn't mind so much, I just needed my pocketful of laughs to help me sleep at night. If there were a few people sitting there to give me their stamp of comedy approval, that was fine with me.

Until one night...

I was assigned a decent spot, eleven o'clock-ish, but my time kept getting pushed back. Some comics went on much longer than they should have. One of the Wayans brothers did a set that went on for almost an hour. Back in my New York Improv days, I didn't mind waiting, but that night, things changed. I felt like I was sitting at an airport and my flight kept getting delayed. I was stuck there, growing tired and frustrated.

By the time I got onstage, it was close to one in the morning. The room, as you might imagine, was spent. There were about six or eight drunk and/or tired people ready to pay their checks. I didn't care about that; it was a familiar sight back in my New York days. In fact, these were the moments, as comics might tell you, where you'd kick down the guardrails and fuck around some. With any luck, you'd stumble onto a new comedy premise or joke. So I did some of my proven, tried-and-true material. I threw out a few notions that I thought might be funny. I even talked a little about my new life in Los Angeles. It felt good. I was at ease. I jumped offstage refreshed. Even in this less-than-accommodating situation, my comedy batteries got charged up a little.

As I headed back to the bar, some faceless Improv comic wrangler/booker appeared out the dark and gave me a consoling pat on the back. He seemed concerned about me. In his mind, he thought I was distraught over what he interpreted as a horrible set. It seemed that he was even worried that I'd consider some sort of self-harm because of what just happened onstage. He had no understanding that I was playing, as I did many times during my ten New York years of standup. Nonetheless, he started to talk down to me as if I were some sort of novice and, as if he were all-knowing, he gently assured me...

"Don't worry, man. You do it a few years, you'll figure it out."

With that, I felt a burning wash through my whole body. I'm not sure if it was anger or disappointment, but my whole being got hot and flushed. I felt dizzy. I imagine it's that feeling of trying to regain your bearings after getting whacked in the face with a tire iron. That clueless dolt thought I was brand new to standup and was welcoming me to the beginning of my journey.

As that false God from the shadows thought he was comforting me, I literally saw the standup comic persona, that spirit, the standup comedy apparition that lived in me since I was fourteen, release itself from my being and float up and out through the roof of the L.A. Improv and out into whatever heaven that comedy souls go to rest. I'm not particularly spiritual. I don't believe in ghosts or any of that sort of thing, but I swear, I saw it!

On stage at the Los Angeles Improv (early 1990's).

That moment marked the end of my standup journey. It had been a long time coming. My instincts had taken me on a different comedy path and brought me to L.A. I was now a Hollywood sitcom writer.

I never did standup again.

Honestly, I don't miss it and I never regretted leaving it behind. In some ways, it was like high school. It was great, I learned a lot, but I'd never want to go back. Well, maybe I'd visit once in a while, but it was no longer a part of my career path.

THE BIRTH OF THE COOL COMEDY

I WAS OUT OF THE standup game, but I was building a nice community of friends among the L.A. comics. Laura Kightlinger, a New York comedy friend, introduced me to Janeane Garofalo. This was right when she was hired as a cast member of Ben Stiller's sketch show on Fox. Andy Dick and Bob Odenkirk filled out the rest of the cast.

Janeane and I became close friends. She was and still is wonderfully smart, hilarious, and a brave standup. Janeane did onstage what I never had the courage to do; talk about yourself, your life, your worldview. Being honest, not hacky, was her modus operandi; no lazy punchlines about McNuggets or familiar observations about pesky air travel.

Janeane was quite astute and I think she felt there was another layer to my humor that I wasn't tapping into. She had a weekly experimental standup-comedy night in a local coffee house and she wanted me in the lineup for her next show. I reminded her that I quit standup, to which she said it was all the more reason to do it. "This is not standup," she said. She was adamant and demanded that I get up on her stage and be brave, crazy, weird and abstract. "Go up and fuck around."

Just like that, I was about to do "standup" again. Janeane brought me to the The Big and Tall Bookstore on Beverly Boulevard in Hollywood, directly across from the famous El Coyote restaurant. The space was a tiny 1990s hipster coffee shop with no stage and no microphone, just a few people sitting at tables, drinking coffee and reading (this was before portable Internet devices). This was a down-and-dirty, naked comedy space.

While this arena was Janeane's comfort zone, I was *un*comfortable, unsure of what I'd gotten myself into. I had a few dumb things planned, stuff I'd never tried anywhere and would never try at any of the established Hollywood comedy hot spots. Janeane had grown tired of those standard comedy clubs, and that drove her to seek out a space more amenable to her comedy style. In her case, it was for the better. For me, I wasn't so sure, but I had nothing to lose except maybe some dignity in front of a few L.A. Gen Xers.

Janeane stood up in front of a few tables of coffee drinkers and just started talking. Confident and on point, she pulled in everyone's attention as she told them of her life and world issues and ideas for fixing them both. This was what I imagined a Greenwich Village coffee house was like during their '60s heyday; poets and social activists needing to be heard. The audience, such as it was, was engaged, laughing, and in the moment. Despite the unfamiliar comedy dynamic, I was liking it. Good thing too, because I was on next. Actually, there were no other comics waiting to go on.

Okay, so I went up, ready to be abstract, odd and playful. I pretended that I had run into someone in the coffee shop who recognized me from my standup appearances on *The Merv Griffin Show*. They were excited to see me and hopeful that I was going to do my famous Civil War routine. I wanted to revive the old bit, I explained, but sadly, I didn't have the props with me. Instead, I went around the coffee shop and gathered a few things to represent my missing props.

Picking through my pile of "props" as I went along, I did voices of several Civil War soldiers in the middle of battle. Each character utilized a different prop. "General, we're losing men!" I barked out. Putting a coffee pot on my head as if it were a Confederate Hardee hat, I transformed into the General. "Send troops to the right flank!" I continued on, using coffee-shop props like sugar packets, cups and napkins as if they were as valid as my usual musket, sword and whatever Civil War prop I used for the bit when I quote unquote "did it on TV."

The concept is exhausting just thinking about all these years later, but Janeane laughed her ass off (she is a very supportive audience for comics). The coffee sippers seemed to like it okay, but for me it was exhilarating to be that odd and idiotic. This new approach to standup quickly opened my mind. I felt as if I had just taken a hit of LSD (although I've never tried it). This mindset helped inform my comedy-writing skills.

Over that summer, Janeane let me get up almost every week to continue the quest to tap into the recesses of my freaky comedy mind. I remember another time when I pretended I was very skilled at the art of throwing my voice. I had a friend offstage toss me a sack holding my ventriloquist dummy. As planned, he flung it at me, and it bounced across the floor. I opened the bag to find the mouth was broken off (all pre-set) and I would have to continue the ventriloquist routine with a busted dummy. In a panic, I first tried saying both the setups and punchlines: "Weren't you telling me earlier that you slept like a log? Is that why I found you in the fireplace?" The dummy would just nod. Then, trying to be helpful, the dummy would whisper the punchlines to me. I'd repeat them. It wasn't working. Then the dummy would talk in a desperate, mouthless mumble. It was all very silly. I eventually honed the bit enough to perform it on *Evening at The Improv*.

The lineups at The Big and Tall Bookstore started to build. David Cross, Ben Stiller and Bob Odenkirk would get up and try a few weird and abstract pieces. A very pretty young woman, who none of us knew, came up wearing a flowing red dress draped over her body. As she recited some sort of poetic diatribe about the oversexualization of women, two men on either side of her circled her while holding the ends of her dress. They slowly unwound it from her body as she continued on. Eventually, she was fully naked as she angrily ranted about how she was giving men what they wanted. I sat there stunned and a little scared. Moon Zappa -- Frank's daughter -- was sitting next to me. We shared a look, shrugged, then she summarized, "Nice tits."

I didn't know it at the time, but we were at the birth of what was to become the new revolution in standup, soon to be called the UnCabaret. To this day, it thrives for those standups who need a space to be brutally honest and comically fierce.

As my new L.A. comedy circles were building, so were my comedy-writing friends. More and more of my New York standup friends were moving into town as well. My housemate, Billiam Coronel, and I decided to throw a house party for all these factions, somehow squeezing two hundred people into our two-bedroom house in Hancock Park. Comics, writers, comedy actors, producers, et al. were jammed from our frontyard, through the house and into the backyard. I happily brought all these people together under one roof and they quickly started to bond. I threw at least one of these parties once a year, forging relationships that continue to this day.

There were times I'd weave my way through the thick of the people crowded in my house and stumble into the likes of Bill Murray, Mike Myers and Quentin Tarantino. Tarantino was taking comedy-acting classes with The Groundlings. Kathy Griffin, his teacher and friend, brought him to the parties, where he bonded with our group.

An old friend, Steve "The Duzer" Scarduzio would be there, and he loved the vibe of it all. The Duzer was a Hollywood nightclub owner who managed The Diamond Club, a block-long dance club on Hollywood Boulevard near Fairfax, across from Grauman's Chinese Theater. The club had a hundred-seater VIP room in the back that included a stage, which he gave over to us once a week to do shows from 6 o'clock until the nightclub opened at 9 p.m. Comics, comic actors, and comedy writers did shows for a private audience of our peers; no regular audience folk were invited. This was one of the first true, full-fledged versions of the UnCabaret. There were no rules except, again, no familiar standup bits. The idea was to be playful, bold and idiotic.

Bob Odenkirk and David Cross performed together for the first time here. They soon went on to create and host the groundbreaking HBO sketch series, *Mr. Show*. One of their first pieces at The Diamond Club was a take-off on improv teams. They continued to take comedy suggestions from the audience, not stopping until it left Bob naked and crying onstage. They later did the piece for HBO's *Comic Relief*, leaving Whoopi Goldberg angry and confused. A young and unknown Will Ferrell was part of a comedy trio who all wore head-to-toe stocking suits as they danced around as some sort of fumbling and overly excited Blue Man Group.

Molly Shannon came on from time to time to develop her clumsy catholic schoolgirl character, Mary Katherine Gallagher. Even then,

Janeane Garofalo and me at The Diamond Club *(1993).*

she'd take hard, backward dives into rows of folding chairs. Jack Black and his partner Kyle Gass "K.G." as Tenacious D tried out new songs. Other regulars included Patton Oswalt, Brian Posehn, Janeane, Andy Kindler, Dana Gould, Kathy Griffin and Sarah Silverman, along with a bunch of us comedy writers.

I did a dopey bit where I'd come out as an insult comic. I'd pick someone from the audience, sit them onstage and roast them, face-to-face. Then I'd show up later in the show and roast a peach on a stool. "Nice fuzz. There's a little thing called a razor. Look it up." I'd come out for a third time to roast Brain Posehn. He was six feet five with long, blond, rocker hair and wearing a sombrero and a loud poncho while carrying a stuffed donkey. So now, after being established as a "master-roaster," I'd go blank. I couldn't generate any kind of insult for this perfect comedy canvas. I'd eventually run offstage, embarrassed.

Most of us, the artists, comedians, producers, actors and managers, ("The Posse," as some called us*)* became close friends. We partied, hung out and broke bread together. Throughout the early '90s, we'd have parties almost every weekend, alternating from house to house. Dave Rath, a friend to all of us and a successful comedy manager, gave up his apartment on most weekends for the more "controlled and manageable" parties of about thirty to forty. I'd get sort of wasted at these gatherings; I didn't do drugs, but I drank enough to get into the flow of it all. I remember a bunch of us wrestling on Rath's living-room floor. If memory serves, I was wriggling around with Moon Zappa and Tarantino was on his knees directing us. He was barking out the moves. "Take her! Take her down. Go!" I remember someone else, who was a little too into the moment, flipping their partner into the wall and breaking through the plaster. Tarantino jumped towards the scene, still directing excitedly, "There's blood! And there's blood! Lots of blood!" I later read an interview in *Rolling Stone* where he talked about these parties. He said he was so high when he left that he didn't remember driving home.

I remember parties on rooftops where we were banging out rhythms on rusted-metal oil drums with hefty mallets. There were giant slingshots sending water balloons into neighboring buildings on Hollywood Boulevard. There was slam dancing, random comedy bits and musical instruments for impromptu singalongs.

I don't remember what I did exactly, but friends would circle around and laugh their asses off, sometimes for as long as ten minutes, as they watched me pretend I didn't know how to close the sliding door behind me, or the time when I couldn't figure out the mechanics of a folding chair. It became my idiotic "go-to" thing at these parties. Everyone, for the most part, was high, so I'm assuming it made my poor man's Buster Keaton routines infinitely more entertaining.

This spectacular phase in our showbiz lives slowly dissolved once Janeane moved away to pursue bigger and better career opportunities in New York City (including *SNL*). She was the driving force, the party planner, the glue that held The Posse together. Others became busy as their careers started to launch. Some went off to become famous. Some found their true loves, got married, and started their families.

Not long after that, I met Denise and we started dating. This brought me into the next amazing phase of my life and career – but more about that – and Denise – later.

I do miss the innocence of those days. All of us were still energized by the folly of youth and the excitement of what was possible. It was our last exhilarating ride before we were to become tethered to the seriousness of the real world and our lives and our careers. It was a seismic shift, but luckily the change was slow and subtle. We didn't know it was over until it was over. By then, we'd found ourselves absorbed into the next chapters of our lives. I was knee-deep, living the sitcom-writer life.

FAILING UP WHILE FALLING DOWN

Coach was a Top 10 sitcom in its eighth year when I was lucky enough to be hired as a writer. A top-tiered network rating in the early 1990s meant the show had around 30 million viewers, so *Coach* was a juggernaut bringing in a ton of money for ABC. The show was, in fact, such a cash cow that money was no object as far as the production budget was concerned. Almost any request from our writers' bungalow was granted. Honestly, it was like working at a vacation resort.

The gigantic rewrite room had comfy, soft leather chairs, a giant screen TV (a rarity in the early '90s), a kitchen and a fully stocked bar. We would often order lunch from top restaurants all around the country. Seriously. The first hour or so of our writing day was usually spent deciding on our lunches. Was it going to be, ya know, crabs from Maryland, sandwiches from the 2nd Avenue Deli in New York or muffulettas from New Orleans? We'd order the day before; the goods would show up the next morning. It was pure indulgence, but fuck it, it's Hollywood. This was one of the few times I actually jumped in on the gluttony that was promised to us full-on network-TV sitcom writers. Besides, it could've been worse; it could've been years earlier when the lunch of choice was cocaine instead of ribs from Texas.

Each writer had his or her own golf cart for easy access from the office to the stage. Since we were on the Universal backlot, I'd take mine for a spin occasionally and tool around the famous movie locations. As an employee, I also got free access to Universal City theme park and priority on the lines for the rides. On weekends, I'd take my cart through the back entrance of the park and spend the day. I'd wave my employee pass and the attendees would usher me up to the front of the line of whatever ride I wanted to ride.

One Sunday afternoon, I went into the offices and grabbed two cart keys, one for me and one for Billiam, my stand up comedian friend and still my housemate. We jumped on our respective carts and tore through the backlot like stuntmen. At one point we skidded up to the Bates Motel movie set (relocated but still standing) and kicked open the door, pretending we were FBI agents looking for Norman Bates. Agents Rowe and Cornell were planning to drag him downtown and book him for murder. On our way back, we got lost in the woods before finally finding our way out, but not before almost getting stuck in the *Jaws* tram-track. Like idiots, we thought it would be hilarious to ride the carts on the tram rails. We assumed that our tires would click on the robotic *Jaws* shark, sending it out to attack us.

We weren't even drunk for any of this.

At one point, we decided we were going to race up the steep hill to Universal City, where we would hit the rides. I was beating Billiam by at least five cart lengths. Cocky, I figured I'd turn and swing back down the hill and circle around his cart so I could gloat. As I took a sharp turn on the steep hill, I felt the cart start to tip. I jumped out just in time as the cart turned all the way over and did a full roll. *Holy shit!* I coulda ended up seriously dead.

The cart landed on its side, a wheel spun ominously as the motor sputtered out. Billiam laughed hysterically at my near-fatal Hollywood cart crash, while I stood there trying to figure out what in the fuck had happened. After lifting the cart upright, I carefully drove it back to the office. Both the cart and I were unharmed, but I couldn't stop thinking about what would have happened if the accident had been more serious. Obviously, I would have been fired. This was a dream job and it would've been so stupid to fuck it up in such an idiotic way.

Anyway, at *Coach*, the first part of the workday was spent talking about dumb shit like awful TV shows, which of our friends was dating who, and why, and what parties were happening that we weren't invited to. Eventually, we'd put our comedy noses to the grindstone. After an exhausting hour or so, we'd stop and have a long discussion about where we were going to caravan for lunch that day -- assuming we weren't having sushi flown in from Japan. The restaurant *had* to have great reviews from the *Zagat Guide* (an actual printed book before Yelp). There were times we'd drive almost a half-hour or so to get to the nearest 4-star diner. When our leisurely lunch was over, we'd go back to the rewrite room, work for maybe two hours and then have a cigar break before working a bit more. Finally, we'd be home before 6pm each night. These jobs and situations are rare in this business. I wanted this one for the rest of my career. We didn't know it then, but *Coach* was in its penultimate season, despite being a Top 10 show.

How'd I get my job on *Coach*, one might ask? Alan Kirschenbaum, the showrunner, hired me. This would be my third series with Alan, one of the others being my second staff job on *Baby Talk*, the show run and co-created by Ed. Weinberger. In reality, Alan was the showrunner there as well, mostly because he was in the room with us every day, which suited me just fine. Ed. was an odd, enigmatic, stoic guy and I had a difficult time wrapping my head around his comedy style. In fact, I was so new to the writing game, I had trouble understanding my own comedy style. His comfort zone, it seemed, was built on chaos. In one rewrite session, he paced the room manically, mumbling out ways the story for an episode could lay out. Crunching on corn chips the whole time and leaving chip trails throughout the office, he walked out of the room mid-thought. We didn't know if he was taking a bathroom break or maybe choking on chips; he just left. We waited and talked a little about the story. A half-hour had gone by and we were ready to pitch further on Ed's idea. We asked his assistant if she knew where he was. "Oh. Ed. went home."

Phil Rosenthal, who went on to create *Everybody Loves Raymond* also worked with me on *Baby Talk* and was now a producer on *Coach*. Phil was the one who, for the most part, was responsible for the fine foods that came into our offices. He was and still is a foodie and would, in fact, later go on to create several food-reality shows documenting his travels around the world as he devoured exotic delicacies from all corners of the globe.

All in all, my life at *Coach* was pretty great. In fact, after one of our cast and crew celebratory drink nights, I met a young sweetie named Denise.

Hollywood is, in some ways, a small industrial town. Its production lots are factories, each churning and producing product for the masses. Hollywood is Waterbury. Denise too worked for one of these factories, Witt-Thomas-Harris, a TV production company that brought America a ton of highly acclaimed sitcoms to the network primetime schedule in the '70s and '80s. She started as a production assistant and then worked her way up the ranks to where she eventually landed a job as an associate producer on their TV hit, *Golden Girls*.

Denise and I met by way of a happy accident at The Money Tree, a small bar in Toluca Lake. What better place for me than a dive bar to meet my future wife? In the '90s, there were a few select bars in town where writers, crew and actors would congregate and have a few tasty beverages to relax after filming that week's episode of each of our shows. Denise caught my eye from across the room. I was attracted to her excitement and enthusiasm as she sat at the booth, telling stories to her friends. Fortunately, I had mutual friends sitting with her, so I sat down and joined in the fun. I kept stealing looks at her cute face. I could instantly tell that she was smart, connected and grounded. She seemed soulful; there was a joy and exuberance about her that was undeniable. We started dating, we were married a few short years later, and we've been together ever since.

With Denise weeks before we were married.

So yeah, life was falling into place very nicely. I felt that all was on track for great things. I didn't have a care in the world, really -- until the time came for me to write my first episode of my first season at *Coach*. This is where many a writer gets to test his or her mettle, while fighting the wrath of unrelenting anxiety. Every episode of every sitcom is a collaborative effort, though it's never really seen as such if your "Written by" is on the cover page. A writer's job is to write a great first draft based on an outline that was built from the input from everyone in the writers' room.

Coach had been about the life of a football coach in a small-town college. By the time I was hired, Coach Hayden (Craig T. Nelson) and his wife (Shelly Fabares) had moved on up to the big leagues where he coached a professional Florida team, The Orlando Breakers. Luther, played by Jerry Van Dyke, was the Coach's befuddled but capable assistant. His character was also known to be a bit frugal, to say the least.

The premise of my episode dealt with the first time they were all leaving Florida to go back and visit their small town in Minnesota, where the show had taken place during its previous seven seasons. I pitched a B-story where Luther figures out that he can get free airfare if he transports a kidney. In the meantime, he's also fantasizing about his favorite funnel cakes in Minnesota and how he's planning to buy a ton of them to bring back to Florida. At some point, the kidney is mixed up with the funnel cakes. Chaos and panic ensue.

The room laughed at this idea. They were excited about it, and it was committed to my episode. Great. We had a starting point. Now, I honestly don't know what else happened in the episode. The only thing I remember was wanting to get it right so Alan and the room would be excited about my first draft and there wouldn't be any major rewrites. After a week or so of sweat, toil and anxiety attacks, I got a first draft done. Alan and the other writers were happy with it, even with the comparatively darker B-story of the lovable assistant coach losing someone's kidney. Great.

The table read was scheduled. By now you know that meant the script would be read by the cast for a small audience of us writers, some producers, the production staff and reps from the studio, as well some random rank and file. However, due to a long holiday weekend, we were actually supposed to skip the table read that week and reschedule it for the next. Most of the writers and other staff had extended weekend plans at some happy fun-time resort and the like. Rescheduling was fine with me, though; I could wait an extra week.

Partway into the week, things changed, and it was determined that there would not be a vacation day after all. Everyone was asked to be in for the table read. Since most of the writers and others had concrete plans and down payments on hotels, they were not going to come in. It looked like we would do this table read with a lot fewer bodies in the room. For most of the *Coach* table reads, the writers got the initial laughs rolling, and now, most of the writers weren't going to be at the table. I wasn't worried though; I felt like the stamp of approval on my script was pretty substantial.

As Alan and I trekked across the lot to the conference room for the read, he reminded me that this was the day that my option had run out. You know, the day when the show creator and erstwhile showrunner, Barry Kemp, decides if I get to continue on with the show or not. No pressure. Nope.

Mommy!

We stepped into the bungalow where the read was about to take place. In the hall, Craig T. Nelson was having a screaming match with Jerry Van Dyke, and it was getting ugly *fast*. I mean, I seriously thought it was going to come to blows. I'd heard stories of these two guys getting into a few donnybrooks like this, but I was told that they were like brothers and these outbursts would typically blow over quickly. This one, it seemed, wasn't going to fizzle out anytime soon. We made our way to our seats at the table, leaving the two stars in the hall to figure out whatever they needed to, while we waited in uncomfortable silence.

Eventually they made their way into the awkwardly quiet room full of fake smiles. They sat down, scripts were opened, my "Written by" for all to see splayed across the cover page on my *OPTION DAY*. Alan started the read with just he and I representing the writers (at least that's what I remember), while most of the other writers were happily on vacation somewhere, floating on rafts, sipping on gassed-up iced teas. Phil Rosenthal, who was usually the one who started the laughs rolling in the room, wasn't there. Fine.

The script could live on its own merits. The printed word would have to be king for that day.

The cast was reading, pages were turning, but there were no laughs yet. Typically, we'd start to hear a chortle or two on the first page. We were three pages in. Nothing. My forehead was getting hot; my mouth began to feel dry.

Oh, man.

More pages were turning. Not one laugh. A few forced chuckles. I was sinking into my chair. Then came the scene where Luther has the idea to transport a kidney to get free airfare. No one said it, but you could hear a collective *"YUCK"* in the room. I don't remember what happened after that. I had gone to my happy place in my head, much like one would do during a root canal. I would've traded a drill in my gums over what was happening in that moment.

The read came to a quiet end and the scripts were closed. All you could hear was the buzz of the fluorescent lights. A tour bus went by outside, the guide warbling into a bullhorn. Barry Kemp mumbled something about there being a lot of work to do. He was wrong. Cleaning out my desk would require very little work.

The walk of shame back to the offices was crippling. Alan was great to me. He explained that because the other writers weren't there and the two lead actors had been in a fistfight just before the read that had basically contributed to what just happened. I wasn't buying it, but I was glad he was trying to comfort me. Alan told me he had a meeting with Barry Kemp when he got back to the offices. I knew what that meant.

I waited in my office, ready to say goodbye to the muffulettas from New Orleans, the cigar breaks, my own golf cart. Alan came into my office to break the news...

"Barry will not be picking you up for the next cycle of the show."

Understandable. *I* wouldn't pick me up after that. Alan reminded me that I was the only other writer in the building. Now the truth is, I could be misremembering this. Another writer or two might've been there. Anyway, we'd have to rewrite the script starting from scratch for a new table read the next morning. Wow. I'm fired, yet I have to stay up all night and write a script starting at page one. Of course, I was going to do it for Alan's sake. Alan was an amazing, loyal and hilarious friend. He'd kept me employed for three different shows in Hollywood; he always stood by me. I was ready to dig in.

We worked into the night. Finding a simple story, each went off and wrote scenes which we later cobbled together, punched up and put into the preverbal mail slot to be rocketed into the conference room to be read, yet again, the next morning -- hopefully, with better results this time, or at least without the preliminary bout in the hallway.

Amazingly, take two of the table read went great. It felt like most table reads. There was great laugh-ratio per page, everyone was relaxed, excited and, quite frankly, relieved. And well, I felt a little better. I mean, at least I was going out with a bang. I figured I could be escorted off of the lot with my head held high.

After the read, I walked back to the bungalow alone, wondering if getting let go from a job like this is was like getting a scarlet letter pinned to my chest. Was it a permanent blemish on my record that would keep me unemployed for the rest of what was left of my career? Was I a has-been before I even had a chance to be a *been*? Alan came into my office. "Let's go outside and have a cigar..."

I stood outside the office quietly puffing on my cheroot. Alan thanked me for taking care of the rewrite with him; he felt that I

Me at Coach *with Crag T. Nelson and Jerry Van Dyke.*

was as responsible as anyone for making that work at the table that morning. He said that, in fact, it's what he told Barry Kemp. He convinced him that I helped with a lot of the heavy lifting for that rewrite. Other writers, he reminded him, were away on their long weekends. He told me that Barry changed his mind; he wanted me to continue on the show, "He's going to pick up your option." A wave of relief shot through me. The roller coaster of those two days had me spinning. I was ready to jump for joy; instead, I took a deep celebratory suck on my stogie. I couldn't thank Alan enough for fighting for me.

I had a great time for the rest of the run of that season. I ended up cowriting an episode with co-producer Scott Buck for Tim Conway as a guest cast member. And that year, for our episode, Tim won the Emmy for Best Guest Actor -- and I had my golf cart for the rest of the season.

GETTING FIRED BEFORE YOU'RE HIRED

I NEVER EXPERIENCE any form of anxiety if I'm working on a series that I can relate to and that I actually watch and laugh at, which is probably why, during the nascent days of my career, I wrote spec episodes for *It's Garry Shandling's Show*. I loved the show, and that love was reflected in my scripts. I'd bet that's why they opened the doors to my writing career.

I never did get to live out my dream of writing for that show. However, in the early 1990s, whilst sitting on my back porch and typing away on my *Seinfeld* spec script (*Seinfeld* specs were required for every writer in L.A., circa 1992-1995), I got a call from my agent. Garry Shandling had just finished a pilot for a new HBO series, *The Larry Sanders Show*, a satire about the behind-the-scenes of a high-profile, nightly talk show. Garry, the cowriter and cocreator, was set to play the host, Larry Sanders. In case you, the reader, haven't seen *The Larry Sanders Show* after all these years, please find it and binge it right now. I'll wait...

The *Larry Sanders* producers had read my script, my agent told me, and they liked it enough to want to meet with me and see if I'd be a good fit as a writer for the show. This was tremendous news! After all these years, my Shandling-writing dream was becoming a reality! I could feel it. I immediately started moving the potted plants off my mantle, clearing space for Emmys. Was I getting ahead of myself? Nah.

I took a deep breath, showered, shaved and headed to what would be my new production offices. I prayed to the comedy gods to bestow upon me the funny, charm and wherewithal to nail this interview and bestow upon me the comedy swagger of a 1970s Burt Reynolds -- or at least a Buddy Hackett.

I waited in the front office. I couldn't sit, I just paced. A producer greeted me and directed me into his office. I was cool and collected as I skipped merrily through the door like a seven-year-old kid. The producer-guy was excited to see me. He gave me a quick synopsis of the show while holding the pilot in hand on a trusty VHS tape. "I'll roll this for you, then I'll come back and see what you think."

What does he *think* I'm going to think? It's going to be fucking great!

I remember watching it and hating it. I mean, I was really hating because it was hilarious, wonderfully dark, and so fucking smart. I was hating it because it became clear that if I didn't land this job, I'd be devastated. Seriously, if I were rejected that day, I'd end up behind my fridge, cowering and weeping like a freshly kicked puppy. I, Mike Rowe, could and should and needed to work on this show. I connected to all aspects of it. I connected to Garry; I knew his rhythms. I studied them. I imitated them. I wrote two fucking scripts of his earlier sitcom. This show was already in my DNA. Sign me the fuck up!

I brought a notebook to the meeting to make it clear that I was a consummate professional comedy writer. As I watched the pilot, I scribbled down key moments that I thought were great and surprising and hilarious. This would help me wax on intelligently to the producers, showing then that I was aware of the nuances of the show.

I even jotted down one or two small notes about a few things that maybe didn't work quite right. Occasionally, in these meetings, they will ask you if you see something that might seem flat or weird or off-kilter. It's not bad to have a few notions in the chamber, so you have something to volley back to him or her. I knew not to bring these thoughts up unless asked. In fact, I knew to avoid this general area whenever possible, but if cornered, I'd keep the thoughts short, light and fluffy.

The producer-guy came back, anxious to hear my thoughts. I was shaking with enthusiasm, yet I was steadfast and professional. I was in a zone and able to embody *The Larry Sanders Show* as if I'd been working on it for most of my comedy career.

He eventually asked, "Anything that seemed like it didn't work?"

There was nothing obviously, but I went to my light and fluffy scribblings. I tossed them out to him thinking it'd help create the illusion that I was astute enough to polish a flawless gem and make it shine just a tiny bit brighter, "You're a little too wide when you shoot the talk-show segments. You should just mock the Johnny Carson *Tonight Show* shots," I suggested. "And maybe fewer close-ups during the doc-style segments." He seemed excited that someone actually had some constructive criticism.

"Yeah. Great. That's great...Let's tell Garry."

"Wha?!"

"Yeah, he's on the set shooting. Let's go down there and tell him everything you said."

Before I could stop him, he was walking me through the lot and onto the soundstage. I didn't know why I was being dragged into this face-to-face with Garry. I trusted that this producer-guy knew what-in-the-Christ he was doing, but shit, man; I really didn't get what was happening. There was nothing I could do but let the undertow of this drag me through the choppy river of uncertainty. I was hoping for a branch along the way so I could grab onto it and pull myself onto the shore and save my life.

The show was in production at that moment, but they were between takes. *The Larry Sanders Show* set was a labyrinth of hallways and offices, and as we made our way through, I ran into Janeane Garofalo flipping through her script pages. Janeane was, as you know, a very close friend as well as a member of Garry's main ensemble. She was excited and surprised to see me there, and I let her know that I was being considered as a writer on the show. She was delighted at the thought.

The producer-guy walked me further to the other side of the stage to the faux talk-show set. Garry was standing there, readying himself for the next take. His back was to us as his makeup person adjusted his face. David Spade was standing by on the set. Apparently he was in this scene with Garry. Spade and I shared quiet hellos. We had mutual friends and we knew each other from parties. Suddenly, the producer-guy yelled out, "Hey, Garry! I have Mike here..."

Garry turned around and sized me up as he tried to figure out what in the hell I was doing there and why I was interrupting his shoot.

"Mike's a writer. He's going to tell you what's wrong with your show."

What?!

Everything got oddly quite for a second -- or was it a lifetime? Not sure. Spade shot me a look, his brow furrowed. Garry looked at me, confused and a little annoyed. He was already done with me: "Yeah. Is that right? Okay."

I was stunned. I felt the wind get knocked out of me, along with the possibility of ever writing for Garry Shandling. The very spirit of me working side-by-side with him flew out of my body and out through the open elephant doors of Studio 23 onto the Raleigh Lot in Hollywood. I watched as it dissipated into the hot California sky where, to this day, it lives somewhere in the thick smog of the San Fernando Basin.

They only way I could get my footing at that moment was to pretend that maybe it was a hazing and it was their way of welcoming me into the *Larry Sanders* fold but, alas, that was not what was happening. I fumphered my way through whatever notes I remembered during my happier times up in the office. I was full-on Robert Benchley in *The Treasurer's Report* (Google it), complete with sweating, hyperventilation, half-sentences and clumsy, quiet thoughts as my voice cracked wildly, much as it did when I had hit puberty. Eighth-grade me was again asking the hottest girl in school for a date.

Needless to say, *The Larry Sanders Show* did not include hotshot young writer, Mike Rowe, on its writing staff.

Sure, that sucked and weighed heavily on me, but the agony of disappointment dissipated over the next day or so. Even back then, early in my writing career, I knew that bullshit situations like that were all part of the Hollywood journey. It's what I had to constantly remind myself; otherwise, I would've been throwing myself off of a tall building once every few weeks.

In the end, I didn't cower behind my fridge (at least not for any measurable amount of time) but I did pull my career up by the bootstraps, dug in, focused and...napped for a few days. But I'd fallen asleep with the comfort of knowing that another writing job would surely come my way at some point. So what if I didn't get to work on the smart, career-changing TV series. Fuck it, fuck that producer guy, and fuck David Spade. (I went after Spade for no reason here, but fuck you, too, for questioning my choices.)

I didn't know it at the time, but a writer-producer job on the smartest, coolest and arguably one of the most prestigious shows in TV history was waiting for me in the not-so-distant future.

MEET THEM BEFORE THEY GO, PLEASE

Most of the old-school comedians I followed, worshiped, and watched on TV with my dad worked in every phase of show business. Comedy stars like Bob Hope and Milton Berle started in vaudeville before going into radio, movies and then television. In my journey through Hollywood, New York and even the Catskill Mountains, I made it a point to meet these historic funny people whenever and however I could. On Bob Hope's 95th birthday in 1998, there was a small parade for him in Toluca Lake, just a few miles from my home in Studio City. I got up bright and early that morning, found a spot on the sidewalk, and waited for the parade, hoping for at least a passing glimpse of ol' Bob. The day was bright and sunny. A decent crowd of well-wishers had shown up, unsure of what to expect. We weren't even sure if Bob was going to actually be in the parade.

A marching band started playing in the distance. It was happening! A cop car blooped its siren as it led a team of show horses through the street. A high-school band clomped by, clumsily playing a farty version of Bob's theme song, *Thanks for the Memory*. In some ways, this charming clunkiness added to the glory of it all. A homemade float advertising some of the local businesses passed by and then, *there he was!* Bob Hope and his wife Delores in an open model T! Ol' Ski Nose sat there in a yellow golf jacket and white baseball hat that was just barely resting sideways on the top of his head, as old guys tend to wear ball caps. Ninety-Five-Year-Old Bob Hope was right there in the flesh, happy to be alive as he waved enthusiastically to the crowd. His car rolled closer, ready to pass by me at arm's length. *This is real!* I was going to get a fer-sure closeup look at Bob "Birthday Boy" Hope!

He was at about spittin' distance from me when a squadron of five fighter jets flew above in formation, leaving behind trails of red, white and blue burnt-up rocket fuel. The marching band switched into a glorious, military version of *Hooray for The Red White and Blue*. What a glorious moment! It was just a fleeting glimpse of a comedy legend, but I was happy, satisfied that I showed up to pay tribute to a guy that's made the world laugh for close to a hundred years.

Later the same night, I went to the local Vons supermarket in Toluca Lake. As I was walking in, a white van pulled up a few feet from the automatic doors. The driver got out, ran to open the door and there, in his yellow Members Only golf jacket was, once again, the one and only Bob Hope. His wrangler/driver helped Bob get down and escorted him into the Vons. Weird, right? Why was Bob Hope shopping at a Vons in the middle of the night on his 95th birthday? I made my way closer to them to see if I could get a sense of what was happening. His wrangler told him, "We'll walk down to the end of the aisle and then we'll walk back out." I heard Bob mutter back in a shaky old-man voice, "Ahhyaa, I don't give-va-shit!"

This had to be kismet. I mean, I wanted to see Bob Hope on his birthday and I was suddenly presented with a chance to get up close and personal. Maybe this was an opportunity to start up a rapport, even get to know him for a sec without the distraction of pooping horses and pesky fighter jets. I thought, if nothing else, since it was his birthday, I could wish him happy birthday. Then I could, for the rest of my life, say that I, ya know, hung out with Bob Hope.

I scoped out the situation and waited for the right moment. I knew he was going to walk in and then be whisked away back into his windowless van, so the clock was ticking. What the hell was he doing? Why did he have to do a lap in a low-rent supermarket? He just had an Air Force salute a few hours earlier, so why did he feel the need to go through the dairy aisle and check on milk prices?

I finally found my moment. I grabbed something off a shelf. I don't remember what I picked up; it was all part of me trying to be casual, like I was in the middle of shopping and I just "happened upon" Bob.

"Hey, Bob. Happy birthday," I said cheerily.

He turned to me slowly, "Wha?" I spoke louder. "Happy birthday!" He turned to his wrangler, "Wha'd he say?" The wrangler, like a dad to his little son, leaned in towards him. "Bob, he's wishing you happy birthday."

"He wha?"

At that point, I was yelling, "HAPPY BIRTHDAY, BOB!" He just stared at me. I shared a knowing look with his wrangler and awkwardly backed off, nodding politely as his wrangler grabbed him by his arm and walked him out the door. So, yeah, if anyone asks, I tell 'em, "Yeah. Bob and I, we were buds. We hung out and went shopping at Von's together."

My dad wasn't quite as old as Bob at the time, but getting older poked at him throughout his life. He was about to turn sixty and he was not happy with that fat number staring back at him and his gray-bearded face. Oddly, at every stage of his life, he saw himself as on the verge of getting old. I recently found an old black-and-white photo of him during his days in the Marines. He was stationed in South Carolina, where he did most of his training before they shipped him off to Korea. The photo was of him when he was young, scrappy, and muscular. He was maybe all of twenty-two years young. The picture showed him with no shirt on, doing pull-ups outside his barracks. On the back of the photo was his scribbled note, "Only 30 chin-ups today. Must be getting old."

I still can't imagine how, on that birthday, the weight of sixty human years was feeling to him. He was always a fatalist. According to my dad, the sky was falling on a regular basis. This is how he saw his day-to-day, and it was part of the colorful backdrop in which I was raised. It likely explains my occasional bouts with panic attacks.

Not long after my parents divorced in the late 1970s, my dad was remarried to Lucy, his secretary who worked in his successful real-estate business. They shared a rolling ranch-style home in nearby Wolcott, Connecticut. The basement was a gigantic paneled rec room complete with a fireplace, a full bar, a Jacuzzi and a fifty-inch, rear projection TV. It was just shy of the size of a banquet room that could fit about a hundred friends and relatives. His then-wife decided this is where his 60th birthday celebration should take place.

I was living in L.A. at the time but I fer-sure was planning on getting back home for the extravaganza. I just needed to find the perfect gift for my dad.

I met up with an old friend, Pat Buckles, who I first knew as a waitress at the N.Y. Improv. All the comics truly liked Pat and her naturally funny, hardcore sense of humor. She especially loved it when comics made her laugh. With a keen eye for what and who was funny, it was no surprise she was promoted to run the shows at the club.

Pat later moved to L.A. where she used her standup connections to become a go-to booker when anyone needed a comedian for their club or TV show. She had told me how she lined up Henny Youngman to perform at a private birthday party.

Wait! THE Henny Youngman? The King of the One-Liners Henny Youngman?!

"I've been in love with the same woman for 25 years. If my wife finds out, she'll kill me."

"Just got back from a pleasure trip -- took my wife to the airport."

Henny Youngman wore loud suits and played *Smoke Gets in Your Eyes* on a screechy violin; his stall while he searched the files in his head for his next line. Henny was around since the days of vaudeville, but my dad and I laughed together like idiots at him during so many of his TV talk and variety-show appearances.

I remember as a 6th grader, pretending to be sick because I didn't want to go to school. My dad, who seemed concerned, moved his arm up and down and asked me, "Does it hurt when you go like this?" Thinking this would help my case, I said, "Yes." "Well then, don't do that!" he said. It was one of Henny's classic one-liners, and my dad used it as a test to see if I was really sick. As you can see, Henny was part of the fabric of my life with my dad.

Now, I was hoping against hope that Pat could again track down Henny to book him for a surprise appearance at my dad's 60th. If you think about it, in a small town like Wolcott, Connecticut, if you saw the local TV weatherman on the street, it would be considered an A-plus celebrity sighting. If I could get Henny to my dad's party, it'd be as if I had The Who show up at *my* 60th.

Pat got me in touch with Henny. He was living in midtown Manhattan, so it seemed possible to orchestrate a town car ride from his mid-town apartment to Wolcott, Connecticut. I did the trip on a bus almost every weekend when I first moved to New York, although Henny, then in his late 80s, might find the sojourn less manageable.

Henny and I went back and forth and eventually settled on a price for his performance. I managed a round-trip town car for him, he needed a meal and a few other easy demands. There wasn't all that much haggling, although I'm guessing Henny's stock in 1990 wasn't all that high. I doubted that I was pulling him from a contractual gig at the Sands in Vegas.

The day before his excursion, Henny wanted to have lunch with me in New York at Wolf's Deli on 57th street. Fantastic! Lunch with Henny, face-to-face, joking around and sharing eggs in a midtown eatery. I'm there. "Okay, kid. Call me. 10:30 in the morning. We'll set up a brunch."

I woke the next morning and dialed up Henny at around 10:40. (These were the days before caller ID and cell phones.) Henny answered, "Hello, Michael?" He was sitting by the phone waiting for my call. We met up at Wolf's Deli as planned. Henny was quite old; there was no longer the "young" in Youngman, although mentally he seemed pretty sharp and up to the task for my dad's event. He came across like all our grandpas; shaky -- most of his scrambled eggs ended up on is lap -- and a little cranky. He went off on a tirade about The Carnegie Deli. The new owners apparently would seat him in the front window whenever he lunched there, hoping he would be a draw to passersby and tourists. Then, he complained, at the end of his meals, they actually made him pay his bill.

"Leo [Steiner, the original owner] never let me pay a check, ever."

He pitched me the idea of shooting a concert performance video of himself doing his best hits, then selling it on a late-night infomercial. Not a bad idea perhaps, but at that point in my career, I didn't have the resources to make that happen.

"Michael, I like you. In fact, I like you so much, I'm going to give you a diamond pin."

That was out of left field, what was he...? Before I could even finish my thought, he pulled out a safety pin with a dime soldered in the middle of it. "Here, that's for you. It's a dime-in-pin."

How did I not see that coming?

Then he mentioned his joke book: "I'll sign one for your dad. He'll like it." He even offered to pick up the check for the meal. If he felt it was important for him to pay, then I should let him, right? But then I looked up a second later and he was at the front counter bargaining with the young woman at the register, trying to get the meal comped because he was comedy icon Henny Youngman. Sadly, there was a stronger chance that the twenty-something employee would know who *I* was before she knew who Henny was. He was not happy as he forked over the fourteen dollars for eggs.

The night of my dad's 60th was filled with celebration, anticipation and excitement. The eighty or so family and friends knew Henny was a surprise guest. My dad, of course, did not. It was a giant sit-down dinner, or as they called it in my hometown, "a time." "We're havin' a time for Johnny on his 60th. Dere'll be a drawin' for a coupla bottles (or 'spirits' as it said on the ticket). Trow me a sawbuck, I'll trow ya in da pot." Waterburians talk fast and a little mumbly, "I'm gonna go too-da store, bick up sometin da eat." It edged into a Brooklyn-Italian sorta tough-guy quality.

As everyone ate pasta, a DJ spun classic Sinatra, Dean Martin and big-band records; all the hits I remembered blasting out of the jukebox during dad's days at the Carousel when I was a kid. When the meal was over, a few close friends and family went up to the microphone to pay tribute to my dad. It was sweet, warm and funny. Then I came up to the mic. I could tell my dad was worried that I was going to pull funny stuff from my standup act. I surmised he didn't want the pressure of worrying about his son bombing in front of everyone he's ever known. It didn't matter; it wasn't part of the plan. After I said my quick, sweet and heartfelt tribute to my dad, I built up to the special guest: "I have a friend from New York here who I think could better tell you how I feel about my dad. Say hello to... Henny Youngman!"

Henny descended my dad's basement stairs wearing his loud suit, his violin in hand and ready. The crowd jumped to their feet, screaming and applauding with unbridled excitement. Even though they already knew he was coming, they still couldn't believe it. I mean, he was their generation's comic.

My dad sat with his arms folded and looked around, confused, probably assuming one of my buddies was going to pop up and do an impression. Henny came into full view at the bottom of the stairs and my dad jumped from his seat like a little kid. I swear he spun into an involuntary pirouette fueled purely by joy, sheer disbelief and surprise. Henny got behind the mic and went from zero to sixty,

"Doctor said I had six months to live, couldn't pay my bill, gave me another six months."

"Rich kid sits on Santa's lap. 'Santa, whaddaya need?'"

"A bum came up to me, says, 'I haven't eaten in two days.' I said, 'Force yourself.'"

His most famous, "People today are crazy...Take my wife. Please."

I didn't watch Henny during his performance, just my dad.

Henny at my dad's 60th birthday party (1992).

He was a wide-eyed boy as he laughed wildly at every joke that Henny mumbled out. He even did the one my dad used to bust me with when I was a little kid:

"Doc, it hurts when I go like this. Then don't go like that."

My dad even heckled a few times and got laughs. After twenty or so minutes of nonstop killer jokes, the room exploded with applause. Henny hung out at the party and mingled. He took me aside and asked me to get the boxes of his joke books from the car, "I'll sign one for everybody." I wasn't exactly sure what he was talking about. I remembered that he was going to sign one of his books for my dad. I carried in three heavy boxes, packed tight with paperback books. He set up a table, sat behind it and readied his pen. Everyone lined up for a face-to-face moment with Henny and a personally autographed copy of his joke book.

Henny was gracious and charming and seemed truly delighted to be there. My dad was on a high the whole night. It was a time he relished and talked about for the rest of his life. Henny called me the next day to tell me that he enjoyed meeting me and my dad and he liked hanging out with my family and my dad's friends. Then he complained a little about the food. He wanted my dad's phone number so he could call and stay in touch with him. He did. They talked on the phone from time to time over the next few years. He even sent my dad a letter a short time after that appearance, thanking him for such a great night.

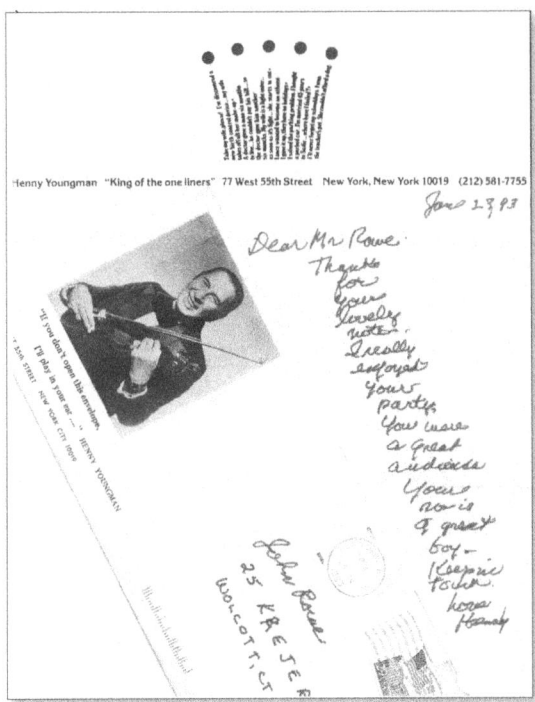

Henny's letter to my dad.

Oh, and by the way, on my call with him the next day, he told me I owed him four hundred dollars for the joke books. I...He didn't... There was no mention of...

"It's for my charity."

I knew he most likely meant it was for The Henny Youngman Foundation, but you know what? He was comedy legend Henny Youngman. He got into a car and rode from Manhattan to a small town in Connecticut where he came to my dad's house and down into his basement to make him and a room full of his family and friends laugh on his 60th birthday, so...

"Take my check, please."

LOST IN A FANTASY

CLEARLY, I DIDN'T limit my career to just writing sitcoms. I loved that I got to write and produce such a wide variety of projects, from game shows to awards shows to documentaries. I was especially excited to write for nightly talk shows. In sitcoms and cartoons, it sometimes takes weeks and months for the material to get in front of an audience. On a talk show, you think of something funny that morning, it's in front of an audience of millions that night.

Writing comedy for Martin "Marty" Short's talk show in 1999 was a dream job. It was one of those *Alice In Wonderland* moments in my career where I felt I was stepping through my TV and into a comedy fantasy world. Marty, along with John Candy, Dave Thomas, Eugene Levy, Andrea Martin, et al. were masterful players on *SCTV*. It was the most consistent and wonderfully smart, silly and hip sketch show on TV during the '70s on into the 1980s. Us comics would gather around the TV at bar at the Improv every Sunday night and laugh our asses off. *SCTV* poked fun at our stand-up sweet spot; showbiz.

The legendary Bernie Brillstein was the producer of *The Martin Short Show*. He was Marty's manager as well. Bernie, as I mentioned earlier, managed the original cast of *Saturday Night Live* and was a colorful figure throughout his long career in Hollywood. When I wrote a screenplay with Bob Odenkirk, Bernie was Bob's manager. We met with him after it was written and in his old-school showbiz way, he laughed as he told us in his cheery gruff voice, "I could sell this in a minute." He picked up the phone and, almost like an *SCTV* sketch, he called someone and told him he had a hot Hollywood project. He hung up and said we had a meeting with the head of Warner Brothers features. We pitched the movie in the meeting and sold the script in the room. That's Bernie.

Bob Odenkirk, George Burns and me.

So Bernie built out this whole talk show for Martin Short and sold it into syndication. Marty was and still is one of the best talk-show guests, period. He comes prepared, he's always captivating, adorable and hilarious. This mistakenly suggested that he would be a great talk-show *host*. It doesn't quite work that way. When the show started, Marty had a diverse cast of amazing sketch actors. Most were unknown, but all were very funny. The show quickly discovered that there's just not enough time to write and produce full-blown sketches for a nightly talk show. I came in right when the cast was let go. They decided that Marty would follow a more basic talk-show structure. Also, for national syndication, the show had to be amenable for the 11:30 nighttime *adult* audience, as well as the afternoon *mom* audience. I came in just in time for a very rough trial-and-error phase. Marty wanted to do a standard talk-show monologue replete with topical jokes. In truth, he is not at his best when he's just himself. He needs room to play and pretend. Marty quickly understood this and shifted to one of his strengths; song and dance! Instead of a monologue, he started every show with a snappy, upbeat song and it was a delightful sight to see. There's nothing better than Marty, with his boyish wink to camera, belting out a swinging cabaret tune. He would transform into his heightened version of jazz/pop singer Tony Bennett; fun, slick, cool, yet extremely silly.

Once we found a handle on how to open the show, we still needed comedy wraparound pieces. This meant simple-to-produce cold opens and desk pieces. Like talk show host David Letterman at the time, we had to find and develop our versions of a *Top 10 Lists* and *Viewer Mail*. Again, Marty's strength wasn't straight refillable talks-show comedy bits, but they'd have to do until we figured out how to find a simple way to do more elaborate pieces. He tried not-so-complicated scenes with former *SCTV* cast members playing their iconic characters. Marty would have lunch with us writers every day and we'd pitch the simplest ways to produce the pieces. The best lunches were when *SCTV* folks were on the show. They'd join us as well, typically in costume and fresh from the studio. Being the *SCTV* comedy nerd that I am, you could not imagine my excitement sitting down and breaking bread with the likes of Count Floyd, Edith Prickly and Bobby Bittman.

I wrote a quick and simple opening piece for Marty to do with Pete Rose. It was a switch on what happened to Pete during an all-star game. A reporter, on the spot, demanded that he apologize for betting on professional baseball. In my piece, Pete, playing a reporter, cornered Marty to get him to apologize for his movie, *Captain Ron*. *TV Guide* somehow ended up writing a nice, short review on the piece.

I wrote another quick opening. It worked fine except it almost killed Marty. Comedian Artie Lange was available for a sketch. I had an idea where we explain that Marty is late for the show. We catch him live on his way to work via a video hookup in the back seat of a cab. His co-host, in the studio, taps into Marty's camera so he could start the show via (yet-to-be-invented) FaceTime. Artie was the driver. Marty, starting his monologue, was harried and bouncing around the backseat as he skimmed through the morning paper, hoping to come up with topical monologue jokes on the spot. They eventually screeched up to the studio doors. Marty ran out of the cab and into the studio. This was all pretaped; the live and in-person Marty was planted at the far end of the studio. He was to make a full-speed run from the outside doors onto the set and in front of the live audience. He sprinted in and entered through a short curtain hanging at the side of the stage. No one knew that there was a metal beam running across the top of the curtain. Marty smacked his head squarely into it at about a thousand miles an hour. You could hear a loud Looney Tunes cartoon *ping* noise as his head made contact. He was clearly dazed, woozy and teetering. He somehow managed to throw it to a commercial. As he gathered himself, he told us that when he hit, there was a flash of white then a second of blackness. He was whisked off to the hospital for tests. Thankfully he was okay.

Marty decided to play it safe and simple and do more desk pieces. The other writers wanted me dead after I pitched a recurring desk bit called, *Things You'll Never See*. It was a dumb but fast and simple premise that was easy to write and assemble, especially when you're in a talk-show emergency situation. It was basically a list of, per the title, things you'll never see, such as Barry Manilow Junior or Donny and Marie at a cock fight. It was such a dumb, lazy and unchallenging premise that the writers wanted me hog-tied and quartered every time we were sent to our desks to write 100 of them.

Each day, we would try to build out new, more sophisticated and clever pieces but, for whatever reasons, none of them would fly. Then, as we got closer to show time, we'd often hear head writer Mike Short (Marty's brother) bark out, "Tonight we'll need, *Things You'll Never See*. Let's go!" I hid in my office and quietly typed away.

Don Rickles was scheduled to make an appearance and I had to meet him. Don was another one of the comedy stalwarts my dad and I rolled off the couch laughing at as he insulted everyone within reach on Carson's *Tonight Show*. His scattershot non-sequiturs were the best: "I got the wife sitting on the back porch with the jewelry, signaling ships…Anyway, gang…" "Give this hockey puck a cookie and tell him to go home."

Marty knew of my affection for Don and he promised to connect us at some point during his visit. Calling someone a hockey puck was a go-to for Don. So, of course, I rushed out and bought a hockey puck for him to autograph.

From the wings, I watched and laughed at Don working the audience. He leaned towards an older couple, "This the wife? Sorry about the accident. Anyway, gang…" I was laughing like crazy. It helped to cover my nerves. I mean, I was going to be talking to *Don*

Rickles, face-to-face, in the next four minutes. The very guy who, on national TV, joked with Sinatra about his mob connections to his face! "Tony Mangano called. You die Tuesday."

I positioned myself in the hallway near the dressing rooms to have the best possible access to Don. I could hear the band in the studio playing through the end credits. The show was wrapped. I stood there carrying the same stress that Jack Ruby probably felt as he waited in the hallway for Oswald to cross his path. The studio doors swung open and Don quickly strolled through, making a beeline for his dressing room. A gaggle of producers and hangers-on and who knows who else surrounded him. I stepped nervously out towards him to get his attention but, *aww shit!* He was whisked through. That was it. Gone.

So there I was, standing alone and forlorn in the hallway, my lowly puck in hand. Everything was quiet. From behind me I heard, "Mike, did you talk to Don?" It was Martin Short. I told him, "Nah, it's okay."

Marty went into Don's dressing room and brought him out into the hall and introduced me to him, letting him know I was one of the writers for the show. He seemed excited to talk to me. He was gracious, engaged and he instantly made me feel like I was one of his inner circle. I asked him about "The Sinatra Story." You may have heard it: Don, on a first date at a fancy restaurant, spotted Frank eating at another table. He snuck over and asked Frank if he could stop by the table and say hello: "It'd *really* impress my date. Please. I'm so lonely." Frank begrudgingly agreed. He stopped by the table and said hello. Then Don snapped at him, "Frank, can't you see I'm *eating?*" Rickles confirmed the story and added that a few minutes later, Sinatra sent two of his goons over. They lifted Don up by the chair and dumped him into the parking lot.

I had him sign my hockey puck. He seemed confused by my request. I wasn't sure why. Maybe I shoulda had him sign a cookie. We talked for so long that the studio was nearly ready to close for the day. Eventually, one of Don's wranglers came over and whispered in his ear, "Don, you get the hangers?" Don said he didn't. He turned to me, "I'm a Jew on a cheap show; I gotta take everything."

Excusing himself, he went into his dressing room and took the wooden hangers. Yeah, that's great. The short Jew's a hockey puck. Anyway, gang.

The Martin Short Show kept chugging along as we got closer to the 100-episode mark. At that point, I had enough showbiz savvy to know when a show was in trouble. The first sign was when aging TV pioneer Steve Allen was booked as an A-List guest. I love Steve Allen more than life itself, but in 1999 it was safe to say that he was not at the peak of his career. If he's the "get" for your show at that stage of the game, there's cause for concern.

Rumblings started floating around the offices that the show was, in fact, in trouble. Bernie gathered the entire staff into the audience and like an old-school Hollywood producer, he gave us all an impassioned speech about how the show was *not* in trouble whatsoever and that we're moving full-steam ahead. I heard the "tell" in his voice. I turned to a fellow writer and whispered, "Clean out your desk." We were cancelled two weeks later.

Even to this day, when I meet my comedy heroes, like Don Rickles, it's always a magical moment for me. I feel like it's my kid-self greeting some sort of imaginary God. I happily put them high up on pedestals. I did it when I met Bob Newhart at an Emmy party. As you remember, I wrote two episodes of his Vermont *Newhart* series to help me learn how to write sitcoms. I thanked him for the boost to my career. He seemed truly gracious.

At another Emmy party, I met Monty Python's John Cleese waiting for his car at the valet. He'd slipped out early, escaping the Governors Ball. I thanked him for *Fawlty Towers* and explained how I try to emulate it in my work. Cleese is tall. He looked down at me and with a slight scowl and answered, rather dismissively: "Very well then," and turned away. Tony DeSena, a friend who wrote material for him and other Emmy presenters that night later told me that Cleese slipped out, because he's tired of hearing writers tell him about how much they like *Fawlty Towers*...

Very well then.

One of my biggest comedy heroes was and still is Albert Brooks. Even as a kid, I recognized his originality and his absurd point of view. In the '70s, he made frequent TV appearances on popular variety shows like *The Flip Wilson Show*, *Ed Sullivan* and *Saturday Night Live*. He was the first, even before Steve Martin, to do comedy about comedy or, as it was later called, "the non-joke." He was wildly different and odd in the best and most hilarious ways. To this day, I rewatch his TV shots and play his records over and over with the hope that some of his funny will wire itself into my brain.

Albert was one of perhaps five comedy icons that I had to meet at some point in my comedy life. The others were and are Woody Allen, Bob Newhart, John Cleese, and Steve Martin. During the writers' strike in 2007, I was stationed to picket at the main gate at the Radford production lot. Every morning, I'd see Albert Brooks circling in the picket line. My guy, my hero, was right there, in this line with us. I tried most days to walk right behind him to eavesdrop on what he was saying to whatever buddy he brought with him that day. The murmur of his voice was unmistakable, with his vaguely southern yet oddly Midwest drawl, "How-rrr yoo, ya doin' pretty guud? That's guud." I was stalking him on the strike line, for sure, but I had to: it was Albert-Fucking-Brooks. I couldn't muster the courage to actually introduce myself to him though, to let him know about the indelible mark he left on my comedy life.

After the strike started to drag on for a few weeks, sympathetic agents started sending multiple trucks full of water, coffee, pastries, pizza and even barbecue lunches. Once one agency did it, all the others had to follow suit. One morning, the head of a low-level boutique agency went above and beyond their call of duty and handed out little tiny boxes of Sun Maid raisins from a plastic Ralph's shopping bag. Each little box had a label stuck on it to promote the agency.

Albert Brooks, circling in the strike line right in front of me, was handed a box. He looked at the label and pretended to be torn and confused as he stared at his handout. That's when he turned around to me. I just happened to be there, as I was every day, but right then and there, I was his easy-access audience. He held up his raisin box and went into a tremendous rant.

"So what do I do? Do I call my agent?...Hello, CAA? It's Albert, how are you? Well, I'm doin' pretty guuud. I'm sorry, I know it's crazy but I'm moving on. I'm leaving you…Well, I got raaaisins. They gave me raaasins. What am I supposed to do? You guys are great, but you never gave me raaaisins…"

I didn't use that moment to introduce myself or start up any conversation; I just laughed my ass off. This moment was more than I needed or hoped for from Albert Brooks.

FUTURAMA AND MY FUTURE

IMMEDIATELY AFTER A successful and satisfying run on Eddie Murphy's animated (Claymation) comedy series, *The PJs*, I was invited to a writers bowling night where we all donated to cancer research. Here we got to mingle with other writers, while basking in the sweet stench of bowling-alley sweat. A sense of community among writers is always helpful and reassuring.

At this particular party, I met David X. Cohen. He, along with Matt Groening, were the cocreators of the highly successful sci-fi comedy animated series *Futurama*. David loved *The PJs* and wanted me to tell him everything that I knew about all aspects of the show. There are, in fact, *PJs* "easter eggs" in episodes of *Futurama*.

A few weeks after this gathering, my agent called and said that David X. would like me to submit a spec script to *Futurama*. They had a position open for a writer. I was flattered that I was still on David's radar.

I tried my best to not get too excited about the possibility of a job on this series. I'd been led down this road too many times. A friend of mine brought me back to earth by reminding me that the entire staff at *Futurama* were all Harvard grads and they only hire their friends from *The Harvard Lampoon*.

David and Matt Groening liked my script enough to bring me in for a meeting. They are both very easygoing, very smart, laid-back guys and all went great, especially when they found out that I had an electronics background and I worked for NASA on the Space Shuttle. That sealed the Mike Rowe-deal right then and there. They were pretty much ready to escort me from the meeting to my new office.

I was excited, nervous, yet ready for my new job on one of the most interesting, sophisticated and smartest shows on TV. I wanted and needed to be here at this point in my career, in a room full of truly smart writers who understood my sensibility. The opportunity more than made up for *The Larry Sanders Show* debacle. This was serious. I had to be clear-headed and focused, so I could take on this new challenge.

As life goes, that was not going to happen. Nothing is ever easy.

Just as I was about to report for comedy duty, my wife, Denise, was about to give birth. Having children was always the plan for us; it was one of the many reasons we decided to get married. We married late in life, at least compared to how it goes in our hometowns (Denise was raised in Memphis). In the 1970s, it seemed kids tied the knot right out of high school. Denise and I were in our mid- and-late 30s when we took to the altar (is that a real phrase?), so we were a little flummoxed when it came time to figure out how the whole "having babies"-thing was going to work for us.

Denise was very determined and focused to make it happen. Not that I wasn't, but she had charts, calendars, websites, books, consultants, whatever it took to perfectly calculate the best, exact time for conception. I somehow have this image of me like a runner in a three-point-stance, ready and waiting to pounce at the perfect moment of fertility. In fact, all of what happened over those months I later turned into an episode of *Becker* starring Ted Danson (I know, everything connects back to showbiz but dude, this is a showbiz book).

We had a bit of a struggle at the start. It maybe had to do with the fact that we were no longer in our 20's, we were a stones-throw away from our 40s. We were worried that the longer it took for the conception charts, graphs and cycles to converge at the exact right time, the less likely we would have our child.

There was no way we were going to give up. Denise put herself on a strict, conception-compliant diet, she sought out acupuncturists, and teams of pregnancy doctors. Then, as we took down our guard for a sec, we were...*not* pregnant with child.

We were pregnant with *two* childs! Twin boys!

This pregnancy felt robust, positive; all health signs were on track from the start. We knew this was going to happen. We knew this was meant to be: Two darlin' identical twin boys in one swoop.

We felt so confident that as we got closer to Denise's 6th month, we discussed baby names. I was joking but kinda serious about naming them Martin and Lewis after the comedy team Dean Martin and Jerry Lewis. Ya know, Marty and Lou, those are wonderfully viable names. They're cool, laid-back, free-spirited, life-is-good kinda names. The more I thought about it, the more the names rang true for my boys -- especially "my" boys with a comedy-writer dad. In fact, a comedy-writer friend, Eddie Gorodetsky, loved this idea so much that he offered Denise five thousand cash to help convince her to sign off on what I eventually decided was a brilliant idea.

My identical twin sons, Jack and Nick, were born on January 30th 2001. We ended up naming Jack after Denise's mom, Jackie, and Nick because to me, it sounded hard and it punched like a tough detective name: Nick Rowe - Private Eye.

They were born just a few scant days before I was to start my job as writer on *Futurama*, one of the most important writing jobs in my career.

Like most new parents, we had no idea what the Hell we were doing. When you're in the thick of it, you realize that all the parenting books suck ass. With tiny, preemie twins, every day was like a three-alarm fire. I seem to remember something like eighteen diaper changes a day. Also, feedings were nonstop. I remember Denise breast-feeding crossed-legged on the floor. She held two babies like footballs up close as they took in their meals. This went on for months. It's one of the reasons I'm sure our sons grew up to be amazingly strong and healthy.

In the meantime, I was working at *Futurama* all day. I had to drive over the hill from Studio City into the Westside, get to the offices by ten in the morning, then work until seven and not get home until close to eight that night. By that time, Denise was exhausted, frustrated, and ready to pass the baby duties off to anyone within view. I, too, was exhausted and spinning from the day as I was trying to find my footing at work. I also know that my breastfeeding capabilities were, at best, limited.

Futurama was a complex and layered show. Some episodes had stories broken out by way of sophisticated math equations formulated on multiple wax boards throughout the writers' room. So, yeah, I was foggy-headed, but all that mattered was Denise needed sleep and someone had to tend to crying twins. I did the best I could, but without being in on how the daily machinery of the baby system worked, I was often lost, confused and overwhelmed. Luckily, Denise's mom, Jackie and my mom, Joanne, were ready, willing and able to fly into L.A., stay with us, and take turns as our pair of au pairs. Both had years and years of hardcore child-rearing experience; they were ready like the cavalry -- confident and prepared. They both took so much of the burden off Denise that we were able to find some stability, calm, and enjoyment in the chaos of wrangling our tiny twin boys.

Jack and Nick, for the first ten years of their lives, got to be a part of the world of *Futurama*. As toddlers, they went to Matt Groening's house for parties. I remember little Jack impressing Matt by throwing up in the middle of his living-room floor. Matt, no stranger to raising little boys, instinctively cleaned it up by hand with a paper towel. So, my son has *that* distinction.

As they got older, they appreciated *Futurama* and *The Simpsons* and got to have intimate talks with Matt about it all. It's how Nick found out why *The Simpsons* were yellow. The answer was shockingly simple: "They're yellow, so they stand out from other TV cartoon

Jack and Nick with their dad at a Futurama *table read.*

characters." My boys would hang out with me at times in the writers' room or sit at the table with the big boys at the *Futurama* table reads.

They got to go to premiere parties and awards shows, and were in a group of the first people to go on the new *Simpsons* ride at the Universal theme park.

Apparently, these experiences seeped into their blood; as of this writing, Nick is a film major at Arizona State, having decided that he, too, would like to be a standup comic and a comedy writer. He's already completed his first screenplay with his writing partner. Jack is studying there as well. He was pursuing a career in sports business and management, but he just recently changed gears. He's been hanging out on TV sound stages and movie locations with a keen interest in the production end of showbiz. I hope they can find a connection that'll help them get a leg up in Hollywood.

Futurama has been, by far, my favorite job in Hollywood. It was one the most imaginative, smartest, highly acclaimed series on TV and it was where I was fortunate enough to work and laugh with a room full of uniquely funny people. In most comedy-writing rooms, we would typically have discussions about bad TV shows, or we'd carry on about everyone's failing dating lives and then toss a series of insults at each other before discussing our lunch plans. At *Futurama*, we would stop the room to discuss such things as viable configurations of the perpetual

Jack and Nick at 18.

motion machine. This would include detailed schematics that illustrated possible real-working interpretations.

David X. Cohen, as a showrunner, was decisive, focused and confident. He was not only great at structuring a story, but he would come up with hilarious jokes along the way. David showed me how a comedy-writing room should be run. Every writer, at all levels (even the writers' assistants) were seen as equals to David. Everyone had the freedom to pitch whatever they felt was funny, and we never felt like our job was in jeopardy if we took a swing or two at a bad joke or idea. He created a relaxed environment that helped generate everyone's best ideas. After some reflection, it turns out that David was actually my mentor. He kept me on the show with him through all of its permutations, starting at their second season at Fox on through to the Comedy Central episodes and the DVD movies. During the six seasons I was there, I, along with everyone on the show, was nominated for five Emmys and multiple Annie Awards.

One of my more cherished moments was when one of my episodes, *Game of Tones* was nominated for a Writers Guild Award. Of course, like all the animation awards of that time, we were up against *The Simpsons*. They would beat us, year after year, no matter what shiny award it was. So yeah, it's an honor just to be nominated.

To this day, when someone finds out I write for TV and they ask me what shows I've written on, I first mention *Futurama*, even though, at this point, it's been off the air for more than seven years.

Burning the 7 p.m. oil at Futurama *with Patric Verrone, Me, David X. Cohen and Matt Groening.*

David Goodman, who wrote with us at *Futurama*, was recruited to *Family Guy* to work with his close friend, Seth McFarlane. This was during the first season that the show came back after its cancellation. *Family Guy* generated record sales with its first season's DVDs, which prompted Fox to take a creative swing and put it back on the air. The rest, as they say, is cartoon history.

During one of the four cancelled seasons of *Futurama*, David Goodman called me and said they needed a strong story writer on staff at *Family Guy*. He asked me to come and meet Seth and see if I'd be a good fit for the show. We met and it was great. Seth was hilarious and we hit it off. I was hired as a producer on *Family Guy*.

I loved the show and I was impressed with the team of writers. They were all smart, funny and a blast to hang with. I'd say that there were at least twenty, maybe twenty-two writers on that staff. *Family Guy* was a high-volume series. There was no real break or hiatus; they needed to pump out twenty-two animated episodes a season.

The *Family Guy* writers were a tight team, and I was struggling to find my voice and confidence so I could crack my way into this band of brothers. One way to do that, I realized, was to come up with episode ideas. I spent many lunch hours in my office scribbling down thoughts and notions with the hope of coming up with three killer premises that I could pitch directly to Seth.

Typically, episode ideas came about through jamming vague thoughts and notions around the writers' room. If something hit Seth in the right way, he'd start building on it and everyone would jump in, while David Goodman mapped it out and structured it as a story on the dry-erase board. Pitching directly to Seth was ballsy and risky, but I had to break through somehow.

After weeks of squirming at my desk, I finally came up with a few ideas that I thought were viable. I pitched them to David and he picked the one that he thought I should lead off with. Basically, the story was about Brian, the dog, starting a Quahog version of Sinatra's Rat Pack. The episode featured swinging big-band songs and all the old-school Sinatra-type accoutrements like tuxes, dames, and lots of liquor. Brian co-opted Stewie onto the team and eventually Frank Sinatra Jr. joined in (played, in fact, by Frank Sinatra Jr.). After much success with swingin' and singin' in clubs all over the country, the overindulgence of booze and inflated egos created a cocktail of chaos.

So yeah, I made a sale. Seth liked it; it played right into his wheelhouse. My first draft was fun to write (although I had no clue how to write a song). It changed up quite a bit as it went through the collaborative process, which happens in varying degrees on most shows. Through it all, the story stayed intact. I was proud of the episode. In a 2019 online article, *Brian Sings and Swings* was on a list of Seth's Top 20 favorite episodes.

I still had trouble navigating my way through the layers of writers and all their personalities and interoffice relationships at *Family Guy*. It felt like the more I tried, the harder it became for me to find my comedy footing. This just happens sometimes. There's not all that much you can do about it except try your best to pitch funny shit in the room. When I was invited back to the third or fourth or whatever reboot of *Futurama*, it seemed obvious that I should move on from *Family Guy* and go back to my familiar comfort zone. So I did go: *Back to the Futurama*.

THE BURNING OF CELEBRITIES

I DESPERATELY WANTED a job writing jokes for *The Comedy Central Roasts*.

As a kid, I'd have to say that the biggest resource for my schoolyard material was the *Dean Martin Roasts*. The roasts aired once a month, hosted by, of course, Rat Pack crooner Dean Martin. He would captain the ship unsteadily at the podium, smiling, sweaty, red-faced and slurring. Even as a kid, I could see he was blitzed on most episodes. I grew up in a bar around drunks. I'd seen it all, so no P.R. person could convince me that Dean was just pretending for showbiz's sake. He was not drinking apple juice.

The roasts were an unrelenting hodgepodge of superstar comedians, celebrities, and politicians. Young me got to see them as their true selves as they each took their shot before a dais of celebrity friends to sucker punch the Man of the Hour with hardcore insults. The showbiz veneer was off; this was how they behaved at Hollywood parties. I sat in front of the TV, a ringside witness to the comedy carnage.

Most of the comedians, actors, sports figures, and politicians on the dais came from my parents' generation, though some transcended and crossed over into mine: Sinatra, Don Rickles, Foster Brooks, Milton Berle, Red Buttons, Jonathan Winters, Dino (of course), Charlie Callas, Jack Benny, and George Burns either roasted or were roasted each week. Ruth Buzzi, even Raquel Welch and Angie Dickinson (you've got some heavy Googling ahead of you) got up to take a few hard swings at the dais. To me, each roast was a lesson in comic performance and timing, as well as an endless font of material for my comedy toolbox. While most of my friends were in their garages and basements body building with free weights, I was a comedy nerd in front my TV, building up my comedy muscles.

A generation later, during my burgeoning writing career in Hollywood, *The Comedy Central Roasts* began airing. A mix of funny, young, up-and-comers took their jabs alongside a few tried-and-true stalwart comedians from the Dean Martin days. These new TV roasts were first assembled by the Friars Club and introduced to the young audience by way of my old buddy, Alan King. When I found out that Comedy Central was going to feature these extravaganzas semi-regularly, I wanted in -- my brain was wired and ready to start firing off some old-school celebrity punches to the gut.

Jeff Ross, an old comedy compadre of mine, was fast becoming the king of the private, untelevised Friars roasts. Gone now, The Los Angeles Friars Club was one of two Friars Clubs, one on each coast. The L.A. club was founded by, among others, Humphrey Bogart back in the 1950s. As of this writing, the New York club lives on, but is hanging by a thread. Back in the day, the clubs were a private social hang for celebs, writers and politicians. Mostly comedians. You could walk in any time of day and in one visit run into old-school comedy greats like Milton Berle, Henny Youngman, and Jerry Lewis. Alas, no women were allowed to become members back then, although Bogart did bring Betty Bacall around without protest. The early private Friars roasts (way before the TV show) were wall-to-wall, hardcore, down-and-dirty, not-for-the-faint-of-heart filthy insults told by the same family-friendly comics I knew from TV. Back then, if the jokes had made their way out of the club and into a fanbase, careers would've imploded.

During the 1980s, young Jeff Ross found his insult groove. Raised by his grandfather, he was the kid who fit right in with the old-school comedy sensibility. He was quickly accepted into their fold, which helped him launch the first roast on Comedy Central. He quickly became a fixture on the dais as the Roastmaster General. Jeff was my friend, so I cornered him and asked him to read a stack of jokes that I wrote and wanted to submit to the producers for the upcoming William Shatner roast. He liked them and got them into the producers' hands. Finally, I thought, those days of hanging out with Dino and the gang in front of my TV was going to pay off in spades. I would basically be living another one of my kid-fantasies. I mean, how were they not going to fall in love with my jokes? Rodney liked my jokes, so did Rip Taylor, so, I'm sure that...You know what? Fuck it; my jokes were rejected. They passed on me.

The lesson here is, don't give up. I figured, *"If Jeff liked my jokes, why not write gags just for him?"* So that's what I did, and he delivered them perfectly. Some stood out; most got strong laughs. After that night, Jeff went to the producers and told them that I wrote some of the stronger jokes from his set. From that point on, I wrote for pretty much every *Comedy Central Roast* from the William Shatner Roast in 2007 to the Bruce Willis Roast in 2018.

It's interesting how the early private roast jokes were taboo and would've ended the careers of any who got caught telling them. Yet the hardcore jokes of the nationally televised *Comedy Central Roasts* are much dirtier, darker and more devastating.

Here are a few of the jokes that I've contributed to the roasts that I adore. Please remember that you've been warned.

This was for *The Roast of Donald Trump* just a few short years before he actually ran for president. I wrote it for Snoop Dogg and he nailed it perfectly -- so much so, that it became a meme during the 2016 presidential election, where it gathered over 20 million hits. It later became the topic of discussion when Snoop made an appearance on Conan's show.

"Donald Trump said he's thinkin' about running for president. Why not? It wouldn't be the first time he pushed a black family out of their home."

This next joke was eventually deemed more shocking than funny. That's why I liked it, as did most of the other writers. It was cut last minute from the Justin Bieber roast.

"Justin Bieber abandoned his pet monkey. He said it grew too big and mean to suck his dick."

Kevin Hart liked this joke and stuck with it until just before shoot night. The joke was eventually seen as too far out of his delivery style. It was cut just before showtime, but it remains one of my favorites.

"Snoop is old. They called him 'Snoop Dogg' because he was a dog with the ladies. Now he's called 'Dog' because he sleeps in the sunspot on the living-room floor."

Sarah Silverman and I were -- and still are -- friends from our New York standup days and whenever she was on the roast, I'd help her shape her set. This is one of the last-minute entries that I got to her the day before she was to appear on The James Franco Roast.

"Jonah Hill is such a Jewy dick, you have to watch his movies through a hole in a sheet."

No one wanted to touch the next joke. It was considered a cheap shot, again -- that's why I liked it. I convinced Wayne Brady to do it for the Roseanne Roast. He later had to make a public apology to Sarah Palin.

"Sarah Palin can't stand Jeff Ross because he reminds her of what Trig's gonna look like in his 40s."

Here are a few more dumb and random jokes that I pulled from the 200 pages of my roast jokes that I've kept over the years. Who knows? Maybe I'll self-publish them. They'd make fer darn good terlet readin'.

"Brad Garrett models himself after his Jewish hero -- Frankenstein."

"Gene Simmons is so old that during his concerts, he no longer spits blood -- he *shits* blood."

"Rob Lowe played President John F. Kennedy in a TV movie. Critics said it was the first time they enjoyed seeing Kennedy get his head blown off."

"Man, Artie Lang is not looking good tonight -- Oh-shit. Sorry. That's Cybill Shepherd."

"Peyton Manning's taken a lot of hits to the head. You have to read about it in his book, *Football Good. Fire Bad.*"

"Farah Fawcett is here tonight for a special reason. She lives under the stage."

I couldn't wait to show my dad my work on these roasts. Again, it was a moment that harkens back to when we laughed at the old-timers on *The Dean Martin Roasts*. After he watched the first five jokes, he dismissed the show with a wave of his hand and grumbled, "Eh, it's too filthy," and left the room.

I ALMOST JUMPED

My first time as showrunner was on the animated Comedy Central series *Brickleberry*. I was hired to run the writers' room and shape the vision and tone of the series for a cartoon about a dysfunctional group of park rangers and a talking bear cub. The show was already up and running for a full season when I came in. The creators, Roger Black and Waco O'Guin, had a clear vision of the show; over-the-top filthy, funny, sick, twisted and crazy. No filters, no editors. Episodes featured, for example, animal-fucking, gruesome murders, misogyny, shitting, and jizz-drinking.

In truth, there was a clear vision for *Brickleberry*, such as it was. It came from the heart, albeit a black heart. The series reflected how Roger and Waco saw their comedy world. It was their worldview and what made them laugh.

Unfortunately, Comedy Central didn't share that view and they weren't laughing. Their intention was for me to go in, push those guys aside, and make the show as much like *Futurama* and *South Park* as possible. No problem, right?

So, here I am, a first-time showrunner, thrown into in an impossible situation. The creators were determined to do the show they wanted and the network was determined I do the show they wanted. During my first weeks in our tiny writers' room (a former editing suite), I pushed my way through crippling anxiety attacks while trying to figure out how to run a writers' room and please a myriad of opposing opinions, all while not letting anyone know that I was shitting my pants.

The first decision I made was to side with Roger and Waco. The show was their vision, and unless they were kicked out of the room, I was going to respect that vision; to make the best of an impossible situation. I took what they wanted and tried to shape it into the best, most coherent and character-driven show possible. I thought

I could make it a little less of a shit-and-fuck potpourri and a little more about what the rangers want and care about. Under my guidance, the first few scripts were, unfortunately, somewhere in the middle: Neither as raunchy nor grounded enough. Put plainly, they weren't working.

Well, that's what happens when you try to please multiple opposing visions. To make matters worse, Tosh of *Tosh.O*, the voice of the snarky little bear *and* a producer, demanded that no one laugh during the table reads. He knew he was in a room with the top animation voice actors in Hollywood and he couldn't bear hearing them get strong laughs on the chance his line readings fell flat. Frankly, his insecurities were sabotaging the show. These table reads were, at best, funereal, prompting the executives to try and squeeze me out of the writers' room while trying out a few highly successful showrunner replacements from *The Simpsons*. Roger and Waco knew why they were there, but they continued to turn to *me* to help shape their episodes. I stayed for the run of the series; the replacements lasted a few weeks each.

Despite the pitfalls, there were great moments of creative triumph. Roger and Waco learned how to shape and build the stories they wanted to tell. I learned, through brutal trail and error, how to run a writers' room.

Years later, I went on to work with Roger and Waco again on their animated Netflix series *Paradise PD*, a show about a team of numb-nuts cops (instead of rangers). I couldn't help but feel a sense of pride for the boys. When we last worked together, they were wide-eyed pups, unsure of how a show came together. Now they were confident, calm, and decisive showrunners. They had become stars, and I like to think I helped them get there. Throughout my run at *Brickleberry*, I stayed on them, showing them the best ways to build out stories and characters, even when they wanted to be filthy, dark and twisted.

From *Paradise PD*, I was bouncing back and forth to another Netflix animated series called *The Trailer Park Boys*. The premise of this show asked the question: What if the TV show *Cops* documented the life of the criminals instead of the cops? Camera crews would follow three close friends living in a trailer park, committing "greasy" and petty crimes throughout the rough parts of Halifax, Nova Scotia. The show is filthy, and funny as fuck. I was drawn to it because, through all of the fucked-up fucking, filth and gunplay, the stories are deeply character driven. The audience cares about these dopes and is moved by their undying brotherhood.

Trailer Parks Boys is another of my favorite comedy-writing experiences. The series existed in Canada as a live-action show for almost twenty years, and they brought me in to help convert it into an animated series. This is that rare case where the small, intimate writers' room is devoid of politics. There are no executives poking at you, and the common goal is to just make the scripts as funny as possible in the little time we have to do so. It's a nice feeling to work on a show where I can utilize everything I've learned in my career to help make it work (in its new format). After the first animated season and a bunch of very positive reviews, the show (as of this writing) has been nominated for a Canadian Emmy for writing.

Just prior to *Trailer Park Boys*, I was asked to develop an animated series for the new YouTube channel. The goal was to write, record and edit eight eleven-minute episodes with a very limited budget and an even more-limited amount of time. I *needed* to take that challenge. With only a small writing staff available a few days a week and an inexperienced animation house, I dug in. Both of the main voice actors were YouTube influencers with large online video-game audiences and zero experience in animation voice acting. YouTube assumed they would just bring their audience of tens of millions onto the series.

I gathered everything I'd learned in animation and just went at it, full torque. I wrote, edited and directed the episodes. I was sort of a one-man band, and I loved it. It might just be the most fun I've had building out a TV series. The show, which was called *The Paranormal Action Squad*, was about two determined, self-trained ghost chasers who worked out of their garage. They were the go-to guys when people in town needed an apparition extracted from their homes.

Unfortunately, the production limitations made their way up onscreen. The animation was flat and the voice guys were good but not great. The scripts were not steller, I had about two days to write each one. Nevertheless, I walked away from that show with valuable showrunner experience. The YouTube executives were very supportive. They couldn't have been happier with the episodes, and they laid out billboards across Hollywood, advertising its premiere, including a four-story-high ad covering the side of a building on the Sunset Strip, right near the old Tower Records on the main drag.

Reviews were fine, but audiences hated it. That is, until it was available for free on YouTube and not part of a $9.99-per-month subscription. Then they loved it.

My show, The Paranormal Action Squad, *on the side of a building on Sunset.*

HEROES IN BLACK-AND-WHITE

When my twin sons, Jack and Nick, were preteens and had fitful nights and trouble sleeping, I'd sometimes pile them into the car and take them on a late-night drive through the empty streets of North Hollywood. They'd talk through whatever they were all a-tizzy about; school, friends, who's dying next on *The Walking Dead*. We'd usually end the night at the now-defunct DuPar's diner in Studio City for a late-night bagel.

One night, sitting two booths away from us was Chuck McCann. It was at least 1 a.m., yet he had his table of friends rolling with laughter. I tried desperately to explain to my sons who he was and how important he was to me as a kid. In the mid-1960s, Chuck and Soupy Sales were there for me, every afternoon. I'd get lost in their idiocy and silliness as I sat on the floor, mesmerized and laughing as I watched them through the blue glow of our family Zenith. During his kid-show TV prime, Chuck was a tour de force. To me, it felt like all he cared about was making little me laugh. He'd magically transform into Little Orphan Annie, Oliver Hardy, a crazy magician, a detective, a reckless chef, whatever. It didn't matter; I was laughing.

I realized that I could play YouTube clips on my phone for my sons right there at the diner and give them a glimpse of who Chuck was. Sure enough, there were a ton of them. They watched Chuck as Oliver Hardy and Dick Van Dyke as Stan Laurel play hapless vacuum-cleaner salesmen. There was a kinescope where he sang *Put On A Happy Face* as he danced merrily through the halls of WPIX TV Channel 11 in New York City. My sons were getting it, I think. Nonetheless, they fed off my own excitement.

Chuck McCann was right there, in person, a few short yards from us. I wasn't sure what to do. I felt I owed him, so I told the waitress I was paying his check. I asked her not to tell him who did it. When he asked for the bill, the waitress spilled the beans and pointed me out. He didn't understand what was going down and called me to his table.

I nervously headed over, my sons in tow. I told him I paid his check because I was thanking him for being there for me as a kid. I explained how I had just showed my sons a bunch of his videos. This touched him; it was very sweet. He responded as Stan Laurel, "That's swell." He kidded around with my sons, then he told them, "Wait right here…" He headed out to his car and came back with his coffee-table photo book. It covered the full breadth of his TV days. He signed the book for them and handed it over as a gift. Then he scribbled out three different phone numbers where I could reach him if I ever wanted to get together for coffee.

Regrettably, I never did call him.

Months later, Chuck was doing a very late one-man show with Q & A at The Steve Allen Theater in Hollywood. I had to go; I had to see him. Ron Lynch, who I knew via my standup-comic friends, hosted the night. He saw me in the lobby and asked if I wanted to go on and do standup before Chuck came out. What? Yes! Of course! It'd been years since I'd performed but yes! I wanted to be on the same bill and share a stage with Chuck McCann.

I scribbled down what I remembered of my act on a napkin, got up before the twenty-whatever people in the late-night audience, and did ten minutes of my old tried-and-true cornball bits and nutty noises. I don't remember how I went over; all I remember was that I went backstage and Chuck was waiting there for me. He gave me a warm hug, told me I was really funny and asked me to sit next to him.

And then we talked. He told me stories about when he did a Right Guard commercial with Groucho Marx. He said that afterwards, Groucho invited him to his house where he gave him a private screening of the Marx Brothers movie, *A Day At The Races*. Groucho gave a live commentary throughout. Late into the night, Groucho's young lady-friend, Erin Fleming, told him he'd been there long enough and tossed him out of the house.

Chuck told stories about his old show and how they did seven separate hours of live TV throughout the week. Typically, after he did his recurring chef character, he'd leave the food around for the crew to eat. After one of those shows, he was on his way home and realized that the chicken in the sketch was weeks old and that his crew was about to eat it. He raced back to the studio and got there moments before the toxic bird was devoured by the WPIX TV crew.

Chuck was about to go onstage. I thanked him and let him know that it was a huge honor for me to share the same spotlight with him. He shook my hand and gave me a heartfelt "I love you." Aw, Chuck...

The last time I saw Chuck was about six months later, again at DuPar's, during the holiday season. Standing alongside a Christmas tree and looking straight out, Chuck stood at attention and belted out *O Christmas Tree* for the benefit of six sleepy and drunk late-night patrons.

My experience with Chuck was a little different from the time I met my other childhood hero, Soupy Sales. Soupy and Chuck had back-to-back kids shows. Chuck's 1966 WPIX TV show from New York, *Let's Have Fun*, came on right after *The Soupy Sales Show* on WNEW TV, also from New York. I'd warm up our big, old, boxy TV, then turn the broken dial with a pair of pliers to channel 5 and futz around with the rabbit ears until the blue static and crackle on the TV screen turned into something watchable. For the next half-hour, I'd sit on the floor and laugh my little butt off. The show was a cacophony of kid chaos. Soupy had his coterie of bold, sarcastic and lovable puppets, growly dogs and screaming, unseen people at his door. They would, most times, smack him dead square in the face with a cream pie to help accentuate the goofy punchlines. It was vaudeville on TV, and I loved it.

In the 1980s, I got to work with Soupy Sales. I was asked to open for his nightclub show at Rascal's, a huge comedy venue in New Jersey. This was such a rare opportunity. I mean, how often will any of us get to work, side-by-side, with our very first hero? For those of you who are not comedy nerds, it would be as if your kid-self rooted for the '69 Mets and suddenly you had Tom Seaver pitching in your Sunday beer league.

I was a little nervous that night as I found my way into our shared dressing room. Just as I entered, he stepped out of the bathroom, his hand covering his nose and mouth. There he was: *Damn, it's Soupy Sales!* He spotted me, grimaced and said with deep concern, "You got any matches? I just took a big shit in there."

I've yet to understand why celebrities feel so comfortable relieving their bowels around me.

ONE FLEW OVER THE WRITERS' NEST

I have to constantly remind myself of my accomplishments in the comedy business. Hollywood has a way of making us creative types feel that no matter how successful we are, we're never enough. There's no resting on laurels in Hollywood.

A screening of my stand up comedy documentary, 50 Years Behind The Brick Wall. *Back row (left to right) Ray Romano, Steve Peckingham, Mike Ivy, Larry David, Me, Marty Rackham, Sue Jaffee, Jon Manfrellotti, John Mendoza, Rick Overton, Judy Orbach, Ned Rice. Front row (left to right) Jonathan Solomon, John DeBellis, Billiam Coronel, Don McEnery, Lou Dimaggio, Sue Kolinsky, Zoe Friedman (our co-producer), Silver Friedman, Pat Buckles. Scott Carter up front.*

With every new project you sign on for, you're starting from scratch. Not only are you building new relationships with fellow writers, you have to prove your talent and dedication to a new army of industry people. You're expected to please the showrunner and/or creator of the project as well as the executives who are poking at everything you're trying to create. They have something to say about everything from casting to wardrobe to the jokes on the page. Learning how to weave your way through the political intricacies and the mind games that come with the job is as important as knowing the craft itself. It's hard, dude.

When I land a sweet writing gig, Hollywood can make me feel that it's a fluke. I'll think that it happened because I was in the right place at the right time, like someone momentarily took their eye off of the ball and hired me. So many of us writers live with the burning feeling that even though we have a job, there's always another writer pacing out in the hall, anxious and ready to take our place. There is some truth to that, metaphorically, I guess, but mostly it's "writers noise." It happens when you're in a high-stress, high-stakes position in a world where you're considered disposable by any one of your long line of bosses. We're constantly living in a fierce tornado whipped up by the collision of the creative mind as it spins into the intensity of the corporate entertainment world. It leaves some of us with a form of writer's PTSD.

On one series, we'd get unrelenting calls from the executives, unhappy with the direction the series was going. They'd give us a full-throated dressing-down, leaving us queasy and feeling lost. By call's end, we'd be regretting our career choice. Years later, when I worked with the same show creators, our new office phones had the same ring tone as the old show. Every time they rang, stomachs tightened a little. They eventually had all the ringtones on the floor changed.

I fumbled around Los Angeles for years trying to find my place in the Hollywood hierarchy. Although I was happy and satisfied, landing nice writer/producer jobs on multi-cam sitcoms like *The Nanny*, *Becker*, and *Coach*, (all great shows), I really wanted to work on a cool show that I liked, watched and was invested in. The truth was, when I'd get into some of the writers' rooms on shows that weren't in my wheelhouse, I'd have a hard time. I mean, I'd truly struggle. I knew nothing about being a young Jewish woman from Queens. I didn't know where to draw from to tell stories about an angry, chain-smoking doctor. There's nothing harder for me than to be writing on a show where my comic sensibilities don't match that of the room. It can get very confusing and frustrating.

When I worked on Eddie Murphy's animated series, *The PJs*, about a middle-aged janitor working in the inner-city projects, I had a handle on all of it. I understood the voice of the show, the rhythm. I somehow knew what jokes would work and which stories would be right for the characters. More importantly, the other writers in the room got my comedic point of view. It was a love fest and I'm always grateful, excited and delighted when I land in these situations. This is where I feel free, confident, and where I flourish. Unfortunately, on the next show, I could easily fall into a situation where I don't connect on any level. There is nothing worse than pitching jokes and ideas only to find my boss or maybe the star of the show squirming and avoiding eye contact.

In the few but unforgettable, soul-crushing times I've been in these rooms, I'd resort to my safety net and start playing around doing "room bits." My go-to was pretending to be outraged by someone else's joke pitch. Standing up in a huff, I grumble about their insolence. In my faux-anger, I pick up what I consider to be my belongings, which would be everything on the table within reach. Stacking my arms with a stapler, a pile of scripts, pencil holders, a coffee cup, whatever, I clumsily storm out, never to return. This was -- and still is -- my icebreaker, famously known to my friends as "the up and away." Sure, it's old-school and dumb, but to me, that's what was funny about it. More importantly, I'm showing everyone my sensibility, physically explaining to them that I can be funny, even though my pitches haven't been (so far). If that doesn't get a laugh, well, then I'm dead. The "up and away" is my litmus test. It's when I know if I will or will not be hanging any pictures and posters on my office wall.

In truth, I'm very proud of much of what I've accomplished thus far in my career. I'm especially proud of a standup comedy documentary I produced (with a lot of help from many) celebrating the 50th anniversary of The Improv. The very institution I dreamt about as a kid trusted me with a project that helped cement the lore, camaraderie, and history of the club. I spent many fun, wild and crazy New York City nights with the comics we interviewed, which gave me a little extra inside scoop on how best to use them. I paired Larry David with Richard Lewis, both close friends for at least thirty years. As they sat together, we got them to ask each other questions about their lives and careers. Then we challenged them to see if they knew each other's comedy bits.

The interview quickly devolved when Richard went after Larry's history of walking offstage at the slightest murmur from the audience. Larry stood by his philosophy: "If people come to see a Broadway show, you don't hear talking. There's no talking in a show!" Richard tried to convince Larry that his standup comedy was in no way equal to a Broadway show. Larry wasn't convinced. I suddenly found myself in the middle of a scene from *Curb Your Enthusiasm*.

For his interview, Jimmy Fallon talked about Jerry Seinfeld and how he was his comedy influence. He didn't know Jerry was in the wings getting ready to be interviewed until Jerry pounced on him from the shadows and mocked him for his praise; a nice, impromptu, goofy moment for the cameras. The show was narrated by Adam Sandler, plus interviews with Sarah Silverman, Ray Romano, Judd Apatow, Bill Maher, Damon Wayans (along with all the Wayans Brothers), Kathy Griffin, and, of course, Budd and Silver Friedman, all talking about intimate moments at the club.

The documentary, *50 Years Behind the Brick Wall*, aired on EPIX, Netflix, Hulu and Comedy Central. EPIX studios paid for the show, so I didn't have final say in the project. The studio wanted it to be a big-celeb marquee show. On-camera choices were made that I had no control over, so unfortunately, some people didn't make the cut and felt slighted and hurt. Sadly, I took the brunt of those decisions from comedians and others who, if I had my way, would've been in the doc. If I'd had full control, I would have loved to explore the comics who didn't make it or dropped out of comedy altogether. I felt it would've been interesting, even fascinating, to find out where they landed in their lives.

I'm proud of the documentary, too, because I threw myself into a situation where I wasn't exactly sure what I was doing. My philosophy is: You have to continually push yourself out of your comfort zone if you want to grow. This is for all aspects of life (and it's why I wrote this dopey book). In the end, there were positive reviews for the documentary in *GQ, New York Magazine* and *The New York Times*, as well as newspapers across the country.

After successful multi-year runs with animated adult comedies, I tried going back to live action, multi-cam network sitcoms. I landed on a primetime series that was up and running and starting its fifth season. After twenty or so years experience in the comedy writing game, I knew, day one in the room, that this show was not going to work out for me. Within one hour of sitting at the table I thought, *"Escape route. I'm gonna need an escape route. How do I get out of here?"*

The writers' room had a palpable, unrelenting and undeniable tension that festered and pulsated like an oozing demon monster from a 1950s horror movie. It'd lie in wait for the perfect moment to attack and devour each and every writer's soul. Each new workday brought anxiety that would build and metastasize through every part of my being. I'd been in a similar room like this before and I knew exactly where it was going.

My first week in, when we were breaking stories and building outlines for the new season, I felt like every joke or idea that was pitched in the room needed to be a solid comedy punch to the gut. If you weren't delivering exactly what the showrunner was hoping for, the idea was met with a giant, angry sigh and a crushing eye roll of disappointment, along with some sort of disparaging comment: "That's what you're pitching, really? Do you hate the show *that* much?" Then the room would sometimes have to stop for a dramatic moment to give him time to recover. If my pitches were off, even by a little bit, I felt like I was one step closer to cleaning out my desk (which is why I kept it empty). I guess this was how he wanted and needed his writers to feel, it was his dysfunctional comfort zone. The stress and tension was excruciating. I did what I could at home each night to recover and rebuild my confidence, but with every new day, as soon as I'd step into the writers' room, I'd feel a wave of dread in the pit of my stomach. I was a deep-sea diver wearing weights and struggling to get back to the surface with zero air left in the tanks. Every day, my task at hand became fighting to be funny while basically drowning.

Due to this happy-happy environment, all the writers, for the most part, were mentally unavailable, uncommunicative and war-torn. Each in our own foxhole, doing our best to survive, there was no sharing of war stories, no comforting hands to hold. How could there be? Everyone was tightly wrapped up in his or her own protective cocoon.

Finally, one day, I had to do it. I jumped out of my chair and pretended to be incensed as I grumbled over someone's joke pitch. I angrily loaded up everything on the table; scripts, coffee cup, full pencil holder, stapler, snacks -- stacking all of it into my arms then storming out with "my belongings" teetering against my body.

My "up and away" was met with silence, then murmurs of concern: "Is he okay?" "What happened?" Not exactly the effect I was shooting for.

Sheepishly reentering the room, I shuffled back to my chair and awkwardly unloaded the props from my arms. I tried to make a joke about how my room bit was intended to be funny while my… voice…trailed off…and turned small. Everyone stared daggers at me, worried that such a bold move might have agitated the king of the room, who just stared out, waiting for it to end.

As I sat back, I happened to glance at the long erase board and saw twenty-two blank numbered spaces across the length of it, one for each episode that was yet to be written. I was suddenly gripped with a brutal and crippling anxiety attack. I'd experienced them before while working on one or two shows in the past. The anxiety was often debilitating, especially when I was knee-deep in an environment where I was expected to be comically precise. I was stuck there for too many months fighting to keep my consciousness and wherewithal from floating out the window, off the lot and into oncoming traffic.

Somehow, the king knew how to push the buttons that agitated the most vulnerable and painful times of our childhoods. I could see it in most of the other writers' faces and in their behavior. Some (including me) would shut down, making sure not to anger "the parent." Others over-performed and became silly, probably their tack for distracting their disapproving parent. Still others played big brother or sister trying to keep family peace at the table. There were those who found calm in prescription meds, while others self-medicated by grazing the snack room all day (me again). Red Bulls and cigarettes were also the drugs of choice for some.

Many's the night I'd get home, sit in my office, turn out the lights and stare through the cracks of my closed blinds at the moonlight creeping in. I'd sip Macallen 12 right from the bottle while blasting the *Apocalypse Now* soundtrack. My whole sense of self had to go to fucking Nam to relax. I lived for the sounds of helicopters swishing around from speaker to speaker while napalm rained down onto the rice paddies. I was Colonel Kurtz; dark, crazed and maybe losing it, as I waited to hear Jim Morrison's dark, guttural refrain, "This is the end/My only friend/The end."

I was Martin Sheen's Ben Willard: "Hollywood...Shit!"

This anxiety is the result of me wanting desperately to be funny, great and the killer writer I sometimes think I am (or that my boss or TV executive expects me to be). When these attacks show up, they keep me from being that guy, which sometimes creates more anxiety, which then builds on itself until I ultimately find myself lost in a tense, dreamlike state. From there, it gets worse, because all the mind-bendyness completely blocks access to whatever funny or cogency I have to bring to the comedy table. The feeling of helplessness can sometimes build on itself so much that, at times, I find it impossible to write a simple grocery list. It's a baffling and chilling phenomenon, and the more I know about it, the less I know about it.

Thankfully, these events only happened a few times over the years, but I'm always on guard, doing what I can to keep that level of anxiety at bay.

The trick is to push through all the insanity; get past the *noise* and keep moving until you find a way to be helpful to the project. If you can't get there, it's not necessarily your fault. If you're in a toxic, dysfunctional situation or on a show that doesn't jibe with your sensibility, there's not a lot you can do about it. Even in the worst cases, don't quit. If you're lucky, they'll fire you and have to pay out your contract. Sweet.

SO WHAT HAVE WE LEARNED?

IT TOOK ME AWHILE to understand and accept that all writers are not created equal. Some can roll into Hollywood from their hometown and, within months, quickly have their movie green-lit. Or they sell a TV series and suddenly he or she is anointed as the new Hollywood whiz kid. It's like the nine-year-old kid who can sit at a piano and play Chopin's Étude Opus 10 No.4 by ear. Some people are just born with those gifts and you know what? Fuck 'em (I say that out of LOVE). The truth is, most of us have to sweat and slave and study and fail and start over and cry and throw up until we discover what, if any, talent we might have. Then we have to develop it, polish it and get our voice out there -- all before we age out of the Hollywood system. Sound fun? You bet it does.

You just have to remind yourself that, along the way, you'll land in a bunch of situations where you'll feel funny, productive, relaxed and at your creative best. Those experiences will remind you that you actually do know what you're doing, and that you do have an original point of view and you do have the talent you always thought you had. It's truly rewarding. (Apologies. My therapist got a hold of my keyboard.)

To this day, I get to share my successes with my mom. Even after all the years of hearing my play-by-play about my misadventures, she's yet to have any deep understanding of how showbiz works. How could she -- how could anyone, really -- if they're not living in the thick of it all?

When I sold my own TV series in 2016, I explained to her that for its premiere week, the network was going to put up a four-story-high billboard on a building on the Sunset Strip to advertise my show. She was proud of me, for sure, but her response was, "All riii. You're getting there." In truth, she was reminding me to keep fighting the good fight and to know that there are no limits to success.

My mom and me.

I'm her only son; she's proud of me and she's always excited and delighted when she sees my "Written by" or "Producer" credit on a TV show, but she feels that the goal for me is to keep pushing and growing until I hit Spielberg status.

Why not?

It's very satisfying that I got to share so much of my early comedy career with my dad. In fact, I have a sneaking suspicion that he lived some of it vicariously through me.

In one of my car rides with him back in Connecticut, he made it a point to show me the house in Wolcott that I was born in. I always knew where it was, but we never actually drove there and stopped right in front of it. I remember my dad sitting in the car, staring at the house and just taking it in. He was, it seemed, watching the movie of his young family in his head. Maybe he was reviewing his regrets, or maybe he was saying a final goodbye to a window of his past. I didn't expect much of an explanation from him; I just watched him relive the moments he needed to revisit.

Now that I was a man and my dad was into his 70s, I did think that perhaps this reflective interlude would instigate one of those movie moments where he would spill his secret of life. But no, our drive back to his house started off quiet and contemplative, then quickly devolved into a volley of awful fish puns. Ya know, just for the *halibut*.

"What'd ya pay a fin for that joke?"
"No. Scale."
"You're giving me a haddock."
I wouldn't have wanted it any other way.

Years later, Denise, my sons and I had to make the trip from Los Angeles to Maine to see my dad in hospice. He was down to his final days and it was time for us to say goodbye. He lived much of his life with crippling back pain, which was what made him, at times, cranky and curmudgeonly. During this last visit, he was so doped-up and pain-free with morphine that he was the happy, spry, joyful and the outgoing dad I remembered from my youth. I sat by his bed for two days and we laughed like idiots. He made sure he let me know how proud he was of me and my family and of my life.

A few nights later, you could see the flame starting to flicker out in him. The nurses readied him for sleep for what turned out to be my last night with him. It was just going to be me alone there at his side to say good night. His wife, Lucy, recommended that I read the Scriptures to him at his bedside. When she left, I put the Scriptures aside and instead, Googled pages of Henny Youngman jokes on my phone. I read them off, one-by-one, in my best Henny-like cadence. My dad laid there blissfully as he smiled a crooked smile while I prattled on with such gems as:

"A man goes to a psychiatrist. 'Nobody listens to me.' The doctor says, 'Next.'"

Jokes like that went on for twenty minutes.

Denise, Jack, Nick and I said our sad and painful goodbyes to my dad the next morning. It happened to be his 80th birthday. Jack, still too young to comprehend exactly what was happening, asked about my dad's birthday: "Will there be cake?" My dad passed away later that week.

I was soon back to work in Hollywood. The Emmy Awards were that week and I, along with the other writers at *Futurama*, were nominated yet again. I was excited, for sure, but not very hopeful. We'd been on this road multiple times and we'd been beaten summarily by *The Simpsons* each time. Nonetheless, it was a perfect Hollywood night out on the town and along with it came extravagant parties and black-tie affairs that I got to share with Denise.

My dad and me.

We were cautiously optimistic as we waited for them to open the envelope and announce the winner for Best Animated Series. This show-biz moment was indicative of so many moments my wife had to endure with me throughout my career: The uncertainty, yet the possibility. We waited for *The Simpsons* to be announced as the winners.

To my surprise, shock and astonishment, *Futurama* actually won. *WE WON!*

I soared up to the stage at full speed. This was a monumental moment that made up for all of those times when I was a kid and didn't win any sports trophies or honors in school, or those times when I was excluded from hanging with the cool kids. I crossed a goal line that I, in my youth, pretended would happen someday. I never thought it would actually come to pass.

I'm not sure what winning an Emmy really means to others in the industry, but to me it felt more than anything like an award to show off to your parents. I knew in my dad's eyes this would've been his version of his son winning a Super Bowl ring. The excitement of running up to the stage and grabbing that trophy was my one true-but-brief moment of being at the top of Everest.

With Emmy in hand, I called my mom from backstage and told her the good news. She, of course, was dizzy with pride and with

Winning the Emmy for Futurama.

her misunderstanding of the business still intact, she reminded me, "There you go. You're getting there."

Yeah, she was right yet again.

I later found myself wandering the lobby of the theater, still clutching my Emmy, looking down at the floor as I navigated my way through the sea of tuxedos and evening gowns. I ended up in a private corner and, in a bittersweet moment, a wave of uncontrollable sadness hit me. I would've loved to have shown my dad the trophy...just for the *halibut*.

Regardless of my experiences in the comedy business, whether good, great, bad or horrifying, each one is undeniably magical to me in its own twisted, dark and exhilarating way.

Those of us who work in show business know that our challenges bring with them the impossible climb up to the top of Mount Everest; but in truth, you don't have to reach the peak of the mountain to enjoy the beauty of the view. And with that -- as I told my mom -- Spielberg can suck it!

Happily, I've gotten to live and experience many of the showbiz dreams that I fantasized about during my days as a teen back in my little factory town in Connecticut. I got to write for and work with and become friends with many of my comedy heroes and legends. To this day, I feel privileged that I'm (metaphorically) able to walk inside the television or movie screen and spend time with the people that inspired me or made me laugh. These are the same stars, comedians and actors who, through humor, helped unite my family and me during the more tumultuous days of my youth. They're the same comedy legends who unknowingly loaned me my first jokes and attitudes and comedy rhythms that I used to win over friends and relatives and eventually got me on stage in front of an audience.

I wrote this book mostly to capture and preserve the wild rollercoaster ride that I've had so far in my long, wonderful and amazing career. These are precious, private, self-reflective moments that, in some form, will live on after me. I have a fantasy that a young kid, too scared to leave his hometown, will find this book, read it, and in it find the courage and inspiration to get on a bus or plane and chase his or her dream. Even if it's just one kid, it will have been time well spent writing this book. My sons have since read it and, as it turns out, it inspired them to pursue careers in show business. ...I guess my work is done.

Reflecting on my writer's life well-lived made me wish I could travel back in time to visit my eighteen-year-old, wide-eyed comedy-wannabe self; the old me standing with the young me, telling him about the fantastic journey that lies ahead. That young and hungry me would collapse with excitement at the idea of this, then he'd collect himself and quickly realize, "Yikes, I'm gonna be fat and bald."

You can't have everything, jerk.

THE END

DEDICATED TO THE MEMORY OF

JANIS "JANE" ROWE

May 15, 1961 – November 27, 2020

MIKE ROWE'S ROOM BITS EXPLAINED

DURING MY MANY Emmy-award-winning seasons writing for Futurama, from time to time I'd pitch a comedy clinker or two in the writers' room. To help right the funny ship, (and ease the pain of my embarrassment) I'd shoot off a quip, bon mot, gag, or whatever silliness that was locked and loaded in my massive comedy arsenal.

Over time, these comedy zingers proved to be so essential and monumental to the entire comedy industry (and some tentacles of science) that it prompted the *Futurama* writing staff to document them. Their hopes were, no doubt, to preserve them in The Smithsonian or perhaps The National Archives, or, at the very least get them framed and hung at a local dry cleaner's. I'm sharing just a few of my one-hundred carefully curated crazy bits so that you, the young comedy writer, could be the life of the party in a professional comedy writers' room.

1. How long was I out?

Save this remark once you've completed a long, rambling pitch. This question takes the blame off of your failure and puts it squarely on a temporary loss of consciousness.

Also accepted: Any mail for me while I was gone?

2. Was that a pitch?

Asking this question will help lift the tension in the room after a fellow writer suddenly overshares and divulges deep, ugly, or sad events from his or her personal life.

3. The "Up And Away."

This happens when someone pitches or declares something so outrageous, it sends you into a rage. Without haste, you stand up and gather everything in front of you including scripts, staplers, pencil holders, cups and books. Once your arms are filled to capacity, you storm out of the room in a huff. For maximum effect, it's recommended that you remain absent from the room for a lengthy amount of time.

4. Hello?

This is called out after your bad pitch creates a long silence. It's to assure you that your fellow writers are OK and they haven't lost consciousness.

5. I opened for them.

This is brought up whenever two words are separated by the word "and." For example, the term, "cut and paste" is commonly used in the writers' room. This gives you the opportunity to remark, "Cut and Paste? I opened for them." It suggests that you've shared the bill with some sort of performing duo, comedic or otherwise.

Also accepted: They handled my divorce (As in: a low-rent law firm).

6. I had that in the Navy.

This response applies to any silly-sounding, polysyllabic word, phrase, or odd last name. For example, if a fellow writer noted that the guest star for that week is Milo Ventmigilia, you would tell them, "Oh, I had that in the Navy." Its intent is to humorously conjure up some sort of exotic and perhaps fatal disease that you'd likely contract while on furlough in the Navy.

7. Sounds like my honeymoon.

This is to conjure up sexual activity when, in fact, it has nothing to do with lovemaking whatsoever. For example, if during a lunch break someone were to exclaim, "My hot dog ripped the bun apart!"

8. He's (or she's) doing his (or her) [ ] bit.

Typically, when you see someone struggling with anything, whether it be a stuck drawer or hard-to-open lunch container, you can point out to fellow writers that this is their go-to reoccurring comedy routine. You'd say, for example, "Oh look, Bill is doing his desk drawer bit."

9. *I was going for speed on that one.*

This is a qualifier indicating that you know you just pitched something godawful but you somehow thought it was better to choose promptness over content.

10. *No further questions at this time, Your Honor.*

It's recommended that you kick back and shout this out with gusto after your pitch. It suggests that it's time to end any additional pitching because you've just handed them the perfect solution. Hopefully, this will distract from that fact that your pitch is far from perfect.

Also accepted: That's lunch everybody!

11. *The Chinese Pitch.*

When reading your pitch aloud off a sheet of paper, you speak in what sounds like Chinese. Then you stop as you realize that your paper is upside down. You sheepishly flip the paper right side up and reread your work in perfect English.

12. *Is she in town?*

This is queried after any set of words that sound in any way like the name of a sexually available woman. For example, "ginger snaps." Despite this being a cookie, of course, it could be considered the name of a stripper. Hence, you wonder if "she's in town" and available.

13. *Is this the correct time?*

This is asked after you pitch a joke or idea that's so dreadful that you tap your watch and bring it to your ear to create the illusion that it's stopped. This gives you an opening to claim that you are extremely late for a previous engagement and must leave the premises immediately.

14. Read that back...

After a long, useless, spiraling pitch, you demand with confidence that the writers' assistant read it aloud to the room in its entirety. This indicates that you are aware of your faulty pitch and you're getting ahead of it before the chiding begins.

Also accepted: I don't hear typing.

15. Dear Mother...

When the comedy room is at a creative standstill, push a pencil through the side of an empty plastic red cup and puff on the end of the pencil as if you're smoking a giant corncob pipe. Then, as if a grizzled sea captain lost at sea, you write and recite a new entry into your journal. Each one starts woefully with, "Dear Mother..." continuing on with something like, "Seas're mighty rough tonight... The crew grows weary as we approach day three of no food and no joke for the act break..."

ACKNOWLEDGMENTS

I first thank my smart, beautiful and generous wife Denise, who lets me spend way too much time in my office typing away at whatever silly thing I'm writing – including this book. Many thanks to my loving mom, who constantly reminds me, in her way, that "great is the enemy of the good." I thank my dad, who was the first person to make me laugh and help me discover the mighty power of humor.

Thanks also go to my sister Tracy, for her undying dedication, incredible skills and super-smarts that helped make this book infinitely better. I thank my sister Janis for being my best comedy audience back when we were kids. Your laugh is energizing.

Steve Stoliar is king for repeatedly fixing, adjusting, shaping, and giving notes on this book. That is no easy task considering my lack of basic book-learnin'.

Many thanks go to Silver Saunders Friedman, who guided and nurtured me through my entire ten-year standup life in New York City. She made the Improv my cozy home away from home. I'm so lucky to have Joel Goss and his lifetime of friendship. Joel was the first to open my brain to the smartest, most sophisticated and silliest world of books, movies, TV shows, comedians, radio shows and on and on. Thank God for my friendship with Scott Buck, who lets me know when I write something that's great and when I write something that's truly awful. I'd also be lost without Eddie Gorodetsky, who hired me for my very first writing gig ever. Over the years we've solved most of the world's problems together.

I can't thank Coco Shinomiya enough for her genius and kind heart. Her design for the cover of this book went far beyond what this dopey memoir deserves. Many thanks to Tom Caltabiano for the use of the photo of me and the gang gathered in my home and especially for the amazing photo of me holding my Emmy. Thanks to Phil Nee for the cover photo of me and my bald head. I thank Carol Hampson for the amazing photo of me and my lovely wife-to-be.

I thank Barry Mitchell, Ned Rice and Steve Skrovan, who read early drafts of this memoir and gave me fantastic, sweeping notes and above all, encouragement. It helped me slog on through to get to the end of this sucker.

Thanks to all of you who, over the years, took a leap of faith and hired me to write funny stuff for you or with you.

Last but hardly least, a double-dose of thanks to my twin sons, Jack and Nick, who keep me motivated, engaged and young. I wrote this for them, so they can better understand all of the treacherous - but mostly glorious - events that can happen when you chase your wildest dreams.

ABOUT THE AUTHOR

MICHAEL ROWE, a former comedian now comedy writer/producer, has been nominated for six Emmys for his work on *Futurama* and *Family Guy* earning one along the way. Mike's also been nominated for two Annie Awards, earning two; a Writers Guild Award, and a Gemini Award. He has earned a WEBBY Award for his original animated series *The Paranormal Action Squad*. His writing has also appeared in *Vanity Fair* magazine. He lives in Los Angeles with his wife, twin sons and a silly dog named Marty Allen.

www.ingramcontent.com/pod-product-compliance
Lightning Source LLC
Chambersburg PA
CBHW060116170426
43198CB00010B/917